Turning Final,
A Life Complete

BY JIM REED LT. COL. USAF (RET)

Order this book online at www.trafford.com
or email orders@trafford.com

Most Trafford titles are also available at major online book retailers.

Printed in the United States of America.

ISBN: 978-1-4269-6319-3 (sc)
ISBN: 978-1-4269-6322-3 (hc)
ISBN: 978-1-4269-6360-5 (e)

Library of Congress Control Number: 2011904844

Trafford rev. 10/29/2014

www.trafford.com
North America & international
toll-free: 1 888 232 4444 (USA & Canada)
fax: 812 355 4082

This book is dedicated to Mr. Gambrell who made the compassionate decision to pass a young cadet who forgot the landing gear on a check ride, or the chapters in this book would not have been written, to my dear mother, Ruth, who loved her son and left this life way too early and to Lou and Connie Reed who took me in as their son and gave me the tools to succeed in life.

TABLE OF CONTENTS

Chapter 1

1933-1952

In the Beginning

Flying has often been described as hours and hours of boredom interrupted by moments of stark terror. But flying is much more than that! This is the story of the human experience, and the humor and terror of a flying career.

*I don't remember being born.

Some have told me they do, and even remember what the delivery room looked like. Perhaps they do, but that's hard for me to believe. My first recollections are from about the age of three or four and marked the start of a three-dimensional adventure that accelerated into an eye-popping, hair whipping, hang-on-tight- ride through 45 years of flying and boating action all over the world.

I now realize that the beginning of life has a wonderful way of hiding what's to come. Each of us moves through our infancy free from the rigors of life. A young child has no sense of the pressures of adulthood and so moves through the early years innocent of the responsibilities and injustices and the fascination and excitement that growing up will bring.

And that's the way it was with me.

I came into the world as James Lawrence Stevens during the depression, on a kitchen table in a house on Coffee Street in Brooklyn's Red Hook section. At that time, the predominant ethnic groups in Red Hook were Irish and Italian. My father was in the Merchant Marine and I didn't see much of him. In fact, I carry in my memory only two occasions of time with him. Both are good memories, but time has erased his features and I cannot now even recall what he looked like.

One day he went away and never came back. To this day I don't know why. During the war, like so many others, his ship was torpedoed and he spent 14 days alone on a life raft, barely escaping with his life before being rescued.

But this was after he left my mom and me.

My mother must have had a difficult time in Red Hook, trying to provide for a young child and herself during the Depression. I know that we spent a lot of time living with other relatives who were able to provide and care for us, and I did not carry into adulthood the difficulties of the events of that time. I suppose that all of us carry the better memories of our childhood into our adult lives.

Some of my recollections of the 1930s and 1940s that I have carried with me over the years:

Grandpa Jim Sweeney sending me (age 8 to 10) to Gabe's Bar on the corner of Wolcott and Conover streets in the evening to get him a growler (a growler was a quart of beer in a white cardboard container with a white cardboard lid and a wire handle), being careful not to shake the growler.

and

Putting pennies on the trolley car tracks so the trolleys would squash them flat. They would be about three times their original size after the trolleys ran over them. Hitching rides on the back of the trolley and being chased by the motorman.

and

The drayage trucks on the cobblestone streets of Red Hook, with their hard rubber tires and large chain drives to the rear axles.

and

The icemen delivering ice from the horse-drawn wagons to the houses, carrying half a hundred pound block of ice on their shoulders into the kitchens of people's houses with their large iron tongs. The smell of the trucks that delivered kerosene for the space heaters in the homes.

and

Stickball and stoop ball played on the streets and in the vacant lots.

and

Going to the Pioneer Theater for five cents every Saturday to see the matinee serials and being disappointed when the hero, who had gone over the cliff in his car to certain death the week before, had really jumped out of the car before it went over.

and

Playing hooky from school and watching the New York Giants and the Brooklyn Dodgers play in Yankee Stadium. Since we didn't have enough money to get a ticket, we would sit on the steel supports of the elevated subway and watch the game from there.

and

Playing in the stream of water from the fire hydrants in the sweltering New York summers.

My next recollection is of my mother and me at the U.S. Army Post at Fort Wright on Fishers Island, near New London, Connecticut, with Sergeant Lou Reed. This memory is strong because of a terrible event that took place there. I recall that we were roller skating one evening and the wind started blowing so hard that it blew us on our skates back to our quarters on post. I didn't know it at the time, but that was the beginning of the great hurricane of 1938.

As the wind increased, the slate on the roofs of the barracks across the street started coming loose, and my mother narrowly escaped death when a two-foot square piece of slate almost hit her head as it hurtled through our living room window. After that, we went below to the basement. In the morning, after the hurricane had passed, we looked outside and the water from the sound several blocks away had come up to our back porch and a refrigerator was floating about. Magazine articles that pictured the devastation and loss of life that took place showed a picture of an ocean-going ship that had washed into a field several miles from the ocean. Because there was little warning of the approaching storm, as there is today, 600 people lost their lives.

Sgt. Lou Reed, now my stepfather, was transferred in 1939 to the Panama Canal Zone. We lived in both Corozal and Fort Sherman and I have some wonderful memories of those times. When we moved to Fort Sherman, at the Atlantic entrance to the Panama Canal, our quarters were right on a small lagoon and the jungle came very close to the back of the house. The adult activity for entertainment was butterfly hunting, and I can recall some delightful excursions into the jungle with nets to catch beautiful blue butterflies, which were plentiful. One day, the maid went under the stilted house to do laundry and found a full-grown crocodile lying next to the washing machine. The Military Police had a difficult time dispatching it.

Each school day the kids were taken to Cristobal by an army boat that looked like an overgrown tugboat. Those were wonderful times, and I loved riding the boat back and forth to Cristobal. This all came to an end, however, when, one evening, my stepfather and I watched as the entire city of Cristobal burned to the ground. Since Cristobal was a peninsula, with only one way in and out, the crowds fleeing the city prevented the fire equipment from getting into the city to fight the fire and the entire city was destroyed in flames. It was a spectacular site for a young child to watch and the visual impression of that monstrous fire has stayed with me through the years.

That was my first contact with the serious part of life.

*Dad was in charge of a gun battery that contained a large gun that protected the Atlantic entrance to the Panama Canal. In preparation for the General's visit, the gun crew had worked all week cleaning and painting the battery to get it ready for this major inspection. They took a break before cleaning up and it was about this time that I showed up. The guys knew me as Dad's son, so didn't think too much of my presence there.

When they all went for a break I found myself alone with the gun.

It's strange what goes through the mind of an eight-year-old. I knew that everyone was working very hard and I wanted to help them, so I started to camouflage the gun with all the different colors of paint I could find. I don't know why I thought the inside of the barrel as well as the outside needed to be camouflaged, but after I did the outside, I started pouring paint down the barrel.

That's when they walked in!

I can remember the details of this incident very clearly because it was brought up time after time over the years as I grew older. Dad said that the General had him in a brace for a solid hour chewing him out. He roared, "How in the hell can I trust you to lead a gun crew when you can't even control an eight-year-old!" With my help, if the war had not come along, Dad might never have gotten promoted.

When the Japanese bombed Pearl Harbor in December of 1941, the strategists feared that they would attempt a bombing or invasion of the Panama Canal, either to gain possession of the canal or to render it useless to us. History has shown that had the Japanese been able to accomplish either of these, the war would have been much more difficult than it was. As a result of this fear, all dependents were shipped out of Panama, and Mom and I went back to relatives in Red Hook aboard the Army transport Hunter Liggett.

During this period Sgt. Reed was promoted to Captain. We stayed in Red Hook until he came back from the Panama Canal and, after a short assignment at the Detroit Tank Arsenal in Michigan, we were reassigned to the Rock Island Arsenal near Davenport, Iowa. Rock Island Arsenal is an island in the middle of the Mississippi River. We had to wait until base quarters were available, so we lived in Davenport for about two years. The house was a two-story, old-style country-type home with a screened-in porch, located in a very nice residential neighborhood. We lived on the lower floor. Access to the upper floor was by an outside staircase in the back of the house and, when we moved into the house, I was young enough that I paid little attention to the amount of traffic that went up and down those back stairs. I'm not quite sure how I found out, but when I got a little older, I realized why so many young soldiers were visiting the second floor. I have to say that there was never a ruckus of any sort that would make the goings on there unpalatable to a residential neighborhood. The folks there were patriotic and probably figured that the second floor contributed to the war effort in some way.

While we still lived in Davenport a sad thing happened that my mother never really got over. She gave birth to twins that were stillborn. She went into a period of depression that lasted until my brother was born several years later. He was a healthy baby, and caring for this new life brought my mother back to us.

During this period of time, Captain Reed was promoted to Major, then Lieutenant Colonel and, eventually, we moved on Post into Quarters #7.

The quarters there were absolutely marvelous. They had all been built during the Civil War era, and were huge. There were five bedrooms upstairs, a beautiful staircase that could have come right out of Tara, and a basement that was built like a French dungeon. The house was located on the second hole of the golf course, and I could hit an eight iron into the Mississippi River from our back yard.

Quarters # 7 Rock Island Arsenal

Everyone had a victory garden, and the Army set aside an area on the far end of the island for this express purpose. Besides the vegetables we grew, the thing that really got my attention was our watermelons. We would check the growth of one particular watermelon each day, and each day Dad would say, "Not quite ready. We'll wait one more day." This went on for days until, finally, he said the day had come. Ready or not, this was the day we were going to bring it home. I drooled in anticipation of eating that beautiful red melon. With knife in hand, we proceeded to the Victory Garden – and the melon was gone! Someone had taken it! We waited one day too long.

*I attended elementary and high school in Davenport, and must admit I was not a shining student. I spent my share of time in the principal's office but did manage to progress from one grade to another at the same rate as the rest of the students. One teacher in particular stayed in my mind over the years – Ms. Purdy. She was a feisty and fiery kind of teacher, and we locked horns on more than one occasion. But however much friction there was between us, I had a great deal of respect for her and carried that through the years. This provided me with one of the most moving events of my life:

I had always wanted to go back and visit Davenport and Rock Island Arsenal. I guess every adult that has been displaced would like to go back and visit his childhood memories. Twenty four years after we left Rock Island Arsenal, I was a Major in the Air Force and had the opportunity to fly into Moline, Illinois, just across the river from Davenport, and do just that. As I toured Davenport, I decided to see what had happened to Ms. Purdy. She was old through my eyes when I was a student of hers, although, looking back, she was probably only in her mid-to-late forties. I was curious to see if she was still alive, having certainly retired years ago.

When I went to the principal's office at J.B. Young Elementary School, I inquired about Ms. Purdy, expecting the answer to be that she retired or died years ago. I was startled when the response was, "Oh, she's in Room 18 and will be breaking for lunch in about five minutes, if you want to see her." I couldn't believe my ears. I waited until all the students had left the room for lunch and then, with Ms. Purdy sitting at her desk, I stood in the doorway. I was startled when she looked up and said, "Why, Jimmy Reed!"

She had not laid eyes on me in 24 years, yet she called out my name. That was truly an emotional moment for me.

We sat there through the lunch hour catching up on each other's lives, and I recounted my years after Davenport and the things I had done as a pilot in the Air Force. I then told her something that I had always wanted to say and now had the opportunity. I told her that the lessons she had drummed into me those many years ago had taken me around the world. She started to cry. I had the feeling that I may have been the first one who had ever come back as an adult to thank her and show her the results of the many years of dedication she had given. I wish every adult could have felt what I felt sitting there in that school over the lunch hour with Ms. Purdy that day. It was a moving experience for both of us.

I have a lot of good memories from Rock Island Arsenal and Davenport. In particular, that's where I took my first airplane ride. After the war, an Army pilot tried to start a business giving rides in a J-3 Piper Cub on floats on the Mississippi River. He charged $5 a piece for a 30-minute ride. My mother, knowing how much I wanted to fly, came up with the money, and I went for a ride with Ritchie Martyn, my very closest friend from Red Hook, who was visiting. The feeling of being in the air was amazing. I knew just as soon as we were airborne and had the sensation of flight that there was no other future for me except flying. We flew by Rock Island Arsenal and, when I held my hand out to wave at Dad, the air stream took my arm back and banged it hard against the airplane.

My first lesson in aerodynamics.

We read in the paper three days after our airplane ride that the piper cub flipped upside down on the river when landing. No one was hurt, but the airplane was lost.

Other memories from that time are:

Sneaking in under the tent flap to see Sally Rand perform in a carnival down on the levee next to the river in Davenport.

Summers on the Cameron's farm, and the bus driver in town not letting me on the bus because I smelled so bad after picking onions all day. Mom had to come and pick me up.

The pusher tugs going up and down the Mississippi River shining their bright spotlights in my bedroom window at all hours of the night.

The cars that fell through the ice trying to drive across the frozen river each winter, generally because people were stupid, and generally they all died.

The squirrels that were everywhere, and the one that crawled up our kitchen screen door each morning to get something to eat.

Playing golf and caddying on the wonderful Rock Island Arsenal Golf Course. We lived on the second hole and I played the inside nine every night before supper.

Playing hot games of Ping-Pong in that French dungeon of a basement with Dad for hours.

The huge catfish that Walt Orthner caught that filled up the bathtub.

Talking the Island Police into delivering the papers on my paper route to the two quarters on the far end of the island so I wouldn't have to ride my bike all the way down there.

The bitterly cold winters.

*During the war I went to a lot of war movies that had airplanes in them. It really bothered me when a German or Jap would get on the tail of one of our pilots and he didn't see them. Then, with everybody shouting on the radio, the pilot would twist and turn to try and see behind him. One day, at about age ten or eleven, and with my Mom's help, I wrote a letter to the War Department in Washington, D.C., telling them that our planes should have rear view mirrors so our pilots could see behind them. I was totally surprised when I got a very official letter back thanking me for my suggestion with the comment that they would look into it. Not too long after that, I started seeing rear view mirrors on the planes in the movies. Aaawww ... You don't suppose ... No. It couldn't be. But in later years, every time I got in a fighter that had rear view mirrors, I thought about that letter.

I had already made up my mind that I would be a pilot. but the old war movies reinforced that notion because it didn't take me long to realize that the Army ground pounders spent a lot of nights sleeping in muddy foxholes eating cold rations, and the pilots always came home to clean sheets and a good meal. After growing up in Red Hook, being a pilot made a lot of sense.

Dad was assigned to Rock Island Arsenal through and past the end of WWII and, in 1949, Lieutenant Colonel Reed was given the job of cleaning up the mess left by the war on Okinawa with the promise that, if he did a good job, his next assignment would be an accompanied tour in Japan. An accompanied tour meant that you could take your family. Mom, my brother and I went back to Brooklyn, only this time we didn't have to stay with relatives. We had our own apartment right across the street from Prospect Park while we waited for Dad.

He must have done a good job because, later in 1949, Mom, my little brother and I boarded a train for Fort Mason in San Francisco. After several days of processing, we sailed from San Francisco to Japan on the troop ship General William O. Darby.

We lived in the Merguro district in Tokyo, and Dad worked in the Dai Ichi Building, on General MacArthur's staff. I would often pick him up after work and frequently saw the great and well-loved General as he left the office after work. There was always a Japanese group of well-wishers to greet him as he left for home. Japan was still an occupied country in those years, and the Allied military people received special treatment. As an example, the Japanese trains had special cars for military which were free. Japan was a much different country from today.

The Japanese had a very difficult time after the war. Granted, it probably was not as difficult as it would have been for us had we lost the war, but they suffered from every kind of shortage. There literally was no fuel for the taxicabs, busses and trucks. They solved this dilemma in an ingenious way.

Almost every car, bus and truck had a stove on the back bumper with a stack of wood or charcoal stored next to it. When the wood or charcoal was burned in the stove, the fumes, which are combustible, were captured, vented under pressure and fed directly to the carburetor. Many times, while riding a bus, we'd stop and the driver would go back and stoke the stove before we could get moving again.

Dad was promoted to Colonel and became Chief of Ordnance in Yokohama, a very important job. He was responsible in part for ensuring the timely supply of equipment to Korea, which had blossomed into a major military conflict. An interesting story developed out of that job.

When it became obvious that we were going to have a war in Korea, the Army went to the big three automobile manufacturers in the United States to get contracts for jeeps, weapons carriers and 6x6 trucks, which were urgently needed to support that conflict. Ford, General Motors and Chrysler, having just retooled and gone back into full production for the civilian automobile market after the Second World War, refused the military contracts, as they saw Korea as a short-term conflict. The Army had a serious dilemma. Where would the vehicles to support the troops in Korea come from?

With typical American ingenuity, someone came up with the idea of going through the Pacific Islands, loading all of the derelict jeeps, Weapons Carriers and 6x6's left after the war in the jungles and beaches onto tugs and barges and shipping them to Japan for rebuild. And that's what they did!

They set up an assembly line, just like you'd find in a General Motors plant in the United States, at an abandoned sea plane base at Oppama, located between Yokohama and Yokosuka. I watched barges loaded with rusty trucks and jeeps come to Oppama, get offloaded and be submerged into a huge vat of acid. They were then taken apart, piece by piece. Each part was rebuilt or thrown away, depending on its condition. Parts that were to be rebuilt were sent to individual shops located all over the area and overhauled bit by bit.

The assembly line at Oppama was turning out brand new jeeps and trucks from those old derelicts at an astounding rate. The scope of the project was huge. There was a separate assembly line for each type of vehicle. As the vehicles came off the line, they went through an inspection and testing period and then were stored until shipped to the race track on the bluffs overlooking Yokohama. Our teen club was located in the same vicinity, and I used to watch the vehicles being placed on the back end of the line as they came out of Oppama. As shipping was available, they would be taken off the front end of the line. The line of vehicles was six across, and normally ran around the entire one-mile length of the race track. Although the project was accomplished under American supervision, the entire workforce was Japanese.

To this day, I'm convinced that the learning experience gained on the assembly lines at Oppama is where the momentum began for the Japanese automobile industry as we know it today.

We almost lost Dad during one of his trips to Korea. He was in a camp on a hilltop when the enemy made an assault and overran the camp. Helicopters airlifted the personnel, and Dad was one of the last out, escaping just before the enemy reached the camp.

*Our Mother died suddenly in 1950, at age 36, in the military hospital in Yokohama. Dad, faced with having two young children to raise, married a wonderful woman who had been working in a government service position there. How fortunate for us that they found each other. My brother and I were taken to her heart as if we were her own children, and that feeling has remained. She brought something special to our lives, and it was a pleasure to watch her and Dad grow together through the years. When Dad's heart started to bother him, we returned to the United States in 1952 and he retired from the Army. Together, they raised my brother.

*In California, as young kids will, I became homesick for Japan and all my friends. At 19 years old, I decided to join the Merchant Marine, with the sole intent of getting back to Japan and jumping ship. I hadn't quite thought about what would happen after that. After going through the Sailors' Union of the Pacific School on Harrison Street, in San Francisco, I got my Coast Guard "Z" card as an Ordinary Seaman and Wiper.

Unfortunately, the West Coast went on strike during that time in 1952 and, with the exception of MSTS (Military Sea and Transportation Service), not a ship was sailing. The strike caused me to abandon my plan to jump ship in Japan and I managed to get on an MSTS ship that was sailing from San Francisco and scheduled to rendezvous with a convoy that resupplied Greenland once a year. I shipped as a wiper, not a very glamorous title, but lots of fun. On this ship, the USNS Chestatee, a combination tanker/cargo ship, the power plants were diesel electric, so I was more of an engine room helper than a wiper.

Because I had just come from Japan, where I had turned 19, I had not yet registered for the draft. I checked in with them shortly after I got back to the United States and they advised me I would have 90 days to sign up in one of the services or be drafted into the Army. I immediately went down and talked to the Air Force. They said that there was a waiting period of 90 days, so I signed an obligation letter that got the draft board satisfied and went ahead and sailed on the Chestatee.

That was a wonderful three months. As it turned out, our condenser broke down and, in the delay to get it fixed, we missed the convoy to Greenland. We were reassigned to service ports on the East Coast, and that also included trips to the Azores and Bermuda. I had spent most of what I had on warm clothes in anticipation of the cold weather in Greenland, so had little left when we started servicing the East Coast.

Most of the sailors aboard the ship were men who had been around for awhile. I was the youngest. There was one other young man, slightly older than I, and we became good friends during that voyage. He had only one leg, having lost the other standing too close to the anchor chain when the anchor let go. As the anchor snaked the chain out, it caught him and tried to take him out the hawse pipe. He stopped, but his leg didn't. After he healed, he got around OK and continued to ship out with a wooden leg.

The only real trouble I got into on the ship in those three months was as a result of starting my jet engine while we were at sea. I had brought along my Dyna Jet, a model airplane jet engine which was a true pulse jet. It developed 4-1/2 pounds of thrust at 400 cycles a second and, when it lit off, sounded like an F-100 in afterburner. When we were about halfway across the Atlantic, en route to the Azores, I made the mistake of starting the engine on the upper deck without alerting anyone that I was going to do it. To compound the error, I unintentionally started it right next to the large intake that blows fresh air into the engine room. Within seconds after the pulse jet fired up, I had cleaned out the engine room. Every man was on deck with eyes as big as silver dollars.

The Captain and I had a little chat. Actually, he talked and I listened.

Chapter 2

1952 - 1955

Aviation Cadets

One ship drives East and another West
with the self same winds that blow
Tis the set of the sails and not the gales
which decides the way to go.

Like the winds of the sea are the ways of fate
as we wander along through life
Tis the set of the soul
that decides the goal
and not the calm or strife

Ella Wheeler Wilcox

*I had been notified by the Air Force that my reporting date was 2nd December, 1952, so, on that date, I went to the recruiting office just off Market Street in San Francisco and signed up. From there it was a bus to Parks AB near Livermore, California, for three months of Airman Basic Training.

When my group of about eight enlistees arrived, we were all given the routine boot camp haircuts and issued our first military clothing, which included a pair of brogans (boots). The Air Force had only become an independent service a few years before (1947) and they were still issuing Army brown brogans that we had to dye black to conform to the Air Force uniform. I was assigned to a standard open bay barracks on the east side of Parks. We had a pretty good group of men, really boys, in my squad, which included a VERY large fellow who had come from a farm way back up in the Ozarks somewhere. He had to be 6′ 4″ and built like a gorilla. His legs and arms were like tree stumps.

It became obvious right away that he, in addition to not being used to the social atmosphere of a lot of people, was a bit slow. Not necessarily retarded, just slow. He tried very hard to become part of the group but it wasn't long before the city guys realized that they could get away with making fun of him without reprisal. They would tell a joke, with him the butt of it, and, when everybody laughed, he would give his "huh, huh, huh" laugh, not realizing they were making fun of him.

I felt sorry for him, until one day he caught on! I was laying in my top bunk when there was a guttural growl at the entrance to the open bay. I looked up and saw this guy from the Ozarks. He filled up the double door, and the look on his face told me that he finally realized what was going on. And **HE WAS MAD!** He cleaned out that bay. Guys were going out the windows and scrambling to stay out of his way. I watched him pick up a double bunk with two men in it and turn it over. Soon, an army of Air Police showed up and took him away. We never saw him again.

That was one of my first lessons in social injustice.

The Korean War was still going hot and heavy and the Air Force was in need of pilots. That meant the Aviation Cadet program was still alive. We were notified that testing would take place at Parks, and I signed up for the testing program.

Since I was about ten years old I had wanted to be a pilot, and joining the Air Force was the way I had intended to make that dream happen. In a way, I guess, I was very fortunate. One of the toughest things in life is knowing what you want to do with your life so that you can develop a plan. So many of the kids today can't figure out what they want to do and, therefore, can't get started with anything. I have always adopted the philosophy that we were taught in flying school when everything was falling apart – Do something, even if it's wrong. So many guys, when they got overwhelmed with a situation, would just sit and ride the airplane to the ground. If you do something – even if it's wrong – the brain gets in gear and starts thinking again. Life is the same way.

When testing for the Aviation Cadet program finally took place, I was pumped. Here was a chance to fulfill my dream. The testing program actually took several days of intense work. There were physical tests, mental tests, interviews, etc. When it was over, there were two days of waiting, and then we were all brought to a room in the testing complex. Over thirty men had applied and been accepted into the testing program and they were all here to get the results.

A short Major got up, read off about fifteen or so names, then told them to report to room 'A'. I was crushed. My name wasn't called. Then he read off about nine more names and told them to report to room 'B'. God! My name wasn't even in the second group, so I knew I had failed.

After all the men from the second group had left the room, he turned to those left in the room and said, "Congratulations. You men have been selected for pilot training." I went into shock! The first group did not make the cut at all. The second group had been selected for navigator training, and, of course, the third group was the pilot group.

Not too long ago, I went back to that building on Parks. It's in a sad state now, as it's abandoned. The windows are broken out, the siding is coming off, and it'll probably be torn down in the near future. But looking back at the chain of events that took place in my life as a result of what happened that day in that building, tears welled up in my eyes.

After that, things were different for me at Parks. I was moved out of the squad to a different barracks. Still open bay, but not quite so barren. The new Aviation Cadets (the official title was actually Pre-Cadets) were given shoulder boards and an officer's emblem to wear on our hats. That was nice, but where were the airplanes? It was explained that because of a backup in entry dates, there would be a waiting period of about three months before we actually entered pilot training.

I was in a group of six Pre-Cadets who were shipped to Vance AFB in Enid, Oklahoma, to wait out our entry into training.

Vance was an Air Training Command, Basic and Advanced crew training base for the B-25 and B-26. The six Pre-Cadets waiting to get into pilot training had no real mission on the base, so they stuck us where we wouldn't get into trouble. They put a couple of us in the Link Trainer Section, and that was fun. The Link Trainers at that time were the stubby little blue and yellow airplanes that rotated on a pedestal and simulated instrument flying. The time I spent there actually became very valuable later on.

Because we were surplus to the base mission, our time was not controlled too tightly and I found out that anytime I wanted to, I could go hitch a ride on an airplane. As a matter of fact, it was encouraged. I flew every chance I got. The first ride in an Air Force plane was from Enid to Biloxi, Mississippi, in the right seat of an old C-45. I was thrilled. But that paled in comparison with riding in the B-25 or B-26. Riding in a B-25 and B-26 was the slickest thing that ever happened to me. These were hot planes! Watching the Instructors go over the training schedules with students primed me for what was to come in my own training in the not-too-distant future.

North American B-25

There were a lot of airplane rides in those three months at Enid. Two really stick in my mind. One was a night flight in a B-25 during which we wound up circling over Oklahoma City. World War II had only been over for about eight years, and advertising with searchlights had become a fad. Not with the kind of small searchlights that they use today to advertise a mall opening or new movie. These were surplus military searchlights, and they were strong and bright. As we flew over Oklahoma City that night, there must have been ten or twelve searchlights that homed in on our B-25, and I got the feeling of what it must have been like in a bombing raid over Germany at night.

One other flight out of Enid that sticks in my memory was a marvelous B-26 flight. I was in the nose of a glass-nosed B-26, and the pilots were buzzing. At 50′ above the ground the rush was exhilarating. What I didn't know was that we were approaching the Grand Canyon. It caught me unawares. When we went over that cliff, I had the feeling that I had actually fallen out of the airplane and was dropping into the canyon.

*The day finally came, and I entered the United States Air Force Pilot Training program, Class 55-D. The first three months were spent at Lackland Air Force Base going through an intense Officer Training program. The Air Force felt that we were officers first and pilots second, so before they were going to trust us with their airplanes and with the authority that comes with rank, we had to be trained and prove ourselves worthy. Looking back, the Air Force was pretty smart.

Real dedication to get through the program was displayed by a fellow classmate. Although he had made it through all of the physicals so far (and there were many), during one physical at Lackland, the Medical Technician determined that he was shorter than the minimum height requirements for Pilot Training. Although the height was a very small amount below the minimum level necessary, the technician wouldn't budge, and so flunked him on height. He was crushed, but managed to talk the technician into letting him retake the height test several days later.

During that period we did everything we could to stretch him. He hung by his arms for long periods of time and used weights to stretch him in bed. When the day came for the retest he was carried to the clinic on a stretcher so that he wouldn't lose the height he gained by walking there.

But it was to no avail. Although he had gained somewhat, he didn't quite meet the height requirement and, again, the technician wouldn't budge. In a last desperate attempt he asked the technician to wait 30 minutes and give him one more chance. The technician agreed and he went outside and got another cadet to whack him smartly over the head with a 2x4 in an attempt to raise a bump that would make him tall enough. The blow brought him to his knees. Whether the bump made him tall enough or the technician finally realized the extent of this cadet's desire to fly, the technician passed him and he remained in the Pilot Training program.

For those who got through Lackland, the next step was Primary Flying School at a civilian contract base. At that time, initial flying training in the Air Force was accomplished through civilian contract schools. Mine was Southern Airways, at Bainbridge, Georgia.

Somewhere along the way, someone told me that when I got to Bainbridge, I should volunteer for the Drum and Bugle Corps. The reason was that the Drum and Bugle Corps got off base frequently <u>and</u> they didn't have to do K.P. That sounded good to me, even though I had never played an instrument in my life. When I got to Bainbridge and they asked for volunteers for the Drum and Bugle Corps. I held up my hand. "What instrument do you play?" I was asked. Although I had never played the drum, I replied, "Why, the drum, of course." I thought, "How hard can it be to beat cadence on a drum?"

Before the tryouts, I got one of the guys to show me how to hold the drumsticks and got a few lessons in beating cadence. I caught on pretty quickly and, before I knew it, I was beating a drum in the Drum and Bugle Corps. The tip was right. We did get off base and travel more than the other Cadets, and there was no K.P.

At a class graduation there was always a parade but, for some reason, to this day I don't know why this one was different. There was a flyover, lots of VIPs in the reviewing stand, and I vowed to myself to do a really good job.

When the command "Troop the Line" was given, we started playing the music. I was right behind the bass drummer, a big fellow carrying a big bass drum. Hundreds of men were marching in time to his beat. He set the cadence. When he beat his drum, every left foot hit the ground. It was so impressive I was caught up in the moment as we approached the reviewing stand. All of the uniformed VIPs were standing at attention with a hand salute, and the civilians were standing erect, with their hands over their hearts. The music was playing. It was a sight, and I was a part of it.

Suddenly, just in front of me, as the bass drummer drew his hand back for another mighty boom, the end flew off his beater and he was left with just a stick. Panic set in. I looked about and hundreds of feet were losing the cadence. Heads started bobbing up and down and disaster was imminent. Whether this had happened before or he acted from instinct I don't know, but after just a momentary few missed beats, he pretended to hit the drum with his stick and boomed the drum with his hand on the other side. Actually, that's hard to do, march with both hands banging a drum at the same time. Anyway, he saved the day and, from then on, I'll bet he carried a spare boomer. I suspect he did pretty well in an airplane if he could think that quickly and didn't panic when things fell apart. Later, I found out that's one of the attributes of a good pilot, being able to think clearly in difficult situations. So often, I've heard people make the comment after a pilot made a good landing, "My, what a great pilot he is." and thought, "There's more to a good pilot than a grease job."

*Bill Keeler was a good friend, and just as aggressive as I was in his flying. Unbeknownst to anyone else, we would meet over a predetermined point and try different things we had seen in the movies. We attempted to dogfight, fly formation and other unauthorized maneuvers in those T-6s. I got to the point that I felt there wasn't anything I couldn't do in the T-6.

We had just seen an Aerial Demonstration Team at a class graduation and we decided to emulate them by doing a loop in formation (we were just learning to do a loop and had no training in formation). We didn't realize that, in formation flying, one aircraft leads and the others follow. We just thought you got alongside each other and flew along. As we went over the top, each of us concentrated on the loop and forgot about the formation. Torque took over, one of us corrected more than the other, and we swapped sides going over the top, inverted, without knowing it.

North American T-6

Coming down the backside of the loop, Bill was on my right instead of on the left. It must have looked impressive from the ground. That did teach us that we didn't know as much as we thought we did and we became a little more cautious.

*One of the most important lessons I learned at Bainbridge had nothing to do with flying. I learned to make my own decisions about the personality of people and not make decisions based on gossip or innuendo. Let me explain.

As training at Bainbridge was nearing its end and all of the other hurdles had been passed, the dreaded final check ride was coming up. This check ride culminated all of the time spent in training so far. If

I passed, I'd go on to the next step in the Pilot Training program, Basic Training, and fulfill the dream. If I flunked ... Well, that would be the beginning of the end. Once you flunk a check ride, it's merely a matter of time before you're washed out.

But I wasn't worried. I got along just fine with airplanes. The T-6 had few secrets from me. I had learned most of her secrets and she had learned a few of mine. During these past months, I had groped through the demanding academic maze, experienced the initial awe of flight and had the thrill of my first solo flight. It didn't matter to me that this check ride decided whether or not I went on to the next level of training and experience the ultimate thrill that a young cadet works so hard for – the coveted Silver Wings and 2nd Lieutenant's Commission in the United States Air Force. I was ready.

While some people had to really work at learning to fly, it seemed to come naturally to me. I guess it's like learning to play a violin. Someone who's pushed into learning the violin, for whatever reason, has a harder time reaching the same level as someone who has a natural talent and plays because he loves it. That's the way it was with me. Academic Training and I were not necessarily good friends, but when I got into an airplane, things just seemed to happen naturally.

But this day was different. This was the final check ride from a civilian Check Pilot. It made no difference to me that Lady Luck had dealt me the toughest Check Pilot of the bunch, Mr. Gambrell, who, <u>rumor</u> had it, took pride in the fact that he had more washouts than any other Check Pilot at Bainbridge. People started coming to me with sympathy. "Too bad, Jim. Mr. Gambrell is the toughest check pilot here. He will flunk a check ride for the smallest of infractions."

On the day of the final check ride, the sky was bright and clear. At the Pre-Flight Briefing, Mr. Gambrell didn't say much. The walk to the T-6 was in silence. During the aircraft Pre-Flight, he said nothing. He got into the back seat and I got into the front. Engine start, taxi out and takeoff went well. The first words he uttered after takeoff were, "Take me to the southeast corner of the acrobatic area at 6,000 feet. I'll tell you what to do after that." Simple enough. But he wasn't going to give me any hints as to what was coming next.

When we arrived at the designated spot, he said, "Give me an 'A' Pattern." An 'A' pattern was a series of climbs, descents and turns, while at the same time maintaining or changing airspeeds as the pattern dictated. Although it looked simple on paper, it was a real test of coordinating and balancing the different control inputs of an airplane. When we finished, he said, "Give me a 'B' pattern." A 'B' pattern was basically the same type of pattern with a different combination of climbs, descents, turns and changes in airspeed and power settings. It seemed to me that I hit everything on the money. After the 'B' pattern he said, "Give me a loop." And I gave him what felt like a perfect loop. The airspeed was right on as I pulled up, releasing a slight back pressure as we were upside down going over the top. The wings were perfectly level with the horizon as we came through and the airspeed was right on when the loop was completed. I felt great. "Give me a barrel roll." And so it went for the next hour and a half. "Give me an Immelmann ... Give me an aileron roll ... Give me a split S." Normally, this was when the palms would get sweaty, the breathing would get quicker and the heart would start pounding. There was so much at stake, and the demands of a Flight Check were physiologically against the human grain. Someone watches every complex maneuver that you do and then decides whether or not you did it correctly. But I was calm and composed.

Finally, the words that I had been waiting for. "Take me home." I knew I had passed. There was no way I could flunk this check ride. It felt like a perfect ride.

As I started back toward Bainbridge, descending to enter the landing pattern, I was resolved to top this ride off with a smooth landing. There was nothing but silence from the back – no words of congratulations or encouragement. But that's OK. I'll be flying jets and he'll still be stuck in this T-6. When I entered the pattern for landing, I was euphoric. As I turned base leg and prepared to turn final, I caught myself whistling. Everything looked good. Landing clearance received from the tower. As I approached the runway threshold though, something didn't feel quite right. The airspeed wasn't bleeding off quite like it's supposed to and ... "OH MY GOD. I FORGOT THE LANDING GEAR!" Too late to get it down. Have to go around. Check prop and mixture - full increase - throttle full - gear up. Hell, it's already up. Call the tower and tell them you're going around. Get climb speed. I could see my future dissolve in a flash. Forgetting the landing gear on a check ride was an automatic flunk.

I waited for the berating and string of comments that I knew would come from the back seat. In those days, instructors cussed out cadets as a matter of course. But there was only silence from the back seat. "He'll wait until I get on downwind and then start," I thought. But on downwind, only silence. After the landing then, when I'm taxiing in. Only silence all the way to the parking area. Well, then, after we get out of the airplane. As I shut the T-6 down, Mr. Gambrell got out without a word and, with his chute slung over his back, he started to walk across the ramp. I hurried to catch up and we walked silently across the ramp towards the operations shack.

Finally, I couldn't stand it any longer. If he wasn't going to talk, then I would. "I guess I screwed that up," I blurted out. Mr. Gambrell stopped, turned to me and said words that have stuck with me ever since that day. "Jim, you gave me an almost perfect ride today, right up until you forgot the landing gear. But, you know what? I learned more about what kind of a pilot you were in that minute-and-a-half when everything was going wrong than in that hour-and-a-half when everything was going right. Anyone can do well when things are going right. The true test of a man's ability is how he performs when everything is going wrong. You found the problem yourself – I didn't have to tell you about the landing gear – and you took the proper corrective action. No, I'm not going to flunk you. You've passed." And that's how I got to be a jet pilot.

I've never forgotten Mr. Gambrell's words, and have tried to use that guidance in my life. This incident taught me to make my own decisions about people and not use gossip or innuendo as the basis for determining someone's ability or personality.

And I've never forgotten the landing gear again, either.

*All through Primary flying school at Bainbridge we didn't lose an airplane. Oh, there were a few T-6s that ground looped and wound up on their nose. And when a couple of guys got lost on the night cross-country, we had some anxious moments. But no blood was spilled. Nobody in our class at Bainbridge got hurt.

There was a story about two cadets from another base and another class who drove over a tall bridge that spanned the Chatahoochee River one weekend and decided to fly under the bridge the next chance they got. The next chance happened to be on Wednesday. What they didn't know was that on Monday construction crews hung cable under the bridge for an upcoming construction project. When the second cadet saw the first one hit the wires, he was able to pull up in time and only one life was lost.

The next step in the Pilot Training process was T-28 and T-33 training at Webb AFB, Big Springs, Texas.

North American T-28s in echelon right formation

Because Class 55-D had not yet come face-to-face with a serious accident, I guess we became a little complacent. I can recall the sick, nauseous feeling that night at Webb AFB when two T-28s had a mid-air when they went belly to belly entering the initial approach to the pattern. Both instructor pilots and both students from the class ahead of ours were lost in that one. Maybe it was because things were getting a bit more complex as we progressed along in training. The birds were getting hotter and the flying was getting tougher. That brought the realization home to all of us that we weren't playing a game anymore.

My first serious brush with extinction came when we were scheduled for a three-ship T-28 day formation flight. The instructor would be with a student in the lead bird, and I and another student would each be solo in our own birds. I was designated #2 and the other solo student, who had been having a difficult time with formation, was #3. During engine start and taxi out, #3 had a minor problem and returned to the ramp. The instructor advised me that we would go ahead and depart as a two-ship formation and orbit to wait for #3.

Takeoff and climb was normal, and we circled in formation for 10 or 15 minutes waiting for #3. When he finally showed up, he began his approach to the formation to join on my right wing while we were still orbiting. As he joined up, my eyes were away from the approaching T-28 and locked firmly on the lead.

The cardinal rule when joining a formation is that if your closure rate is too fast, never, **never** throw up a wing to slow your closure rate, although it is a normal human tendency to do just that. The procedure is to drop down and slide under the formation and go back and try it again.

If you throw up the wing to stop the closure rate, you lose sight of the formation and then have no idea where they are. And that's just what #3 did. Thank goodness the instructor was watching him. As he approached the formation wing up at a high speed, the instructor yelled, "**SPLIT!**" He went up, I went down and #3 went through the formation right where we had been. That was my first wake-up call!

Once we got into T-33s, we were semi-accomplished formation pilots, or at least we thought so. Andy Clark, himself a 2nd Lieutenant not too long out of flying school, was our instructor. He was a pleasant fellow, a good pilot, and I felt lucky having him as my instructor in 'T-Birds'. He did have one idiosyncrasy, however.

When returning to Webb after a formation flight, he loved to put the formation in echelon right, role inverted and drop the speed brakes upside down. The T-Bird had a natural tendency to pitch up when the speed brakes were dropped and, if you were in formation, you had to anticipate the pitch up or you'd have serious problems.

Once, when I was #4, flying on the wing of #3, we were echelon right, had rolled upside down and dropped the speed brakes. Number three pitched up (because we were upside down he actually pitched down) and out when his speed brakes extended and tried to regain position in the formation coming down right on top of me. His speed brakes were inches from my canopy and so close I could read the writing on the hydraulic lines in the speed brake well. I pushed the stick forward and fell out of the formation, narrowly avoiding a mid-air.

A few minutes after something like that happens, the strength drains out of you and I suppose you go into some mild state of shock. Andy Clark got us all back together and, with rubbery knees, I got back into formation and we landed at Webb.

After I was back into the parking area and had shut down the engine, I tried to unbuckle the seat belt and get out of the airplane, but the latch wouldn't move. After several minutes of struggling, I called a mechanic over to give me a hand. He then struggled unsuccessfully for several minutes before he gave up and went to get his tools. The little ball that holds the latch in place had somehow jammed and the mount bolts that hold the seat belt to the seat had to be disconnected by the mechanic before the belt could be removed. Because we sit on the parachute, had I ejected as a result of collision with #3, I could never have gotten out of the seat, the chute would not have deployed and I would have ridden the seat all the way to the ground. That's when I got nauseous!

Lockheed T-33 – The "T" Bird

*When it came time for my night solo checkout in the T-33, my regular instructor, Andy Clark, was not available, and I had a substitute Instructor Pilot, Lieutenant Fox, a hotshot who had just come back from flying F-84s in Korea. So it was a thrill when, on my first night flight in the T-Bird during the local area orientation, he broke from the staid and standard training schedule with the question, "Hey, Cadet Reed, have you ever seen a Chinese Immelman?" I had never even heard of a Chinese Immelman and replied in the negative. So, as the tip tanks ran out of fuel, we never did acrobatics with fuel in the tips and, with me wondering what was coming, he started his dive to build up the speed to 450 knots.

Here I must explain that the T-Bird was not like the jets of today. Today, the fighters can start from a cruise speed and use power to go over the top. In the T-Bird, you had to accelerate (dive) to achieve about 450 knots then pull a steady four Gs to insure that you could make over the top before you ran out of airspeed.

Anyway, the hotshot pulled the four Gs but, instead of going over the top, he stopped while going straight up, rolled the bird 180 degrees and continued to pull it over on its back, rolling out at a very low airspeed. A normal Immelman is designed to get the maximum altitude with you winding up in the opposite direction from where you started. A Chinese Immelman achieves the maximum altitude ending up in the same direction in which you started.

I was impressed not only at the maneuver and the skill, but also that he was able to pull the airplane over the top at such a low airspeed. We then headed back to the field and I successfully completed the three compensatory night landings prior to release for solo.

Normal Immelmann

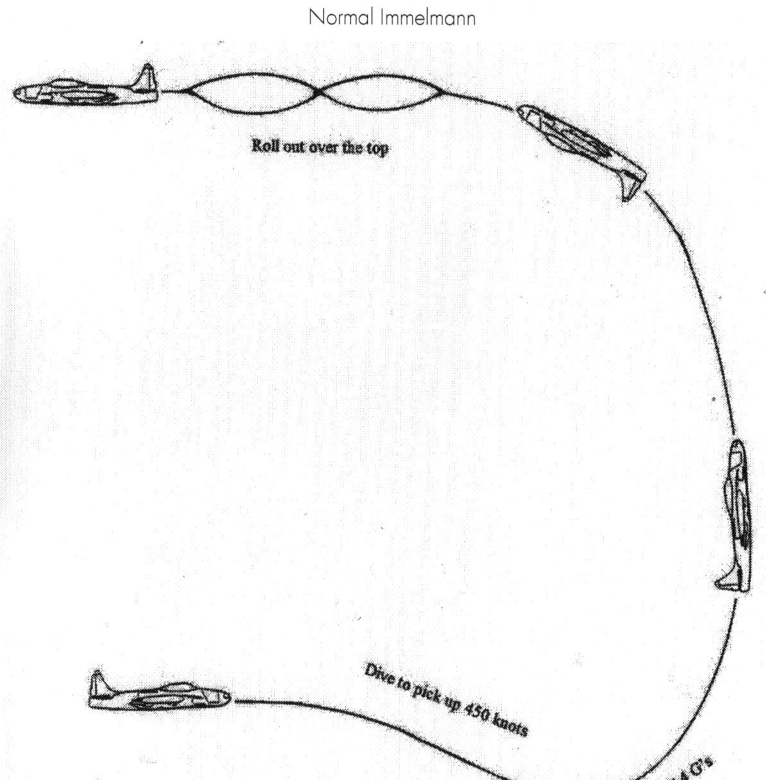

Of course, during my night solo, the first thing I did when the tips ran dry was to try a Chinese Immelman. I started the dive, got the 450 knots and pulled the four Gs. The problem was that, during acrobatics, I was used to a horizon. Out there, at night in West Texas, there was no horizon. The few lights on the ground in the mid '50s looked just like the stars in the sky and, as a result, instead of stopping straight up, I wound up overshooting straight up and had to pull the bird a much greater arc to get on my back.

As I tried (upside down) to pull the nose back to where I thought the horizon was and stop the airspeed from decaying, I ran out of airspeed before I got there. The first thing to happen was that the airplane started shuddering, then snapped violently three times. I don't know if I passed out from shock, fear or from hitting my head on the side of the canopy, but the last thing I remember was that I was in a flat inverted spin with a large city way over on the horizon (probably Ft. Worth/Dallas) going round and round and the sound of the engine spooling up as I advanced the throttle.

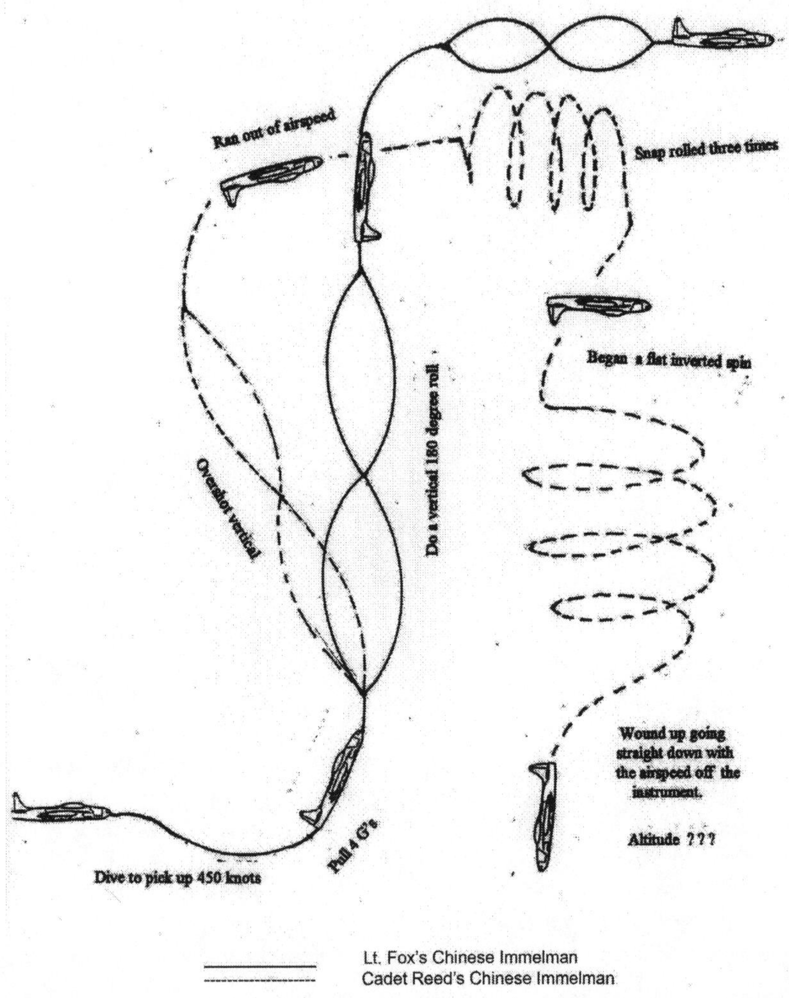

When I woke up, I was going straight down at full throttle with the airspeed off the instrument and not knowing how high I was. Things were happening so fast, the instruments were a blur. I pulled back hard on the stick until the nose came up and I started climbing again. With things back under control I flew in a straight line with wings level for a long time. To this day I don't know at what altitude I pulled out or how close to the ground I came. It could have been fifty feet or five hundred feet or five thousand feet. I just don't know. If I could have seen my face in a mirror, I'm sure it would have been pure white. It was difficult to bank the airplane to turn back to the base.

I didn't say a word to anyone, as night acrobatics were illegal.

*When Class 55-D graduated from Webb AFB at Big Spring, Texas, our new assignments were posted on the board. I was disappointed to get assigned to F-86Ds at Perrin AFB, Texas. The F-86D was an all weather interceptor and I wanted an air- to-air fighter assignment. Actually, I should have felt lucky. A lot of the new graduates got assigned to B-52s and spent their entire career standing alert in the Strategic Air Command (SAC). Once you got into B-52s, it was almost impossible to get out.

A number of the new graduates had to wait several days before their assignments came in and, when they did, one of the guys got an F-86 day fighter assignment in Europe, the assignment that I wanted. He wasn't particularly hot on day fighters, and even less enthused about going to Europe. He was from Texas, so Perrin AFB turned him on. It wasn't too difficult to talk him into swapping assignments. Since I was going to be married five days after graduation, I called Colleen, my fiancée, and asked her if she was willing to go to Europe after we were married. She said yes.

And that's how I got to France.

Chapter 3

1955 - 1958

Toul-Rosières Air Base and Évreux Air Base, France

I'm often asked what Pilots do. I reply that some Pilots go around making little piles. They pile it here and they pile it there. The trick is to make sure that you are not the one that makes one of the little piles.

A small group of newly commissioned pilots went to Europe together. The ride across the Atlantic in the MATS C-118 was a real experience. As we passed through Ernest Harmon Air Base in Newfoundland and Keflavik, Iceland, we got our first look at what the real Air Force looked like outside the training environment. Upon arrival at Rhein Main Air Base, Germany, all of us went through a processing center and received orders and transportation instructions to our new bases.

Something happened during this process that changed the unit that I was going to be assigned to without my knowing it.

Second Lieutenant Bill (Spook) Medellin and I were told to get on a train and go to Toul-Rosières, France, to our new unit. I still thought I was going to fly the F-86. Toul-Rosières is an agricultural area in the Northeastern part of France. We arrived in Nancy, a large city close to Toul, just before midnight on January 5th, 1955. I had heard that the Wing of F-86s were being high flighted over and would arrive on January 6th. The base sent a car to the train station in Nancy to pick us up and we got to the BOQ just after midnight, in muted excitement at what I thought was the arrival of my fighter squadron the following day. The weather that night was miserable with freezing rain and intermittent snow and sleet.

The next morning, Spook and I hot-footed it over to Base Operations in anticipation of the arrival of my new squadron. What we didn't know was that the squadron was being high flighted to France OK, but their destination was Chaumont, not Toul. Someone had changed my orders when we arrived in the European Theater and I was destined to join a C-119 Squadron located at Toul. To further compound the confusion, the weather played a significant part. All of Europe was in the weeds, except a few bases in Northeastern France, but a storm was moving west, off the Alps, towards these bases. This is what happened, as it was explained to me years later by retired Colonel Paul Bell, USAF, who at that time was the leader of the third flight of F-86s.

The wing, consisting of 24 F-86 Fs, departed Prestwick, Scotland, for Chaumont, France, on the morning of January 6th, 1955, with Marseille, in Southern France, as the alternate. They departed in flights of four aircraft at about 15-minute intervals between flights. The Wing Commander was in the first flight and, upon arrival over Chaumont, was given the weather as 3,000 scattered, 8,000 broken and 15,000 overcast, with good visibility. As the first flight began their approach, it started to snow and the ceiling and visibility started going down fast.

When the second flight showed up over Chaumont, they were cleared for the approach and given the same good weather. However, by this time, the Wing Commander had gotten to the tower and passed the word that the weather was deteriorating and that they had better hustle on down.

By the time the first two aircraft of the third flight made their approach, the weather had deteriorated below minimums and the lead and his wingman barely made it in, holding about 10 degrees heading correction to stay on final approach to compensate for the strong crosswinds that had begun to blow. The second element of the third flight made a missed approach and were diverted to Toul. On the approach to Toul, the weather there was going down fast, with snow falling at the rate of two to four inches an hour. The lead of the second element got to minimums and went around, but the wingman saw the field, made a tight 360 at about 200 feet and made it in.

Lead, being just about out of fuel, took it up and ejected in that blizzard. For the rest of the aircraft that were en route and committed to land somewhere in Europe, it was pure panic. They scattered. Some went ahead and diverted to Marseille and some landed in Germany. Some were not far along in the flight and were able to return to Prestwick.

There was a hell of a party in the Toul Club that night to celebrate the successful recovery of the pilot who ejected and the one who landed.

The next morning, Spook and I, still thinking that I was going to join the F-86 Squadron now going to Chaumont, went to the Wing Adjutant, Captain Lloyd Deets, to ask for transfer orders. He said that Spook and I were permanent members of the C-119 unit there and no transfer orders would be issued. Spook knew all along that he was being assigned to a C-119 unit, but I did not.

I explained that, when we graduated from Webb AFB, I was told that if I signed for an extra year in the Air Force beyond the original four year commitment, the Air Force would guarantee that I would attend an advanced flying school, i.e. F-86s in Europe. Spook and I had both signed the extra year commitment to ensure that we would be sent to an advanced flight school. Deets explained that the wing had received a message just that morning designating the C-119 outfit there as an advanced flying school and, by us checking out in the C-119, the Air Force had met their commitment.

And that is how Spook and I got into the C-119 in France.

Fairchild C-119
This photograph was taken with the formation west of Évreux, between Évreux and the Normandy Coast, while preparing for a night three-ship formation training flight.

Actually, although at the time the disappointment of not flying the F-86 was devastating, looking back on it, flying the C-119 all over Europe was the best thing that could have happened. We got to see a lot of the world we wouldn't have seen in the F-86 and had a truly challenging flying experience.

*A few days before Spook and I got to Toul, the Wing lost a C-119 on the island of Corsica in a scenario that speaks of the primary elements that can contribute to a serious accident: Crew Coordination and Communication.

It seems that one of the birds was inbound to Rome, Italy, from France, to remain overnight (RON) there and proceed on a long leg the next day. The crew was calibrating their fuel gauges by letting the fuel run down until they were almost out of fuel in that tank. They did this by watching the fuel gauges very closely and, as the fuel approached zero on the gauge, they waited until they got a fluctuation in fuel pressure, indicating the tank was empty, before they changed to the fuller tank. Many crews have used this method to find out where the tank really runs out of gas, but you must be alert and responsive to do this safely.

This is how the story was told to me.

As they passed over Corsica with both tanks on the inboard to calibrate them (you should only do one tank at a time), the entire crew was dozing, both pilots in the seat and the Crew Chief in the cargo compartment. As they passed over the east shoreline of Corsica, the pilot opened one eye briefly and noticed an old German dirt fighter strip close to the coast. Several minutes later, and with everyone still dozing, the left engine sputtered and quit. The pilots came alert and, noting the left engine torque dropping to zero, feathered the left engine and started a turn back to Corsica.

After regaining his wits, the co-pilot, realizing that they had run out of fuel on the inboard tank for that engine, switched both of the fuel selectors to the outboards, which were full. It then should have been a simple matter of a little cockpit discussion, restarting the left engine and everyone keeping quiet about the incident.

Unfortunately, the crew chief, asleep in the cargo compartment, heard the left engine quit, woke up and probably thought, "Those pilots have let the left engine run out of fuel," and, without saying anything to anyone, went to the cockpit and switched the fuel selectors (already on the full outboard tanks) back to the inboards, which were empty. Needless to say, shortly after that the right engine quit and, in the confusion that ensued, the pilot feathered the right engine and they became a glider with 10,000 pounds of pipe in the cargo compartment.

A C-119 doesn't do real well as a glider, but they did make it back to the old German strip, which was about 3,000 feet long. With both engines feathered, they had no hydraulics for lowering the landing gear (fortunately it free-fell to the locked position), for flaps or brakes and no reverse thrust. They touched down about halfway down the strip doing about 140 knots (final approach speed probably would have been about 100 knots), ran off the end of the runway across a field, pulled up and over a man on a donkey and hit in a stand of trees, coming to rest with the cockpit completely broken away from the main fuselage. It was a miracle that none were injured in the crash and the 10,000 pounds of pipe did not come loose. I was told that the only place that four humans could have survived in that plane was where those four men were.

*About six months after Spook and I got to Toul-Rosières, the Wing moved, lock, stock, and barrel, to Évreux Air Base, about a 45-minute drive west of Paris. The Air Force moved everyone's personal trailers and we set up a very nice trailer park on base there. The 780th and 781st were on the main part of the base and the 782nd, our squadron, was on the far side of the field, requiring a short drive to get to the hanger and the B.O.Q., where the bachelor officers lived. Each squadron was equipped with 16 C-119 aircraft and supported various airlift requirements of the 322nd Air Division all over Europe and Africa, including England and the Scandinavian countries.

*Since we arrived at Evreux in 1955 and the World War Two had only been over for about 10 years, during our training flights over to the Normandie coast we could see that there was a lot of the equipment used during the invasion, still resting there.

Most of the buildings in the town of Evreux were new because Evreux was one of the sites where the Germans launched V-1 and V-2 Rockets from that targeted England, so we beat them up pretty badly.

We had one pilot in our wing who had bombed Evreux in B-26 raids during the war and now was back flying C-119's out of Evreux Air Base.

*Each of the squadrons participated in an annual Base Carnival that was held in one of our aircraft hangers. On this particular day, I had been to the carnival in the 780th hanger on the main part of the base.

As I left the hanger, I noted a C-119 on final approach with an engine feathered. A Pilot I knew was on a test hop at that time and I surmised it might be him, so I stood idly by to watch the landing.

As it turned out it was my friend and they had, as part of the test hop, shut down the right engine and were unable to get it out of the feathered position, so were returning to the field on one engine. As he approached the field I saw the gear come down and, although the left main and nose gear appeared to be all the way down and locked, it was apparent to me on the ground that the right main was not all the way into the locked position. I watched as he brought up the power on the left engine and executed a single engine go-around. As it turned out, he then could not get the gear to come up. A C-119 will not do well, even empty, on one engine with the gear down and, by the time the crew tried in vain to get the gear up, they were out of runway, going down and looking for a field. They disappeared over the 782nd hanger on the far side of the field and I knew the open field that the pilot was probably shooting for.

Because it is a high winged airplane, you always crash landed the C-119 with the gear down because the weight of the wing and engines could collapse the fuselage. The second best option, if you couldn't get the gear down, was to try and land with all gear up on a prepared surface. The worst option was to have one main gear not down. In that event, the wingtip would dig in, the fuselage would collapse and the airplane would most likely roll up in a ball.

I was going to be the first one to the wreckage. I sped in my car at 70 mph around the perimeter road, closely followed by the Air Police, who were also trying to get to the scene. When we got to the field, instead of the charred and twisted wreckage that I anticipated, there was the airplane, sitting on all three gear and the crew outside scratching their heads.

"What happened?" I asked.

"I don't know," my friend said. "We were on one engine and got an unsafe gear. When we went around, the gear wouldn't come up and the bird wouldn't stay in the air, so we headed for this field. As I started my round out, the gear horn quit and we got three green lights."

Investigation showed that, without knowing it, they had caught the right main gear on a telephone wire that was strung across their landing path. We surmise that the gear hooked the wire, pulling it back against the hydraulic pressure that was trying to put it down and, when the wire broke, the gear snapped to the locked position. That accident, which should have happened but didn't, had one of the happier endings.

*MSGT Wilson was the 782nd Line Chief. He did everything the right way, and ate Pilots for breakfast. So, one cold winter day, when he directed the maintenance guys to close the hangar doors to keep it warm inside, he was a bit perturbed when, sometime later, it wasn't done. We could get two C-119 aircraft in the hangar at a time if they were placed exactly right. To assist in their placement, lines were painted on the hanger floor with markings where the two main gear and the nose gear should be. When he started to chew on the man that he told to close the hangar doors, the man replied, "Sarge, I did what you told me, but the doors won't close." Sure enough, both aircraft were exactly on their marks, but the nose of one aircraft stuck out too far and would not allow the doors to clear for closing. This was a real mystery and required an answer. The final analysis revealed that the airplane blocking the door had been manufactured by Kaiser Frazier and was slightly longer than the Fairchild C-119. We could not find any specific place on the plane that was noticeably different, so I suppose it was just a little here and a little there.

*Several other Aviation Cadets from Class 55-D went to Europe at the same time as Spook and I. Two of these were Lloyd Wolford and Ray Nath who were assigned to Germany. Some months after we had gotten comfortable flying the C-119, we were saddened to hear that Ray was killed, along with many others, as a result of a formation mid-air collision over the Black Forest in Germany. It seems that while flying formation, one of the airplanes lost an engine, causing a swerve that caused them to contact Ray's plane. Both airplanes crashed into the Black Forest, one with a load of troops on board.

close formation

*I've heard a lot of explanations about the meaning of "savoir faire", but I believe that one day I stumbled on the true meaning. We had a ten-ship gaggle of C-119s headed for Wheelus AB near Tripoli, Libya, flying in a line of about 10-minute intervals between aircraft. Our route was over the Tunis Radio Beacon in Tunisia. Just past Tunis lay an ugly looking squall line. Since the Air Force had just come out with the rule that you could not knowingly fly into a cumulonimbus (thunderstorm), and there was a whole sky full of them up ahead, the lead diverted into Tunis to spend the night and go on in the morning. Of course, we all followed him and, pretty soon, we overloaded Tunis Approach Control.

Normally, the guy in Tunis Approach Control just took position reports and passed them on. Now, suddenly, he had ten birds in the holding pattern, in the weather and was trying to get all of them instrument approaches. It became obvious that he was getting screwed up when he tried to descend the top airplane down through everybody in the holding pattern. We then took over and started coordinating and clearing ourselves, i.e. the guy on the bottom would make the approach, call field in sight then the next guy would descend and call out of his altitude down to the approach altitude and everyone would call in sequence that they were dropping down to the next lower altitude. We never heard a word from the controller. I think he was relieved to get relieved.

Since this was a French AFB, we all headed for the billeting office after we got the birds squared away. I was one of the last to get a room and, with key in hand, proceeded outside down a quaint covered walkway to my designated room. I looked in startled amazement as I opened the door to find a guy and a gal on the bed, a French Officer's uniform hung on the bedpost, both naked and in the middle of **THE** act! Two startled faces turned to look at me as I stood openmouthed in the doorway. Naive as I am, I acted properly embarrassed, apologized and started to back out of the door. The French Officer, seeing my USAF flying suit, raised up slightly, waved his arm and said politely, "Please, come in." I declined, and quickly backed out the door. Since that time, I have always used that French Officer's coolness as a true description of what savoir faire really means.

*I don't recall the occasion of our meeting but, while stationed at Evreux I met an Air France Pilot who lived just a short way from the Air base and we became friends. He invited me over to his place, not far from the air base, where he had French homebuilt called a Bebe Jodel. He had built this low wing airplane, taken the air cooled engine out of a Volkswagen Beetle and bolted it on the front end of his Bebe Jodel which he offered to let me fly. I was excited to fly it and he explained that the airplane had no brakes so that in taxiing you had to get enough airflow both in movement and prop wash to turn the airplane. He had a small hanger/barn and several acres that provided a runway for this small airplane to operate. All of the instruments were in meters and kilometers and when I tightened the Sam Brown belt that he had for a seat belt on this small open cockpit plane, it was very, very loose.

I took off and climbed up to just over 914 meters which, what I thought, was about 3,000 feet and slowed the airplane to do a stall, so I would know what airspeed to fly final approach. When an airplane is certified in the United States it must give you a physical warning as you approach the stall. The stick must shake or you get a burble from the elevator, just something to let you know you are approaching a stall.

On this French home built, there was no warning. As I slowed the airplane, with the nose high, the airplane suddenly stalled and the nose snapped straight down. I came clear out of the cockpit and finally got to the end of that very loose Sam Brown Belt, but then could not reach the short control stick. As the airplane built up speed I knew that the nose would come up sharply which would force me back into the cockpit and then I started wondering where the control stick was. Fortunately I got back in the cockpit without having an unpleasant meeting with the control stick.

I found this photo of a Bebe Jodel in a French museum. This may be the very air plane that belonged to my Air France Pilot friend that I flew so many years ago because the colors appear to be familiar and I don't think there were that many around.

*One day I was dispatched to Neubiberg AB in Germany, near Munich. The mission was to drop 360 troops in one day with one airplane. Since I could drop 40 troops at a time out of the C-119, this meant that I would have to make nine trips over the Drop Zone (DZ). When I landed at Neubiberg, I was met by a fiery Army Colonel who quickly told me that I **WILL** drop **ALL** of 'his troops' that day. This was the last day that 'his troops' could qualify for their jump pay, and he promised 'his troops' that they would **GET** their jump pay. "Do you understand that, Lieutenant Reed?" I told him that I would do everything I could and, short of a mechanical problem or weather (which was OK at the time but forecast to get a little sloppy), we'd get it done.

The tower gave us free use of one of the runways and I started the process. The turnaround time from load to takeoff to the DZ and back was about thirty minutes. After the third load, the weather started to deteriorate and low clouds started moving in, threatening the mission. The regulations were very specific: The DZ had to be in sight when troops were dropped and the weather conditions had to be Visual Flight

Rules (VFR). When I told the Army Colonel that the weather didn't look too good, he corkscrewed and reminded me that **HE** had promised 'his troops' they were going to get their jump pay and **"BY GAWD THEY WERE GOING TO GET IT**." and 'his troops' "**DIDN'T MIND JUMPING IN THE CLOUDS.!**"

Now, I had dealt with a lot of Brass under difficult conditions before and I really wasn't intimidated by the Colonel. I did, however, want to ensure that these GIs got their jump pay. They really didn't get paid very much so the jump pay was important.

When we flew the next load I got a brilliant idea. While we could still find the DZ visually, why not get Neubiberg Radar to track us to the DZ and mark an X on their scope when we drop? That way, even if the clouds moved in they could vector us to the DZ and call the drop. And that's what we did. The radar guys caught on quick, and we even had the opportunity to test it for a couple of runs before the weather socked in. It worked perfectly. "Hell," I thought. "I've discovered something new that will change the concept of dropping troops."

About the eighth load, the weather had moved in, the ceiling had dropped to almost nothing and I was solidly in the clouds on an Instrument Flight Rules (IFR) clearance from approach control. The radar guys were doing a great job vectoring us to the DZ and now would come the true test, an actual drop IFR by radar. As we approached the DZ, I had my finger on the drop switch that would launch the 40 troopers out the back doors. We had gotten clearance to drop from the DZ Control Officer and I started to apply pressure on the switch as radar gave us the countdown to drop. Suddenly, over the radio came, "**NO DROP - NO DROP - NO DROP!"** I quickly took my finger off the jump switch and called the DZ control Officer. "What's going on?" He explained that five H-21, twin rotor, Helicopters were just passing over the DZ. Apparently, they had gotten caught out in the weather and were on the deck trying to sneak back under the low ceiling. I went weak. I had almost dropped 40 troops on top of five H-21 choppers. Wouldn't that have been tragic?

Then I realized why the regulations were written the way they are. We might not always understand why, but somebody does. I might add that eighty of the Colonel's troops didn't get jump pay that Month. I wanted to ask the Colonel why he had waited until the last day of the month to get his troopers their jumps, but then thought better of it.

*Three or four of our crews on separate missions were scheduled to

RON at Rhein Main on the same night and we had planned a get together at the Rhein Main Officers' Club. As I prepared to depart Erding AB, just northeast of Munich, in mid-afternoon, I was looking forward to the relatively short flight up to Rhein Main and an evening at the club with the guys. So I was disappointed when the left engine wouldn't start and the crew chief's verdict was that the starter had died. A new starter would have to be flown in, which could take a day or two. I wrestled with the situation.

I had heard of engines with bad starters being started by rolling down the runway on one engine, getting enough airflow over the dead engine to turn the propeller, and getting it started that way. But, for some reason, at Erding that didn't seem too feasible. While I was in Base Operations trying to figure out the next step, a young pilot stepped up to file a flight plan. I asked him what he was flying and he replied he was going back to his home base in his F-86D. The wheels started turning. I explained my situation to him and asked if, when he fired up for departure, he'd mind if I taxied out on the runway behind him and try to start my bad engine with his jet blast. He said, "Sure."

I followed him out on the active runway and, as he ran up his engine as high as he could without skidding tires, I closed the gap between us, milking the feather button in and out, trying to find the best blade angle to start the engine. As I got within about 40 to 50 feet of his tailpipe, the propeller began to turn very slowly, but not enough to start the engine. I tried different prop angles by milking the feather button, hoping that I could speed up the rotation, but no use. Finally, I got a call from the F-86D pilot. "Hey, I'm burning up a lot of fuel and I've got a long way to go. Can't stick around much longer." I reluctantly replied that it didn't look like it was going to work, thanked him for his efforts and said he had better go ahead and take off. When he released his brakes and cut in the afterburner, that dead engine started spinning as if the engine were running. The magneto and fuel got on in time and the engine started.

We made it to the club in time that night, and the only repercussions of that incident were from Captain Van Dyke, the Maintenance Officer, for "endangering his airplane and exposing the landing gear and all the wiring in the wheel well to excessive heat."

I don't know how Maintenance Officers find out about everything, but they do.

I explained to him that during the whole process I had the pilot's window open and had my hand out in the jet wash and it didn't get too hot for me to hold my hand in it. Inspection revealed that there was no excessive heat and nothing was damaged. And, unless it's ever disputed, I will lay claim to be the first pilot (most likely the only one) in the Air Force to start a Pratt and Whitney 4360 from the jet blast of an F-86D! Buddy starts between C-130s later became a standard procedure when they had a starter out. Some years later, at Kwajalein, I started a Marine C-130 with the wash from a DHC-4 Caribou. That may have also been a first.

*Although I'd heard stories about the terrible locust swarms in the United States, I had never seen one. I guess the irrigation and development that had taken place, along with modern pesticides, have removed the locust as a threat to the agricultural industry in our country. So it was with interest that I heard people at Nouasseur Air Base, just outside Casablanca in French Morocco, excitedly talking about a locust swarm that was coming.

Nouasseur was a routine stop for our planes and I was there on Temporary Duty, (TDY) to coordinate a gaggle of about ten planes that we had coming through. Since I was near Base Operations, I started over there to see what was cooking. In the distance, I could see the swarm as it approached the base. Inside, they even had the swarm on radar. I had checked out a 35-passenger bus that I could pick up the C-119 crews in when they landed and, as I drove across the ramp, the swarm, which was now overhead, descended to the ramp.

I had always thought locusts to be about the size of a grasshopper or perhaps a little bigger. These were huge, about five or six inches long, and their undersides were reddish/blue in color. They covered the ramp and I could feel the bus skid as I drove over them. I watched a mechanic working on the tail of a straight wing F-84 slap at a locust that had landed on the back of his neck then turn and look up at the swarm descending on him. He crawled up the tailpipe of that F-84. I went around picking up mechanics on the flight line who were anxious to seek refuge in the bus. Andy Clark, my old instructor from Aviation Cadets at Webb, was just taking off in a T-33. He made an early turn-out and managed to escape the swarm. Two F-86s taxiing in required engine changes because the pilots didn't get the engines shut down in time and suffered a massive ingestion.

*We never worried about ice buildup on the C-119, even though we flew in a lot of it in those days. Nowadays, with jets and turbo props, you spend most of the time above the icing level where it is too cold for ice to adhere to metal. Generally speaking, you won't pick up structural ice if the outside air temperature is below minus 20 degrees centigrade because the moisture is too cold and hard to adhere. But the temperatures at the altitudes we flew were just right for icing

But I had no worries on a night flight from Adana, Turkey, to Athens, Greece. Just a routine flight over the Mediterranean, along the coast of Turkey and a cold beer in Athens. Although heavy ice was forecast, we had eight 200,000 BTU heaters that provided hot air to all leading edge surfaces and the windshield. In several years of flying in heavy icing conditions all over Europe there was never a situation in which I felt uncomfortable in that old C-119. She could handle it.

As we slogged through the dark and stormy night en route to the cold beer, we had not a worry until an overvoltage spike burned out the points in all eight heaters and we were left with nothing. Then things started to get interesting. It gets mighty lonely out there in a situation like that. The wings, tail and windshield immediately started to collect ice. I could feel the airplane getting heavier, and we still had a long way to go. The crew chief was frantic in his efforts to relight the heaters, but with no luck. Two things happen when you start to collect ice: first, you get heavier, and second, you destroy lift. Eventually we were at climb power just to hold altitude.

Why do these things always happen at night?

As things were getting pretty grim and it looked like we weren't going to make it, the clouds started breaking up and, eventually, descending over the water we got below them, which stopped further ice buildup. But could we make it to Athens? Finally, out of the co-pilot's side window – the forward windshield was completely blanketed with ice – we could start to see the lights of Athens. As we passed by the airport to set up for a right base and final approach, we opened both side windows and, having no forward visibility because of the ice buildup on the windshield, the co-pilot and I both landed the airplane each looking out his window as far as possible. We carried the speed on final just above the burble to the stall at 140 knots instead of the 95-100 knots it should have been.

Boy, the beer tasted good that night.

*On another mission, we were airlifting the materials to build the DEWLine (Distant Early Warning) across Turkey, part of the radar sys-

tem used to detect missile launches from Russia. We departed Adana, Turkey, for Diyarbakir with two C-119 aircraft. I was 3,000 pounds over the maximum allowable weight because of a 6,000-pound and a 4,000-pound roll of cable that had been loaded on board and the requirement to carry enough fuel to go from Adana to Diyarbakir and return. To be legal, I should have downloaded the 4,000-pound roll of cable.

But, what the hell. I was invincible.

Although the airplane will fly at 3,000 pounds above the maximum allowable weight limitation on two engines, that limitation is based on the airplane being able to fly in the event one of the engines fail. En route, we elected to do a little low level flying and, as I pulled up to about 1,500 feet to get over a rise ahead and let the other aircraft join up for a formation flight to Diyarbakir, I lost the scavenge pump in the right engine. When I shut that engine down I found, to my dismay, that, because of the overweight situation, the airplane would not hold altitude and we were descending at about 100 feet per minute.

There wasn't even a decent place to crash because of house-sized boulders everywhere. I saw a dried up riverbed (I later determined it to be a tributary to the Euphrates River) and, when I got to about telephone pole height above the ground, dove into it, hoping to get more speed and possibly the ability to climb. When a C-119 is slow, it has additional drag caused by the flat bottom. Changing the aircraft pitch attitude with higher speed might reduce this drag.

We didn't pick up any additional speed, and now I was below the banks of the riverbed on one engine, but at least there were no large boulders around and it was more suitable for a crash landing. The riverbed turned and, when we came around the bend, I was shocked to see a wall directly ahead. We had flown into a dead end. As we approached the wall I started to pull up, which would lose airspeed, and in the process guarantee that we would crash on top, regardless of what was there. As I started up I told the co-pilot to stand by on the gear and then got this hair-brained idea to try a restart on the bad engine. Nine out of ten times with a Scavenge Pump failure, the main bearings seize and the engine freezes, making a restart impossible.

With no communication between the co-pilot and myself – there was no time – we put everything back on line and I pulled out the feather button, not knowing what would happen. The engine turned over fired up and, with zero oil quantity and zero oil pressure, I ran it at full throttle until it froze up. But that poor engine got us to five hundred feet and 150 knots before it froze, and by then we were on a long downslope, similar to that coming in to Albuquerque from the west. We just followed the downslope to Diyarbakir, turning final at about 100 feet. The crew chief had a jug of booze on board and we emptied it before we left the airplane.

They changed both engines on that bird because we had exceeded the maximum time at military (maximum) power on the good engine. Maximum time at military power, as I recall, was two minutes, and we ran the good engine wide open for about 45 minutes. I heard later that there was talk of a ceremony and recognition of the crew when we arrived back at Évreux, but while we were en route back to the base in Old Shaky (C-124 Globemaster), on which we had hitched a ride, the Commander found out that I had been over the maximum allowable gross weight and had been flying low when I lost the engine. No ceremony, no recognition.

For about ten years afterwards, every time I tried to relate this story to someone, I'd start to shake and could not continue.

*From a strictly personal point of view, flying the C-119 all over Europe in those days as a young pilot had several advantages over the pilots flying missions there today. One was that the airplane did not have the speed and range that the birds of today have and, therefore, you were frequently required to spend the night in some pretty exotic places, such as Rome, Athens, Casablanca, etc. Communication with our routing command, the 322nd Air Division, was primarily through the unreliable High Frequency radio, and quite often there was no communication at all. Therefore, we were regularly left to our own devices and had the authority to divert after our primary mission was completed and deviate as necessary to carry high priority cargo from one Air Freight area to another. This led to a lot of good RONs at some very neat spots.

The U.S. Navy 6th Fleet was stationed in the Mediterranean during this same period, and our paths would frequently cross at such places as Athens or Naples, and, being a boat nut, I never missed an opportunity to visit the aircraft carriers when they were in port. This led to establishing relationships with the Navy guys in the Operations Center, and they provided the frequencies necessary to contact them when they were underway. The real advantage to all of this was that I was often able to get radar monitoring and diversion around thunderstorms through some of those lonely night flights around the Mediterranean. Those visits to the Navy ships were always exciting events for me and, later in my Air Force career, I managed to talk myself into four week-long cruises at different times aboard such carriers as the Hancock, Coral Sea, Enterprise and Ticonderoga.

I recall a week long cruise in 1960 aboard the Coral Sea from Alameda NAS, near San Francisco. While on board, I managed to talk the operations people into letting me fly right seat in an A-3D on one of their two-hour sorties. An A3-D is a twin jet bomber, reputed to be the largest operational aircraft routinely operated from an aircraft carrier. As we sat on the catapult, weighing about 67,000 pounds (as much as a fully loaded C-119), it was the only time in my life I REALLY wanted to get out of an airplane. I knew that there was no possibility we would get airborne in the available runway of about 600 feet. But, somehow, we did. While we were airborne, an F-8U fouled (crashed) the deck on the Coral Sea and we had to recover back to Alameda and wait out the investigation and cleanup.

By the time we got the OK to come back to the ship it was nighttime, the fog had moved into San Francisco Bay and Alameda was practically zero-zero (zero ceiling and zero visibility). We took off with me in the right seat again and headed for the Bay Bridge. As we rolled down the runway, I couldn't help but think of the T-33 that ran into the bridge years ago, killing both pilots, and hoped that the guy flying this big bird knew enough to max rate the climb until we got on top. He did, and we cleared the bridge with oodles to spare. What I didn't realize was that I was about to encounter one of the most exciting and terrifying experiences of my flying career – a moonless night trap in an A-3D aboard an aircraft carrier.

After establishing the traffic pattern at 500 feet, we turned from base to final and flew into a black hole. With the entire ship blacked out, there was no reference except the orange meatball (the reflection of an orange light in a gyrostabilized mirror that gives the pilot a visual glidepath to follow) and a very thin and dim row of centerline pencil lights submerged into the deck. Talk about disorientation! With one eye on the altimeter and the pucker factor increasing incrementally as the altimeter decreased, we finally crashed – the Navy guys call it landed – onto the ship. It was a flying experience I'll never forget. Those trips aboard the carriers made me realize what great pilots Navy guys are.

Oh, sure, there's interservice rivalry, and we in the Air Force always thought the Navy pilots were sissies when they pitched out at an Air

Force base and disappeared over the horizon in their landing pattern. But after watching them perform (I've seen a Navy pilot bring an A-3D aboard the Coral Sea in weather I wouldn't attempt on a 12,000 foot runway) I'll salute the Navy pilots every chance I get. I've a great deal of respect for what they do and how they do it.

There's a saying among the Naval Carrier Pilots that goes something like this:

Three good things for a Naval Carrier Pilot are:

1. A good Landing
2. A good Bowel Movement
3. A good Orgasm.

With a night trap aboard an Aircraft Carrier, you can get all three!

*Châteauroux was located in Central France and was one of the main transfer points for cargo coming into and out of the European Theater. As a result, we made many trips to Châteauroux in our travels about the continent.

On one trip, I was given the task of airlifting the remains of six bodies from a base in Germany to Châteauroux for further shipment back to the States. The coffins were each in individual blue/grey wooden shipping boxes and were manifested. There are certain rules in the handling of remains, i.e., you can't stack anything on top of them, accurate transfer documents must be maintained and, among other things, they must be handled with respect.

As we flew from Germany to Châteauroux, I looked over the manifest. Among the remains was a dependent wife, a dependent son and an Army Lieutenant Colonel, none of them related. I wondered what circumstances had led to their death in a foreign country so far from home.

When I landed at Châteauroux, I parked in front of the Air Freight office and went inside to check on my next load. While talking to the Air Freight people, I glanced outside at my aircraft. They had opened the large clamshell doors and were pushing the coffins out onto the ramp and letting them fall to the ground. As I watched, horrified, one man tipped a coffin over. Furious, I ran to the airplane and started to chew on the first guy I came to.

"What the hell are you doing with these remains?" I demanded.

"Remains?" came the reply. "Lieutenant, these are truck axles."

Sure enough, although I had signed for six bodies, someone had mistakenly loaded six truck axles on my plane. The containers for the truck axles looked very similar to the shipping boxes for the coffins. A check with the base in Germany revealed the remains were still in storage there.

*One Armed Forces Day I made a trip to Chatêauroux and had the opportunity to spend a little time and enjoy the Armed Forces Day Show. Since dropping troops and equipment from our aircraft was one of our primary missions, I was particularly interested in the parachute display that they were preparing. They intended to inflate one of the large cargo chutes that are used to drop such things as trucks and road graders. The chutes are huge and the Sergeant in charge was searching for something to tie down the chute to when they inflated it and, since there was a 10 to 15-knot breeze blowing, he wanted something substantial. He borrowed one of the very large forklifts from Air Freight, made sure that the chute was well tied and proceeded to inflate it.

When the chute inflated it started to move the forklift, and the further it went the faster it went. With a group of very excited Air Force Troops chasing it, the chute with the forklift attached started across the field. It crossed the ramp, went across the active runway through the fence and started out across the French countryside, still with the Troopers trying vainly to catch it. At last, when the forklift went into a shallow ditch, the forks dug in and stopped the journey. I'd have paid $50 just to read that incident report.

*During one of the many crises that occurred in Lebanon, the 322nd Air Division was tasked to move Swedish troops from Stockholm to Naples, Italy, to be in position for possible deployment to the crisis area. I was the last C-119 in a group of ten aircraft to support this mission, with Colonel Evans in charge of the operation.

Taking off from Évreux, we proceeded to Stockholm. En route, the weather, which was already tight, dropped below minimums and we were forced to divert all ten aircraft to Oslo, Norway. That evening in Oslo, it was early to bed to be ready for the long flight to Stockholm and then down to Naples the following day.

The next morning, after filing the flight plan, I showed up at the airplane, bright-eyed and bushy-tailed. To my surprise, the crew chief had both engines running and the interior of the airplane all warmed up. The reason he started the engines ahead of time was because the outside air temperature was about 15 degrees below zero and, at those temperatures, if the exact starting technique is not used in the Pratt and Whitney 4360 and the engine doesn't start during the first firing, moisture gets into the plugs and refreezes, making it impossible to start the engine. This requires the mechanic to pull and clean the spark plugs – and there are 56 of them in each engine. So, in those temperatures, the mechanic had a vested interest in ensuring a good start. I had no problem with that.

I jumped in the back to change into my flying suit and told him he could shut the engines down while I made the pre-flight and we'd get underway.

"No sweat Lieutenant," he said. "I've made the pre-flight. We're ready to go."

Although highly irregular, I was impressed with such efficiency. The weather on takeoff at Oslo was about 200 feet overcast, with half-mile visibility and a relatively short runway. As I started down the runway, the last airplane off in this ten ship gaggle, I scanned the engine gauges to ensure everything was normal. Approaching flying speed, I glanced at the airspeed and was horrified to find that both the pilot and co-pilot airspeed were sitting on zero. My first thought was that they had iced up, so I reached up to confirm that the pitot heater was on. The pitot tube is what gives the pilot the speed of the airplane through the air. There were no distance markers on the runway at Oslo and, knowing it was a short runway but not knowing quite where the end was, I continued the takeoff.

With zero airspeed on the gauges I poked my head into the overcast and climbed based on a rate of climb, pitch attitude and power that I knew would give us enough airspeed to fly. As we climbed above the overcast into the beautiful blue sky, my fears were realized as I looked out and saw that both pitot covers were in place, causing the zero reading on the airspeed indicators. With Stockholm weather in the weeds, I had no appetite for a low visibility approach and landing with no airspeed. That sounded like a suicide wish.

We tried everything we could to get the pitot covers off. I had heard that by leaving the pitot heater on that you may be able to burn them off. But these were heavy canvas covers that had been painted over many times, and there was no hope of burning them off. I even thought of using the long pole that held the clamshell doors open, in an attempt to push them off by holding the pole out the pilot's window, but then realized if I lost the pole back into the engine, the problem would be much worse if we had to shut that engine down. So, a dejected crew proceeded to Stockholm and, on arrival over the Radio Beacon, found the weather to be right at minimums, with lots of snow on the runway.

I had found that Copenhagen weather was good and called Colonel Evans in the tower to advise him that we had an engine acting up and running rough and I was apprehensive about making an approach in such low visibility with a suspect engine (just a little white lie). I said that I would prefer to land at Copenhagen, repair the engine and come back to Stockholm.

"Jim," he said (he called me by my first name, which really impressed me), "this is really an important mission and, if at all possible, it would be better if you could land at Stockholm and repair the engine there."

Well, we all talked about it and the crew was willing to take a chance on me if I was willing to make a zero airspeed approach under the snotty weather conditions that existed. We formulated a plan of what we would do as soon as we got on the ground and, with great reluctance, I started the approach. Stockholm had a funny approach at that time. Only one part, the localizer, was available for the Instrument Landing System (I.L.S.). The localizer enables the pilot to fly through the clouds right down the centerline of the runway. There was no glide path, and the altitudes you should be at on final approach were designated by bearings from a radio beacon as they intersected the localizer.

I'm sure that we had adequate airspeed when we put the gear down and started down final approach. I wasn't going to be slow. The approach worked out OK, and when we broke out it was very difficult to see the runway because of the heavy snow layer that had been accumulating through the night. After touchdown, I went to full reverse, which put us zero-zero in blowing snow, got to the end of the runway and stopped. I told the tower that we had an unsafe nose gear indication (another little white lie) and that I was sending the crew chief out to put the nose gear pin in. Of course, while he was out there, he took off the pitot covers so we wouldn't have them on when we taxied into the parking area where the rest of the crews were.

In reality, the approach and landing with no airspeed indication into those dreary weather conditions did not seem that difficult. I attribute that to the fact that I had so much recent time in the airplane, had a great deal of confidence in the airplane's performance, and I felt comfortable with the power settings that would give me specific descent rates. I would guess that, if it were known, our airspeed on final would have been within five knots of normal.

After we taxied in we even removed the cowling on the engine that was supposed to be bad and were elated to find out that we had pulled the ruse off. No one suspected a thing. So I patted myself on the back until about six months later when, at a party in the club at Évreux, Colonel Evans came up, put his arm around me and said, "Jim, that was a hell of a job you did at Stockholm, landing with the pitot covers on. I watched you through binoculars from the tower."

He could have had me severely disciplined for a number of reasons, but instead saw a feat of airmanship that he admired. I reflected on the T-6 incident with Mr. Gambrell and realized that it takes more than just trying to survive - it takes luck! In both of those incidents I was lucky to have people about me who were understanding and compassionate. Our world needs more of this.

* Several of the pilots, including myself, were selected to be maintenance test pilots. Whenever there was an airplane that had maintenance performed on it that required a test flight, we would fly it. This included periodic inspections where the airplane was literally taken apart, the parts inspected and then the airplane was put back together.

The model C-119 that we flew had an elevator gust lock that that would hydraulically lock the elevator when you put the props into reverse after landing. The elevator on the C-119was huge and without the lock it would flail around very aggressively when you went into reverse to the extent that the pilots couldn't hold it and the elevator would hit the stops. The hydraulic lock prevented that.

There was a switch installed on the throttle quadrant that was activated by the throttle when you placed the throttle into reverse. As the lock engaged there was a noticeable flicker on the hydraulic gauge located just forward of the co-pilots knee. I got used to expecting that flicker of the hydraulic needle when I put the throttles into reverse.

On this particular test hop, the airplane had been through a major inspection and I had been assigned the task of test hopping it before releasing it back to the squadron as operational.

Everything checked out OK prior to takeoff and we started our take off roll down the runway. The procedure is, you start advancing the throttles, making a power check at certain manifold and torque setting and finally get to maximum power for take off. As I was approaching take off speed I pushed the throttle to maximum power and out of the corner of my eye noted that familiar flicker of the hydraulic gauge forward of the co-pilots knee. I jerked back on the yolk and sure enough the yolk was locked. Thankfully we had room to abort the take off.

Inspection revealed that the switch that engaged the elevator control lock had been improperly installed, so that when you reached maximum power the lock would engage.

*There were a lot of stories that came out of that C-119 tour in France that happened to friends of mine, and some are probably worth telling here.

Scott came out of Madrid one dark and stormy night. Our normal route back to France was to go north on airway Red 10 out of Madrid until we got to the coast at Bilbao, then a right turn to San Sebastian, which was marked by a radio beacon, call sign SS (we called it Sugar Sugar). At Sugar Sugar we changed from Madrid Center to Bordeaux Radio, turned left and proceeded to Bordeaux. Since Navigators were only on board for overwater flights, many pilots had the Radio Operator pick up that duty when there was no Navigator aboard.

Such was the case on this night. They made the turn at Bilbao OK, but when the Radio Operator got the needle swing at Sugar Sugar and told the pilot to turn north with his new heading to Bordeaux, his voice was apparently lost in the thunder, lightning and turbulence that they were experiencing at that time. As a result, the turn to the north never took place and they flew the entire length of the 11,000-foot Pyrenees mountains at night, in the clouds, at 6,000 feet. They began to suspect something was wrong when they couldn't pick up Bordeaux either on their ADF or on VHF radios.

Just about the time they reached the East Coast of France and would have started out over the water, a break in the clouds revealed a town and a runway below. Scott pulled off the power and descended through the openings in the clouds in a desperate attempt to get to the runway and stay visual. As they were descending, the keeper of the airport, who was finishing his duty day, turned off the runway lights, got on his bicycle and started home. Scott circled the town until the keeper returned to the air field and switched on the runway lights. That's when they found out they were in Perpignan, France.

One of the stories worth repeating came out of Naples, Italy. Seems that one bleary-eyed morning at Capodichino Airport, a Navy Pilot took off in an F-8U with the wings folded. Now, only the wing tips fold up in the F-8U, but the ailerons are in the part that folds. Fortunately, even though they were in the folded position, the ailerons continue to work and the guy was able to get the bird off the ground and back again in one piece. I heard that the Navy tried to hush this story up, but when Chance-Vought, the manufacturer of the airplane, heard about it, they shouted it from the rooftops. I certainly would have liked to see the expression on that pilot's face when, after takeoff, he looked out and saw that his wings were in the folded position.

In the maritime industry, local knowledge is so valuable. That's why they put bar pilots on board vessels entering harbors, to advise the Captains of local conditions that could affect the ship. And so it is in an airplane. Local knowledge is invaluable. If you are familiar with an approach, have made it many times, know the frequencies and can anticipate what's going to happen, you will fly a much safer approach. That's why the airlines require pilots to have route checks for routes they will fly. Not only does it give them an opportunity to become familiar with the route and associated approaches, they are required to demonstrate proficiency at being able to accomplish the approach. We tried to do that in our wing, but it was not always possible as there were so many destinations. Our pilots became very experienced with making first-time approaches and with the language problems associated with flying in foreign countries. During the winter, European weather can be very demanding. I have flown missions through England and Germany where I've made six or seven legs that required takeoffs and landing at minimums and have never seen the ground until I was over the threshold on landing and lost it as soon as I rotated on takeoff.

Night Formation

One of the major problems that exacerbates the difficulties for new crews flying in Europe is the language used by controllers both at terminal facilities and in enroute centers. Although English is generally used throughout most countries, it takes a while to get used to the different dialects and accents.

Another problem that could be potentially hazardous is the different altimeter settings. Some countries use the Queen Nan Howe (QNH) altimeter setting, which will display the field elevation on the altimeter when the aircraft is on the ground. Some countries use the Queen Fox Easy (QFE) altimeter setting, in which the altimeter will read zero when the aircraft is on the ground. You had better be aware of which altimeter reads what or you could have serious problems.

A stateside crew, TDY to Europe, were relatively inexperienced with the approach to Rhein Main Air Base as they started down in heavy weather. When cleared to descend on the Rhein Main Radio Beacon, a terminal facility serving the airport, the Co-Pilot tuning in the radio misinterpreted the radio beacon to be the Rudesheim Radio Beacon, an en route facility for an airway but located in the Rhein Main area. The

Rhein Main Beacon was in a flat area, but the Rudesheim beacon was in the hills.

The pilot, thinking he was making an approach to Rhein Main, began his descent. The radar guys weren't quite as well equipped as they are now and they missed what was happening. Just before they hit the trees in the vicinity of the Rudeshime Beacon, the pilot happened to look up, saw the trees and threw full power to the bird in an attempt to climb. He didn't quite make it and ricocheted off the trees. He managed to stay airborne, hollered Mayday and got radar assistance back to Rhein Main.

The following pages give an example of the Radio Facilities book that was our primary navigation tool before the expanded navigation sheets came out. Imagine trying to navigate on a dark and stormy night with pages in a book as shown below. Note the absence of VORs in 1955

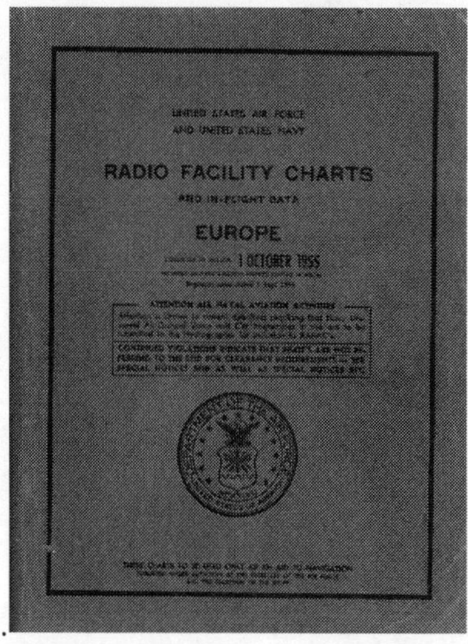

RADIO FACILITY CHARTS

EUROPE

1 OCTOBER 1955

Lighting in aircraft cockpits is never the best, and trying to read that small print in a congested area was very difficult. I'm not sure how the guys flying single pilot aircraft did it. This all changed when the new Letdown books and the High Altitude and Low Altitude charts came out.

There were very few Visual Omni Ranges (VORs) in 1955 when I started flying in Europe. They were limited primarily to the larger cities, so our navigation and approach aid at many airfields was the Automatic Direction Finding (ADF), a primitive system by today's standards. At

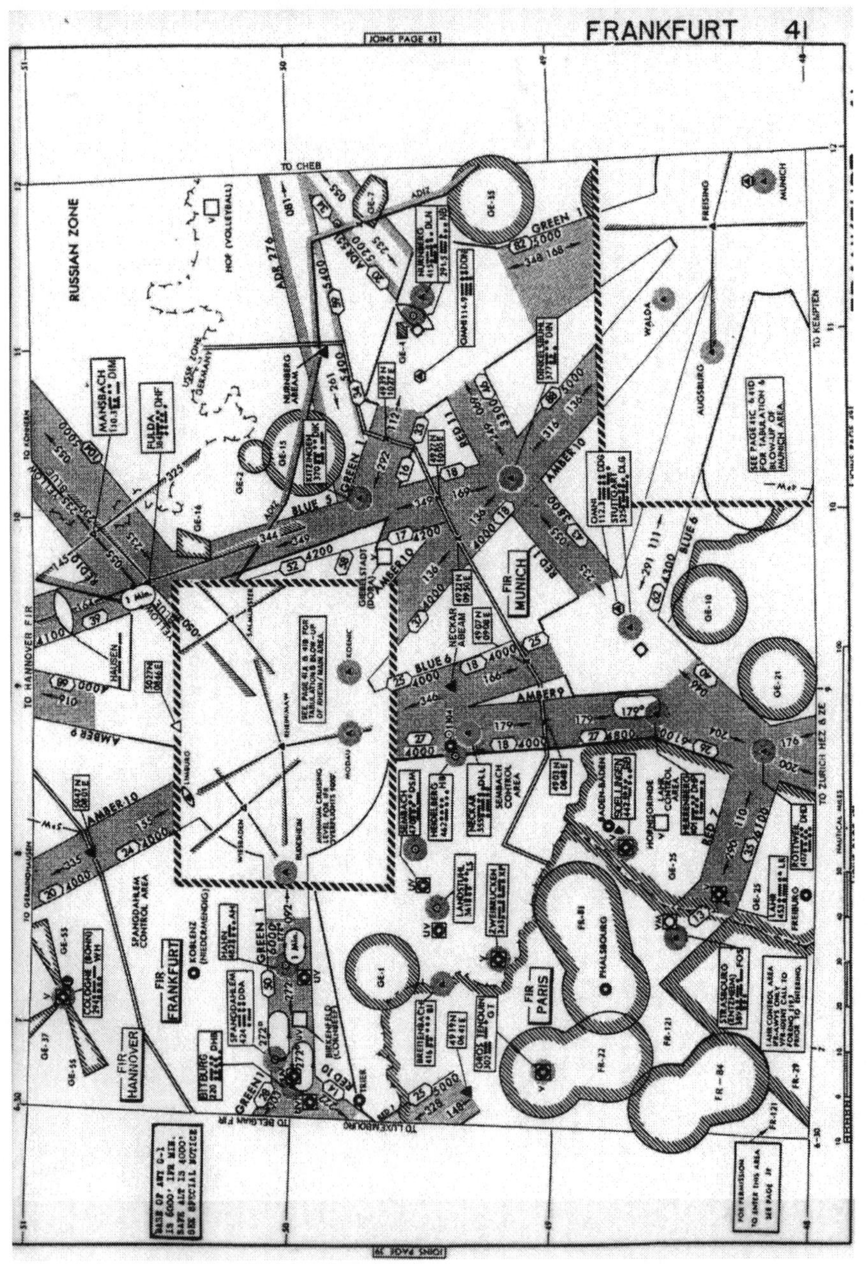
FRANKFURT 41
JOINS PAGE 43
RUSSIAN ZONE
FIR MUNICH
FIR FRANKFURT
FIR PARIS
FIR HANNOVER
JOINS PAGE 39

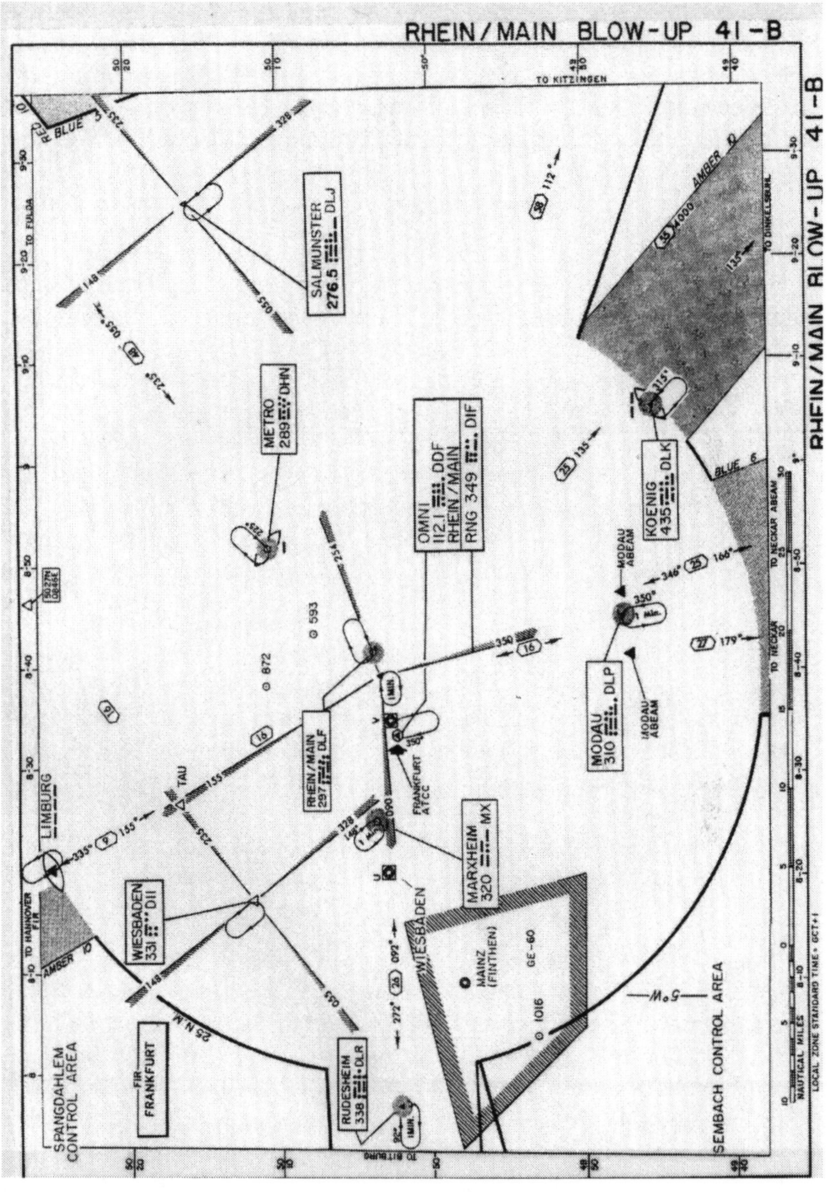
RHEIN / MAIN BLOW-UP 41-B
SALMUNSTER 276.5 DLJ
METRO 289 DHN
OMNI 112.1 DDF
RHEIN / MAIN
RNG 349 DIF
KOENIG 435 DLK
MODAU 310 DLP
RHEIN/MAIN 297 DLF
MARXHEIM 320 MX
WIESBADEN 331 DII
RUDESHEIM 338 DLR
LIMBURG
FIR FRANKFURT
SPANGDAHLEM CONTROL AREA
SEMBACH CONTROL AREA
FRANKFURT ATCC
MAINZ (FINTHEN)
TO KITZINGEN
NAUTICAL MILES

times, the needle would lead you to a thunderstorm instead of the station you were tuned to. And in places like Rome, the Range Leg could make several turns out over the water. One thing that flying environment did was keep you sharp and your proficiency level high. Your attention level was always in the airplane and not on a ski slope or a beach somewhere.

*We frequently flew to Wheelus Field, just outside of Tripoli. It was a long haul from the Continent, and we were ready for a relaxer when we got there. Usually, just as soon as we hit the ground, it was a quick shower then head for the club. On this particular trip I was a little slow, and the rest of the guys had left for the club while I was still getting ready. A messenger came into the BOQ with instructions to capture the first sober pilots he could find to take an emergency medical air evacuation to Germany. It seems a truck had backed into an Airman and crushed his chest against a building and he needed an immediate operation. The closest place capable was a hospital in Germany. The next thing I knew, I was flying a C-119 north from Wheelus with the patient under an oxygen tent and a load of doctors and nurses on board.

We had to stop at Marseille for fuel and, when we were about 30 miles out, I called the tower to let them know we were an Air Evac on a long, straight in approach. Meantime, I could hear a B-26 calling for landing clearance there. He called downwind, base and final and each time the tower said they didn't have him in sight, but to continue. Finally the call came from the B-26 that he had landed at Istres, a military field just a short way from Marseille, by mistake and would be right over. Apparently, this B-26 landed at Istres, realized his mistake, did a 180 on the active and took off without even contacting the tower there.

As it turned out, we conflicted, he on base and me on a long straight in final and he started arguing about who was going to land first. Finally, I lost my cool, told him that I was an Air Evac and directed him to give way. He did, and made a 360 while I landed. As I pulled off the runway and started to taxi into Base Operations, I watched as he touched down. When the nose wheel on that B-26 came down, it collapsed, banging the nose hard on the runway. The glass in the nose detached itself from the airplane and went up over the tail. There was a man in the seat, in the nose, and he appeared to be holding his legs up as the airplane ground away below him.

I attempted a quick turn around to get the patient to the hospital in Germany as quickly as possible, but when I went to file my clearance, the young Captain who was the Base Operations Officer said the field was closed pending investigation of the B-26 crash. I explained that I was an Air Evac and had a dying man on board who needed to get to the hospital as soon as possible. He said they would have to wait until the photographers had finished taking pictures as a minimum, and that could be some time. I told him that I was a Tactical Aircraft and could take off on the dirt alongside the runway, but he would have none of that.

At that time, I was a White Card pilot and had to have my clearance signed by the Base Operations Officer or his representative in order to have authority to fly. When he refused to sign my clearance I told him that this was an emergency and I was going anyway and would take off alongside the runway with or without his approval. As I started towards my aircraft he called the fuel trucks and directed them to stop refueling my plane, but when I got there and checked the fuel, they had already loaded enough on board to make the trip, so I fired up and started out.

Marseille was a joint use military/civilian field, so the Base Operations Officer didn't have control of the tower and, as I taxied out, he finally reneged and told the tower that he would pull the B-26 from the runway, which he did. We waited a few minutes, and he came out and signed my clearance they yanked the B-26 out of the way and we took off on the runway. I've often wondered what would have happened had I taken off in the dirt without a signed clearance. The young man was alive when we arrived in Germany and I later learned that the operation was a success.

A side note to this story. Several years later, at Randolph, all of the KC-97 Instructor Pilots had gone to the snack bar for coffee while we were waiting for the weather to clear enough to get to takeoff minimums. I wound up telling that story and one of the instructors, who was a good friend of mine, whispered to me, "Jim, that was me flying that B-26."

*Marignane Airport, at Marseille, was a routine stop for our C-119s either bound for Mediterranean destinations or returning to the Continent. On one trip, I was making the routine fuel stop there and following a C-46 on final approach. As the C-46 turned off the runway ahead of me, I heard a gruff voice on the radio say, "Marseille, where do you want me to park this damn airplane?" They gave him directions to the parking area, which was close to where I parked. I hadn't seen a C-46 in some time, so I walked over to this one, which was still in the old camouflaged paint scheme, stuck my head in the rear door and asked if there was anybody home. A voice up front said, "Come on in." The C-46 is a tail dragger transport built by Curtiss that looks similar to a C-47/DC-3, but a bit larger.

I stepped into the cargo compartment, walked past a huge steel auxiliary fuel tank that had two 55-gallon drums of oil tied to the front of it and noticed the hand pump and oil lines that ran through the broken windows to each engine. In the cockpit was an old gentleman who appeared to be in his late sixties or perhaps early seventies. He was the only soul on board that airplane.

"Where you headed?" I asked.

"South America," was the reply.

He told me that he had bought 11 of these C-46s at a little strip about 100 miles north of Calcutta for $2,500 a piece. They had been sitting there since the war. He was flying them back to South America, where there was an outfit that was rebuilding and using them as airliners there. I didn't ask him how much he was selling them for.

I looked into the cockpit and nothing appeared to be in operating condition. Both airspeed indicators were stuck on 140 mph and the rest of the gauges were either missing, broken out or obviously in a poor state of repair.

"The oil quantity gauges don't work," he said, "but I've calibrated my oil consumption and, when I think they need oil, I trim up real good, run to the back and pump like hell, then run back and recover." Apparently the autopilot didn't work either. When I asked how he navigated he said that he just headed west until he hit land, figured out where he was, landed at the first field he could find and paid a $50 fine to the FAA for not having a co-pilot. Then he picked up a co-pilot and headed for South America.

He said that he kept a couple of mechanics in India to get the planes ready for the trip and change out the hydraulic seals that had dried up since the airplanes had been sitting without maintenance for about 11 years. He said he'd like to have company on the trip across the Atlantic and asked if I would like to go. I was happy to have other commitments!

*Departing from Rabat Sale, a French Air Force Base in Morocco, we developed a slight problem in the C-119. As we ran the right engine up for the pre-takeoff runup, pieces of hot metal started coming out of the engine and falling to the ramp. The crew chief surmised that we were grinding up the generator. This was confirmed by the wild amperage noted on the right ammeter. With some experimentation, I found that as long as I kept the engine at idle or slightly above, everything seemed to be OK. There was absolutely no maintenance at Rabat Sale. If we shutdown, we could be there for several days waiting to get a part, and Rabat Sale is not a place that I would prefer to spend several days. With Nouasseur a bit over 60 miles away, it was tempting to depart Rabat with the right engine at idle, or slightly above, feather it soon as we were airborne and fly to Nouassuer on one engine.

I had practiced single engine takeoffs at Évreux (just for the hell of it) and found that with an empty airplane and just a little help from the other engine, a single engine takeoff could be made successfully, although it was a little grabby at the rectum when you got to the end of an 8,000-foot runway. Évreux had 7,900 feet of runway. Rabat Sale had 8,000 feet. I figured that the difference in temperature would make up the extra 100 feet. And, besides, if we really needed the other engine, it would be there, running just above idle.

We started our takeoff roll from a high speed taxiway that gently curved onto the runway at the approach end. With takeoff power on one engine, it's impossible to keep the airplane going in a straight line. The curve in the high speed taxiway allowed the airplane to turn to the right with full power on the left engine and, by the time we actually got on the runway, we were doing about 60 knots and, between the rudder and nosewheel steering I was then able to keep the airplane going straight. I may have momentarily nudged the right engine a bit as we approached the end of the runway. I pulled it off as the end of the runway disappeared under the nose and, as soon as the gear started up, feathered (shutdown) the right engine. Actually, once you get the airplane cleaned up, an empty C-119 does pretty well on one engine.

With the right engine shut down, we proceeded to Nouasseur, contacted the tower and, as the regulations require, declared an emergency because we had one engine shutdown. The base responded, the fire trucks rolled and we landed without incident. We didn't tell them the rest of the story.

*We learned about more than just instrument flying and weather during those years flying the C-119 all over Europe, Africa and the Near East. One time, I was on a trip across the Mediterranean with another pilot, named George. As a routine, if both pilots were qualified, we would switch seats, although the Aircraft Commander was still responsible even though he might be in the right seat. On this particular flight I was designated the Aircraft Commander and this leg had George in the left seat.

As the flight progressed, we ran into some bad weather that had some very active cumulonimbus in it that we couldn't avoid. Anyone who has flown at six to eight thousand feet, stumbling from one thunderstorm cell to the next without radar, will know the terrifying feeling that the human body is subjected to when you penetrate a cell. There is a noise, a deep rumbling, accompanied by the roar of rain or hail, which can be deafening; and the colors become dreadfully dark in the middle of the day; with turbulence that can slam you into the seat one second so hard that you can't move and the next second drive your head into the overhead circuit breaker panel, accompanied by blinding lightning and frightening thunder. It can truly be a horrific event.

The twin booms on the C-119 have a great deal of flex, and I have witnessed their movement from the cargo compartment and been surprised at the amount of flex, even in light turbulence. Always in the cockpit, I have mercifully not seen their movement in severe turbulence, but can imagine that they must look like an orchestra leader's baton during the 'Flight of the Bumble Bee.' Anyone who has watched the flex of the wing or engines on a modern jet during turbulence will know what I mean.

My eyes were glued to the instruments as George tried to keep the C-119 upright in these turbulent and difficult conditions. Suddenly, I noted that we had gone into about a 45-degree bank to the right and George didn't seem to be correcting it. I glanced at him and was amazed to see him sound asleep, head on chest and eyes closed. As I desperately took the controls and recovered the aircraft to some semblance of upright, I thought, "What a hell of a guy to be laid back enough to fall asleep in these conditions. I've never met anyone so cool."

Some time later, back at our home base at Évreux, I recounted that story over coffee to some of the other pilots in the squadron. It turned out that George had done the same thing to several other pilots when they were faced with difficult situations, of which we had many in that flying environment. We put the pieces together and realized that every time things got stressfull, George would fall asleep. Someone must have gone to the Operations Officer because the next thing we heard, George was at the Flight Surgeon's office and was determined to have a form of narcolepsy. The type that George had was the type that uses sleep as the body's defense mechanism to deal with stressful situations.

George was fortunate that he was in a crewed airplane and there was another pilot along. This made me think about the number of unexplained crashes of single placed fighter aircraft that I had become familiar with over the years. I wondered how many of them might have occurred with pilots who had the same problem as George.

*Whenever we were out in "The System" we were under the Operational Control of the 322nd Air Division and were required to stay in touch with them, making periodic reports while airborne. Therefore, we were required to have Radio Operators (ROs) on all flights out of the local area, as the High Frequency radios we used were old-fashioned, and frequently the only contact was with C.W. (Carrier Wave: use of a key device to send Morse Code). When newer single sideband high frequency (HF) radios came out that were Pilot-friendly, the Air Force discontinued training Radio Operators. Because of this, and because we still had the old radios in our birds, the 465th TCWg became very short of Radio Operators. To solve this problem, they minimally trained Crew Chiefs to act as Radio Operators when the real ROs were not available.

On a flight from Nouasseur to Algiers, we were approaching Oran and I kept hearing the HF Dynamotor spooling up as the Crew Chief tried to get out his Ops Normal report, as we did every thirty minutes. I finally went to the interphone and asked him if he was having trouble getting his Ops Normal out and was startled when his response was, "Yes, sir. Some guy keeps cutting me out yelling "MAYDAY! MAYDAY!"

I immediately went to the HF radio and talked to a Navy P-2 that had lost an engine, was having a tough time holding altitude in those hot desert temperatures and was trying to make it into Oran. He wasn't too far from us and we got a visual on him and followed him into Oran, where he made a successful landing.

Apparently this minimally trained Crew Chief, who, as I recall, came off a farm in Iowa, had never been trained on, nor even heard, the term "Mayday."

*One of our Pilots got a lesson in communications from the Italians on a flight into Aviano Air Base in Northern Italy. Aviano was an F-100 base nestled in the foothills of the Italian Alps, and we routinely flew there on resupply missions. On a dark night, when Aviano was inundated with weather, which required that a GCA (Ground Controlled Radar

Approach) be used almost to minimums, one of our C-119s started an approach. The GCA unit had recently been turned over to the Italians and the final controller was giving his final approach information in broken English with a heavy Italian accent. As they progressed down the final approach, the aircraft (I'll use AF 1234 for the call sign) started to fall slightly below the glidepath.

The final controller told the pilot, "Air Foosa Onea Tow Tree Fowa, you falla slightly below da glidepath. You pullem up please."

Whether it was turbulence or weariness or inattention, the pilot didn't make the correction as fast as he should and actually went a bit lower on the glidepath.

The controller, knowing of the foothills on final approach got a little more urgency in his voice. "Air Foosa Onea Tow Tree Fowa, you falla below da glidepath. You pullem up please!"

Again, the controller waited and, when he saw that the pilot was not making the correction back to the glidepath as quickly as he thought he should, he announced, **"Air Foosa Onea Tow Tree Fowa. You no pullem up you gonna busta you ass!"** That got his attention and he made an immediate correction.

*The British can be a little testy at times. All of our en route clearances from centers were conducted on VHF radio. We didn't have the infinite crystal capability that we enjoy today and our radio operators carried with them a valise that was full of VHF crystals to be used in the European environment. Considering that we flew into all of the countries on the European Continent, Finlandia, the British Isles, Africa and the Near East, and each country had their own concept of frequency use, we had to have a lot of different crystals in the bag.

On one flight going from France to England in particularly heavy weather, I was handed over from Paris to London Center and gave them the particulars of my flight. They acknowledged and shortly thereafter told me to contact London Center on another frequency. After a quick scan of his available crystals the radio operator stated that we didn't have that frequency on board. I advised London of this, expecting them to give me another frequency, of which they had many. Instead, to my shock, this very calm and authoritative voice came back and said, "Please leave the airway." I thought, "Where in the hell does he want me to go? Here I am, IFR over the channel, airplanes all around and he wants me to leave the airway." I started to argue. He was adamant. "Please leave the airway." No clearance, no nothing. I made a ninety-degree turn until I thought I was off the airway in uncontrolled airspace and then started to orbit, wondering what I was going to do next. Finally, after a few minutes, he came back, gave me a clearance back on the airway and a new frequency, which we mercifully had. He had simply wanted to make a point, and he made it. If we didn't have the exact frequency that the Brits wanted us to have then by God we weren't going to fly on their airway. I thought that his approach was a bit extreme and that he could have endangered our aircraft as well as others. I brought the message back to our squadron in France and it caused a complete review of all of our crystals.

*When the 465th Troop Carrier Wing started to transition from the C-119 into the C-130, each of the pilots was given the opportunity to make the transition if they were willing to extend their European tour for another year. With two on the ramp and one in the hangar, my wife and I wanted to get back to the States and the grandparents, and so did not extend. As part of my Permanent Change of Station (PCS) I had the opportunity to ferry two C-119 aircraft from France back to the States. I took both aircraft from France through the Azores and on one trip went North through Argentia, Newfoundland, and on the other stayed south and went through Bermuda. It amazed me that Argentia was closer to the Azores than Bermuda. I always thought of Newfoundland as being so far north, and I guess it is, but for some reason I just pictured in my mind that it should be further away from the Azores than Bermuda.

Both flights went well except for the leg from the Azores to Bermuda. The computed fuel reserve for that leg was 1.5 hours. It got my attention when the Navigator announced that we were 45 minutes late to the halfway point. If we had the same error on the second half of the leg we would arrive in Bermuda with dry tanks. I'm not quite sure what happened, but we made it up on the second half of the leg. Both fuel and time were right on the precomputed numbers. Our Navigator had jumped in the jug in the Azores the night before and, with the fuzz that existed in the cockpit, I believe he probably misplaced the halfway point.

Chapter 4

1958 - 1962

Randolph Air Force Base
San Antonio, Texas

**Find the inner child within yourself
Then kick its little ass
and get moving!**

*My arrival at Randolph AFB to be an instructor in KC-97 Tankers was faced with some trepidation to be sure. I had no four-engine time and no background in aerial refueling. The Commander, Lietenant Colonel Claude McIver, obviously felt the same way. His policy was to interview all new pilots along with their Form 5 flying record. When I showed up with my Form 5, he said, "There must be some mistake. You have no four-engine time and no tanker time, I can't use you as an instructor." I could see us getting transferred after I had gotten all moved into our quarters. With two young babies and Colleen pregnant with the third, I didn't want to go through that again.

I spent the next thirty minutes convincing this man that I was the world's best pilot. I pointed out that I had extensive experience on all the KC-97 systems, including the engine, because they were identical to the C-119, of which I had just spent three years flying all over Europe. In my eyes, the KC-97 was just a four-engine C-119. I could get my refueling experience by going through the school. He said that there were 27 long, memory item emergency checklists that I would have to know verbatim and be able to react to instantly. I could tell that I was losing the battle. But that changed when I said, "Colonel, let me go through the school and, if I can't hack it, I'll know it before you do, and I'll come and tell you." That apparently sold him and I went through the school.

Since the instructors there were all old, experienced heads, I was the only First Lieutenant Instructor Pilot in the Wing. I think the Commander realized he did the right thing, giving me the chance he did, when our crew won the top crew award two years in a row. One of the smart things they did for a relatively inexperienced KC-97 Instructor Pilot like myself was to give me a strong Flight Engineer. Master Sergeant Elmer Webb was a dream. What he didn't know about the KC-97 wasn't worth knowing.

Several years later, when I had grown comfortable in the KC-97, I was selected to host a tour of a KC-97 for a group of VIPs who were touring our unit. It provided me with one of my more embarrassing moments. I don't recall the exact glowing words that were used when the Commander introduced me to this group of Senators, Generals and other high ranking Air Force officers, but it was something like, "Lieutenant Reed is one of our most proficient pilots," and the words 'Hot Shot' may have been used.

Boeing KC-97 Stratotanker

We boarded a bus and proceeded to the flight line and to the aircraft that had the tail number I had been given for the tour. Arriving at the aircraft, we all got off the bus and I noted that the entrance door to the aircraft was closed. In all the hours that I had flown the KC-97, the door had never been closed when I arrived at the airplane because the airplane had always been prepared for flight. I put my hand in the small opening that I thought might be the handle for opening the door and, try as I might, with all the VIPs waiting and watching, I could not figure out how to open that door. What I didn't know was that there was a little latch inside the handle that had to be depressed to turn the handle and open the door. Finally, and with a very red face, I had to send for a mechanic to open the door. So much for being a 'Hot Shot.' I could tell you anything you wanted to know about the KC-97, except how to open the entrance door. That was an embarrassing moment.

*We had two basic types of sorties with the KC-97 aircraft. One was a straight five-hour transition mission in which we trained crews in normal and emergency procedures, which usually included lots of touch-and-go landings. The other was a ten-hour Navigation/Air Refueling mission that also included transition time at the end. In either case, both the instructor and student crews received a grueling workout on every mission. On one of our ten-hour Navigation/ Air refueling missions, we were passing over Louisiana at about 17,000 feet when the Instructor Navigator decided to give the student some training in lowering the nose gear manually. The uplock release and hand crank to lower the nose gear in place was located in the "Hell Hole" just behind the pilot's seats. This was a two-foot-by-two-foot opening in the cockpit floor that went to a compartment housing all of the radios and associated electronic equipment for the airplane. After the student navigator descended into the Hell Hole to freefall the nose gear and crank it into place, he appeared again, head and shoulders sticking out of the opening, and declared, "I can't turn the crank. It keeps hitting the deck and won't turn."

"Here, let me do it," the Instructor Navigator said. The next thing I knew, the Instructor Navigator's head was sticking out of the hell hole declaring, "I can't turn the crank. It keeps hitting the deck."

Elmer Webb, the Flight Engineer, said, "Here, I'll show you how to do it." Sure enough, he had the same problem. The nose gear was down, but not locked, and Elmer was standing in the Hell Hole with only a thin piece of aluminum between him and Louisiana, 17,000 feet below. He called to me and said, "OK, Lieutenant, I'm going to stand on the hand crank while you put the gear down electrically." So, while Elmer stood on the hand crank, I placed the gear switch in the down position.

I could hear the gear motor whine as I watched Elmer get pushed up about eight inches and then dramatically drop back into the Hell Hole.

He thought he was going out the bottom to Louisiana and his arms had dug into the deck, hanging on for dear life. After we retrieved Elmer from the Hell Hole and started a turn back toward Randolph AFB in Texas, we investigated this unusual phenomenom. What we found was the entire nose gear area had bent and broken aluminum and the actuator that held the gear in the locked, over-the-center position had broken loose from the mount and was simply hanging there. What this meant was that although the nose gear was down, there was nothing to lock it into place. One little bounce on the runway would cause a collapse. I contacted the SAC Command Post at Randolph, apprised them of our situation and asked for foam on landing. At that time, foam was the acceptable method of landing with gear problems. The Command Post said that they would prefer I land at Kelly AFB rather than Randolph and they would make arrangements for the foam and fire gear. The landing was basically uneventful, but the pucker factor was high as we came to a stop on the four-foot strip of foam that was spread for the nose gear. We found out later that on the previous day's mission, one of the Wing people had made the final landing of the day on an alternately wet/dry runway, cocked the nose wheel on a wet spot, and then hit a dry spot, causing the damage. They failed to investigate or write up the damage and we found it in flight. That doesn't say much for Post Flight and Pre Flight inspections.

On another Navigation leg that took us over Louisiana, we were approaching New Orleans when New Orleans Center called and asked if we could provide assistance. I told them we could. They said there was a vessel on fire about 80 miles south of the New Orleans V.O.R. The crew had called in a May Day and were huddled on the after deck fearing an explosion. The Coast Guard was getting underway and they asked if we could get a good fix and a visual surveillance of the situation. I said we would, and immediately called the SAC Command Post at Omaha, Nebraska, to advise them we were breaking our Navigation Leg. Actually, the only reason I called them was because the Wing was graded in the performance of the navigation leg and any unauthorized deviations resulted in a bad grade. I was surprised when the Duty Officer called back and asked if I had over-water gear on board. I said no, as we had not planned an over-water flight. However, we had four engines, the aircraft was performing well, we were responding to a mayday and we would only be eighty miles from shore. A few seconds later he came back and directed us to continue our navigation leg and not go to the boat. I was amazed. Here we were, in perfectly good shape in a four-engine aircraft and they were directing us to deny assistance to a mayday.

When I reluctantly told New Orleans Center that we would have to decline assistance, they got a single-engine T-28 to fly out and get a position on the vessel. Life is full of learning experiences. This one taught me to act first on your own intuition and tell the powers that be after it's over. More often than not, the powers that be would prefer it that way also.

*Our Strategic Air Command (SAC) refueling tracks in Texas ran north and south. On one refueling mission in south Texas that paralleled the Rio Grande River, we were in position as the B-47 we were scheduled to rendezvous with started down from altitude to join up for a practice refueling mission. Suddenly over the radio, on our SAC, VHF, refueling frequency, I heard a female voice talking in Spanish. After listening for a few minutes, I gave the voice a call in English and was surprised when I got a response in English with a heavy Spanish accent.

It turns out that the woman talking on this SAC refueling frequency was a dispatcher for a trucking company, which her father owned, in the Mexican town of Piedras Negras, right across the Rio Grande River from Eagle Pass, Texas. Just by chance, their dispatch frequency was the same as this particular frequency for our western most refueling track. We struck up a conversation and every time I would get the western refueling track we would have a nice conversation and she even invited me to come visit and have dinner.

The SAC Command Post was very interested in our conversation because they could only hear my side of the discussion.

* Takeoff times at Randolph in the KC-97 Training Wing were critical because he Wing was graded on each training mission meeting it's initial on time takeoff.

On this particular day I was Tower Officer at Randolph AFB where our KC-97's were stationed.

One crew was ready to taxi out to meet their on time takeoff, but the flight lunches had not yet been delivered to the airplane. On a 10 hour mission the crew really needed to have those flight lunches. When the time came that they had to taxi, the Aircraft Commander made the decision that they would go ahead and taxi and if the flight lunches don't show up in time, they will go ahead and takeoff to make their on time departure then come around the pattern and land to get their flight lunches.

They got into the run up area, did their run up and prepared to takeoff. The instructor scanner, in the rear of the aircraft, noticed a pool of liquid under the left main landing gear and advised the pilot that it could be hydraulic fluid. The pilot advised the instructor scanner to deplane and check it out. The KC-97 is a two deck airplane with the crew all on the upper deck. The Instructor Scanner proceeded to the lower deck, deplaned and found that it was just a puddle of water and started back in to the lower compartment. When the Student Scanner reported that the Instructor Scanner was back on board he reported that to the pilot.

Just as the Instructor Scanner on the lower deck was starting to crank up the entrance door, he noticed the flight lunch truck driving up and deplaned to get the lunches.

It was at this time the Pilot, having been told that the Instructor Scanner was back on board and being anxious to make an on time takeoff, added power to make a rolling takeoff.

The Instructor scanner ran to catch up with the KC-97 now taking the active runway, managed to get on board and tried to crank up the entrance door. In his haste the articulated rod that holds the door bent the wrong way and he had to lower the door to get the articulated rod to bend in the right direction.

As the KC-97 proceeded down the runway and took off I noticed that the aft entrance door was in the fully extended position with the Scanner desperate to get it up and closed.

Once airborne the wind forces prevented him from cranking the door closed and they came around the pattern, landed with the door open and picked up their lunches. They then departed on their mission without further incident.

Since there was no damage or injuries, that was one of those incidents that was better off not reported.

Some people will do anything to entertain themselves. One story that circulated was that a KC-97 Instructor Crew (no names) decided that they would like to be the first crew in history to shut down all four engines on a KC-97 in flight and turn it into a glider. It was a well planned maneuver, although illegal and foolhardy.

First, they were all sworn to secrecy. Second, they discussed in detail the events that would take place. At about 18,000 feet they would start the Auxiliary Power Unit (APU) and get it on line. This is necessary because the feathering motors used to feather and unfeather the propellers are high-load electrical motors.

Because she was a tanker, the KC-97 was different from most airplanes. The battery, in a sealed container, was disconnected in flight from the main aircraft electrical bus when the main gear oleo strut extended on takeoff. Although electrical power would be available from the engine-driven generators to feather the engines, unless the APU was running and online, there would be no electrical power to unfeather the first engine and get an engine-driven generator back online. So, with everything ready, APU online, the pilot started to feather the engines: first, #1, then #4, then #2, then #3. All four engines were feathered. It got awful quiet as they became a glider in that monster.

As the ground drifted closer, and everyone was getting nervous, the pilot reached up and pulled out the feathering button to start #3. That's when the APU current limiter blew and all the lights went out. Without electrical power there was no way to get the first engine started. Wasn't this going to be a lovely accident report? Panic ensued!

With no way to get the battery back online, things looked grim. And then, one of those silent heroes who appear just as the lion is about to bite showed up. The crew chief, who was along for the ride, remembered that they had left some heavy wire on board from an earlier maintenance job. He and the Flight Engineer removed the sealed battery cover and physically jumped the battery to the main aircraft bus, providing enough power to get the first engine unfeathered. Few people to this day know that story, and even fewer know their names.

Republic F-84 G 'THUNDERJET'

*There were 10 F-84 Gs assigned to our Refueling Wing, and I salivated at the chance to strap my young butt to one of them. These F-84s were equipped with refueling receptacles and were used to provide training for refueling crews when SAC Bombers were not available. So I was absolutely delighted when my request for a checkout in the F-84 was approved. After I studied the Dash-1 Pilot's Handbook, filled out the appropriate questionnaire and got some ground training, I was ready to go. A chase pilot accompanied me on the first flight. Now, I had heard stories about this guy who was going to fly chase on me, but didn't pay much attention to them. After we got to altitude, he suggested that I run the airspeed 10 or 15 knots past the limiting Mach (maximum speed for the airplane). Every airplane has its own idiosyncrasy as you push it to its maximum speed. We used to do this in the T-33 to demonstrate the aileron buzz that you got when you exceeded the limiting Mach in that plane, and I thought that was what he was trying to demonstrate to me. What I didn't know was that in the F-84, when you got past the limiting Mach, you experienced elevator reversal. That is, the stick inputs were reversed. When you pulled back you went down, and when you pushed forward you went up.

As I pressed beyond the limiting Mach I didn't notice any aileron buzz, so no big deal. But when I tried to pull back and slow the bird back to the other side of the limiting Mach, the nose started down. Normal human tendency is to do the thing that has always worked. Pretty soon, even with the power off, I was going straight down 50 or 60 knots over the red line with this guy's voice laughing over the radio. Texas was coming up mighty fast and the trees were starting to get bigger. The thing that got me out of it were the speed brakes. When I popped them, they got me back on the other side of the red line and the airplane started flying properly again. He and I had a little chat back on the ground.

*Things were a little different from now in those days. As it turned out, I was current and actively flying five different types of airplanes during that period. I was instructing on the side in the C-119s at Brooks AFB. The reserves were transitioning from C-46s to C-119s and welcomed the help. Then I was flying the F-84 and T-33, instructing in the KC-97 at Randolph and flying the L-20 in the AeroClub. In addition, I would go to Kelly AFB, also near San Antonio, and hitch rides in the B-52 and F-102 on the test hops. Kelly was an overhaul facility for those aircraft. Our instructor pilots used to pull tower duty to monitor operations at Kelly when we had KC-97s transitioning there.

One day, while I was pulling tower duty, a C-46 pilot called for Taxi/ Takeoff. The tower cleared him to Runway 15 and he proceeded to taxi out and complete his runup. When the runup was completed he called, "LOG AIR 534 ready for takeoff." The tower cleared him for takeoff and the C-46 taxied onto the active. The Kelly Runway 15 is 11,550 feet long and 300 feet wide, and that C-46 looked awfully small on that big runway.

When he started his takeoff you could tell something was wrong, even as far away as we were. There was a lot of rudder movement and the airplane started veering from the centerline. As it progressed from centerline, it got all of our attention in the tower. We watched in amazement as it left the runway, rudder flailing, and then returned to the runway only to transition clear across the 300 feet, left the runway on the other side and proceeded to disappear in a cloud of dust while executing a loose ground loop.

Then, over the radio in a slow, calm and clear voice epitomizing a white-haired old Captain with decades of experience, we heard, in a very slow drawl, "Kelly Tower, this is LOG AIR 534. That last takeoff was a little sloppy. We'd like to go back and try it over again." All of us in the tower busted up laughing and, of course, the tower chief advised him to hold his position and sent the Airdrome Officer out to check them over. They appeared to be sober. It seems that someone forgot to lock the tail wheel and it got away from them in the crosswind.

*Reese Air Force Base at Lubbock, Texas, was an Air Training Command (ATC) Training Base. As I had business there one day, I scheduled a T-33 (T-Bird) to fly there in the morning, conduct my business and then fly back to Randolph that afternoon. I had a very important function to attend that night, so I had to get back to Randolph by about 1700. I was approached the afternoon before the trip by an old Master Sergeant who had found out through the scheduler that I was taking a T-Bird to Reese. He said that he was going to retire in a few weeks and had some very important business to take care of at Laredo (also an ATC base). He asked if it would be possible for me to drop him off at Laredo on my way to Reese and pick him up on the way back. I did a quick mental calculation on time/distance and decided I could work it into my schedule. But I did emphasize to the Sergeant that I had a very important engagement that evening at Randolph and that he would have to assure me that he would be at Laredo Base Operations ready to go no later than 1600. He promised that he would be there at exactly 1600.

The next day, I dropped him at Laredo, as planned, and flew up to Reese. When I was finished, I went by Laredo to pick up the Sergeant, pulling into Base Operations there at about 1530. At the appointed hour, there was no sign of my passenger and I started to get anxious. I had insisted that he leave me a phone number where he could be reached and so I called him. The line was busy, and stayed busy for the next thirty minutes. I didn't feel as if I could just leave him there. Since the telephone number was an on-base number, and the base phone book wasn't too thick, I went down all of the quarters' phone numbers and found the one he had given me. This gave me an address.

I called the head of the Air Police, explained my dilemma and asked if he could send someone over there to find out where the Sergeant was. He said he would. I went back out to the bird and sat on the wing waiting to see what would happen. It wasn't too long before the Sergeant appeared between two Air Policeman, who were escorting him out to the plane. They explained that the Sarge and his buddy were having a party and had taken the phone off the hook. I was mad! I had gone out of my way to help this guy and all he wanted to do was party with his buddy. Besides a lot of extra time, he had caused me to miss my important engagement that evening. I really became uncorked when he smiled and said, " Well, Lieutenant, you gonna chew me out now?" I knew that a Lieutenant chewing out a Master Sergeant within a few weeks of retirement was worthless, so I strapped him in the back seat and took off for Randolph.

Staying below 10,000 feet, I leveled off and told him to take off his oxygen mask and get out his hat.

"Why do you want me to do that?" he said weakly.

I yelled, "Take off your oxygen mask and get out your hat!"

When I could see in the mirror that he had removed his mask and had his hat, I started to aileron roll that T-Bird. I'd roll it to the right for a few minutes then I'd roll it to the left for a few minutes. I corkscrewed that T-Bird, first one way, then the other, all the way back to Randolph Pretty soon I could hear him heaving over the hot mic. I went to 100 percent oxygen up front so I couldn't smell anything and continued to roll. The objective in getting him to take out his hat was to give him something to heave into. But the hat filled up long before he was through and, unfortunately, he dropped it. You can imagine what that rear seat looked and smelled like when we pulled into the parking area at Randolph. And he was really, really sick. The rule is, if you mess it up, you clean it up. As bad as he felt, the T-Bird Line Chief made him stay and clean up every bit of that cockpit. I knew that chewing him out would do no good, but there's more than one way to skin a cat. I don't know where that old Sarge is now, but I guarantee that he remembers that ride.

*For those who are faint of heart or weakened by the sight of blood, it may be best to skip over the next few paragraphs:

At one time, the policy for crash landing in a single-engine fighter was to blow the canopy prior to touchdown. This was a result of incidents where the canopy jammed during the crash and the pilot couldn't get out and away from the aircraft to escape the ever-potential fire. And so it was when a straight-wing F-84 took off and flamed out just as the pilot started gear retraction. As soon as he realized what had happened, he slammed the gear handle to the down position, but the aircraft settled back to the runway before the gear had time to extend. Realizing he was going to auger in, the pilot blew the canopy and slid off the end of the runway across the perimeter road and into the barbed wire fence around the road. With the F-84 on its belly, the barbed wire rode up over the nose, up and over the windshield and came into the cockpit, catching the pilot in the mouth. The airplane came to a stop with the wire taut, having cut through the pilot's cheeks back to the connecting points of the jaw bone. He was alive, but his head was pinned to the seat by the barbed wire.

When the fire department showed up, one of the fireman looked into the cockpit at the pilot, still alive with his eyes rolling and blood spurting from the incision the wire had made, saw the taut barbed wire coming out of his jaw and ran to the truck for the wire cutters. The problem was that in his haste, and without thinking, instead of making the wire cut at the pilot, he ran to the closest point, which was a fence post, and cut the wire there. What would have been a very uncomfortable experience became a major medical problem as the stretched barbed wire twanged through the pilot's mouth.

*A Mechanic on the KC-97 flight line was standing on a maintenance stand working on a Pratt and Whitney 4360 engine and couldn't quite reach a place he needed to get to. Normally at this point he should have gotten off the stand and used the hydraulic mechanism to raise the stand higher to a position that would enable him to reach his work. It was more expedient, however, to just stand on the safety rails and brace himself with his other hand on the engine. And with his greasy boots on, that's just what he did. A finger will slide between two cylinder hold down bolts, but a finger with a ring on it won't. When he slipped and fell to the ground, his finger stayed on the engine and, to make it worse, it was still connected to the man by the now stretched tendon that runs from the finger to the elbow. I'm not sure where they cut the tendon, but for months after that (and with the victim's permission), the safety officer kept the finger in a jar of formaldehyde on his desk.

*I was pre-flighting a T-33 for a test hop one morning, and as I approached the tail of the aircraft, I heard a loud **'KABOOM'** from the row of aircraft in the line behind mine. I looked up in time to see a seat with a man in it blowing through the canopy of a T-Bird. The seat continued up to its full height, however, the occupant apparently hooked on something and flopped over to the ramp. I ran to the aircraft and found a mechanic lying on the ground with his right knee missing and his right arm held on only by pieces of skin. Instantly, people gathered and we tried to make him as comfortable as possible until the medics showed up.

It turned out that the mechanic was an Explosives Ordnance Disposal (EOD) Master Sergeant who had been in EOD his entire career and was going to retire in six months. Since the EOD guys do all the work on ejection seats, he was in the process of installing an ejection seat modification that had come out. The procedure called for the right armrest to be raised, which arms the ejection seat and exposes the ejection trigger. The procedure also specified that the gas lines to the expander tube should be disconnected prior to raising the armrest to prevent an accidental ejection. But the mechanic had done many of these modifications and found that it was a lot quicker to just raise the handle, be very careful, and not fool around with disconnecting the expander tube lines. While he was hunkered down in the cockpit, one of his men walked up beside the airplane to ask the Sarge if he could go to an early lunch. When the Sarge raised up to respond, the tool holder on his belt caught on the ejection trigger and off he went. His butt was several inches above the seat when the seat caught him. As he started up, his right arm didn't clear the side railing and was torn off. He and the seat went through the canopy and the thing that probably saved his life was that his knee caught on the metal former that the leading edge of the canopy attaches to. This prevented him from staying with the seat through its full travel. Although he survived this accident, he was both physically and mentally changed. Where he had once been a hard-slogging, beer drinking tough guy before, he entered retirement as a meek, withdrawn and wistful man.

Although somewhat gory, I believe it's important to relate stories such as these because that's the way we learn. In the Air Force, I found that pilots seemed to talk to each other about aircraft systems and accidents and situations that had happened to them. That was a great learning tool. Later, when I got involved in civilian aviation, I found that pilots didn't converse so much with each other about those subjects.

I missed that.

Addendum to Chapter 4
Concerning Master Sgt. Elmer Webb:

I have previously mentioned in this Chapter that due to my relative inexperience with the refueling mission and the KC-97 aircraft that the 4397th Air Refueling Wing Operations assigned me a very strong, very experienced, Flight Engineer, Master Sgt. Elmer Webb.

Over the four years that we flew together, we became very close friends and I had a great deal of respect for his character and professional ability and believe he had the same for me. When the KC-97 school closed down in 1962, we went our separate ways. I believe Elmer retired while I went on to other endeavors. After retirement from the Air Force we eventually wound up for our first of two tours at the Kwajalein Missile Range from 1980 to almost 1986

When we returned to the states after our first tour at Kwajalein, we received a notice that the 4397th Air refueling Wing reunion would be held at Randolph AFB and the list of attendees included Master Sgt (ret) Elmer Webb.

Since I had not seen Elmer in over 25 years we elected to attend the reunion. It was great seeing Elmer and when he asked me what I had been doing, I recounted the past years finishing up with the six years at Kwajalein. When I said Kwajalein his eyes got big and he told me the following story which he had never mentioned in the four years that we flew together:

During WWII he had been a Flight Engineer on B-24's in the Pacific in the Pacific Theater. After our forces captured Tarawa in that bloody battle, his unit flew to Tarawa in preparation for the invasion of the Marshall Islands, specifically the Kwajalein Atoll.

His crew was picked out of all the crews, to make a low pass down the runway just at daybreak on the morning of the invasion and drop a string of bombs that would close the runway and deny its use to the Japanese planes during the ensuing battle.

And that's what they did. Making a night takeoff from Tarawa, they arrived in the vicinity of Kwajalein and at daybreak, made a low level pass down the runway dropping a string of bombs that denied the Japanese the use of the runway during the invasion.

Neither of us would know that 36 years later, I would be flying off that same runway, which by then had been upgraded to modern standards.

Point of note: The modern runway at Kwajalein is tilted slightly to allow rain water to drain into catchments between the runway and taxiway as a source of water for the island. It is then pumped into and stored in 15 one million gallon storage tanks.

Chapter 5

1962 - 1966

* Yokota Air base, Japan

Often, some of the toughest decisions in life are:
Which bridges to cross
and
which bridges to burn!

In 1962, when the 4397th Air Refueling Wing was disbanded and my next assignment was to KC-135's at Minot North Dakota I was sorely disappointed. So, when one evening, about 2100, I received a call from the Wing D.O. that the Wing was to submit four names for an overseas assignment, he asked if I would like to volunteer? The only thing they knew about the assignment was that it was overseas and it was an accompanied assignment which meant that families were also allowed to go.

I said I would be most interested and please include my name.

As it turned out, of the four names submitted, my name was selected for the assignment and that is how I became an Airborne Operations officer. After a 30 day TDY to McClellan AFB for briefings and training, my first assignment was to Eielson AFB Alaska, just outside of Fairbanks, in August of 1962. I was a young and eager Captain.

The Russians had started a very aggressive Nuclear test program and we were very busy with a 24 hour schedule. The senior officer at the detachment and the only other Airborne Operations Officer was a Lt. Col. We pulled 12 hour shifts.

Our job was to develop tracks for aircraft to search the atmosphere and collect particulate and gaseous samples from nuclear tests.

At our disposal were a myriad of aircraft that included: RB-50's, WC-135's, B-47's, B-57's and U-2's. These aircraft would pick up gaseous and particulate samples of the atmosphere which would be analyzed by our in house lab and then sent to McClellan for additional analysis.

Sometime around early to mid October, the Lt. Col. had a problem and was pulled out (transferred) in a hurry and I was then the sole Airborne Operations Officer at that unit running a 24 hour operation. Apparently there was no replacement available for the Lt. Col.

Late on the 26th of October, 1962, I assigned an upper level track to the U-2 unit. The track was very simple and very basic: From Eielson AFB to as close to the North Pole as the Pilot could get, then return to Eielson.

As you fly North from Eielson AFB there is a certain point that your compass becomes useless. To help solve this problem aircraft have a Directional Gyro that somewhat holds the heading but, as with all gyros, it has a precession error so it cannot be completely relied on.

At this time modern navigation systems such as Satellite Navigation or G.P.S. were not around.

The way the U-2 pilots solved this problem is that, when they made the turn at the north pole, they would look through a small window where they had pre computed the position of a certain star and kept that star in their window until the compass started working again.

In this case, the pilot turned at the pole **but homed in on the wrong star.** Instead of turning 180 degrees to head back to Eielson he turned short and headed for Russia.

This in itself would not normally have been that critical but the time was October 27th 1962, at the most critical time of the Cuban Missile Crisis when President Kennedy and Premier Krushchev were nose to nose.

Recorded in the War Room Journal and others. See below :

Around 10:15 to 11:00 A.M.: A U-2 from a SAC Base in Alaska strays into Soviet Airspace over the Chukotski Peninsula on what was reported to be a "routine air sampling mission" The U-2 Pilot apparently enters Soviet airspace as a result of a navigational error. The pilot radios for assistance and U.S. F-102 fighter aircraft in Alaska scramble and head toward the Bering Sea. At the same time, Soviet Migs take off from a base near Wrangel Island to intercept the U-2, which eventually manages to fly out of Soviet territory with no shots being fired. Alaskan Air Command records suggest that the U.S. Fighter planes are armed with nuclear air-to-air missiles. According to one account, when Secretary of defense McNamara hears that a U-2 was in Soviet airspace, "he turned absolutely white, and yelled hysterically, 'this means war with the Soviet Union."

President Kennedy's laconic reaction upon hearing of the incident is simply to laugh and remark "there is always some {son of a bitch} who doesn't get the word. (War Room Journal,10/27/62; Chronology of the Cuban Crisis October 15-28, 1962,

11/2/62. P.14; Interview of David A. Burchinal, 4/11/75.pp. 114-15; Hilsman 1, p.221; Sagan 2 pp. 117-18; Air defense Operations, ca. 12/62)

This is an excerpt from an article written by Michael Dobbs in the 22 June, 2008 issue of the Washington Post:

"By contrast, historians have given scant attention to a much more frightening moment -- the accidental overflight of the Soviet Union by an American U-2 spy plane amid the swirling tensions of what White House aides called "Black Saturday," Oct. 27. Capt. Charles "Chuck" Maultsby was on a routine mission to keep an eye on Soviet nuclear tests when he took a wrong turn at the North Pole and ended up in Soviet airspace on the most dangerous day of the Cold War. Air Force chiefs failed to inform Kennedy and McNamara for an hour and a half that they had a plane over the Soviet Union, even though the Soviets sent MiG fighters to shoot Maultsby down and the Alaskan Air Command responded by scrambling nuclear-armed U.S. fighter-interceptors."

When the U-2 Pilot, Chuck Maultsby, saw the lights of Wrangel Island he knew he was not where he was supposed to be. Reports are that he could see the contrails of Russian Fighters trying to reach his position.

President Kennedy got on the hot line to Premier Krushchev and told him that we have a lost U-2 pilot over your country on a weather mission and he is not-repeat-not a hostile aircraft.

When the morning sun started rising in the east and his compass finally started working Chuck headed east where he was met by a couple of our F-102's that escorted him back. He had made the longest U-2 flight ever, and ran his fuel down to zero, flamed out and had to dead stick in with his face mask frosted over.

It was my understanding that Chuck was standing in front of General Powers, then the SAC Commander, the next day, explaining what had happened.

Another potential career ending event took place when I was sent with a small Air Force contingent, to Pago Pago, American Samoa, in conjunction with the upcoming nuclear tests in the Tuamotu Archipelago. Pago Pago is actually a small town on the island of

Tutuila, America Samoa. The island is about 26 miles long with a hogback of large jungle covered hills running down the center of the island.

Pago Pago is pronounced Pongo-Pongo. The 'G' in Samoan always has an unseen 'N' preceding it.

Pago, Pago was only a backup location in the event the upper air winds reversed themselves and went west. I had 2 WC-135's and 2 Long Wing RB-57's on site, to launch if that were to occur.

After we got settled in at Pago Pago I got out the charts, did some plotting and figured out that a WC-135 could just make the route from Pago Pago to the border of the published hazard area and return which would provide the best samples. By launching the WC-135 several hours before the event was to take place, he would be on site as the effluent left the hazard area and we could pick it up. The timing was critical for several reasons. Because of the fuel requirements we only had the minimum of time on site. There was no reasonable alternate for Pago Pago so everything had to go as planned, to the minute. A good weather forecast was an absolute.

The flight went off perfectly as planned, we got fine samples in a very short time and the bird started back toward Pago Pago. Then things started to go south.

To this day I'm not sure where he got it but the Aircraft Commander (A/C) got a weather report that Pago Pago weather was deteriorating, which was not true. The weather at Pago Pago was beautiful and forecast to stay that way.

But the WC-135 Aircraft Commander after receiving that incorrect weather report and knowing he would be low on fuel with no alternate to go to, decided he'd better get some fuel and diverted into Papeete, Tahiti.

The airport people and especially the controllers and tower people knew exactly where the airplane had come from and what it was doing. They knew that if possible, the French government would like to impound the airplane.

They searched in vain for someone who had the authority to delay or impound the bird.

With his Air Force credit card, the A/C took on enough fuel to make him feel comfortable then took off with minimum ground time, before they were able to find someone in authority.

The reason they were not able to find someone in time is that it was Bastille day (the French 4th of July), all Government Offices were closed and people were scattered about at parties.

Yokota Air Base is located just west of Tokyo, in the Kanto Plains area. At that time, Tachikawa Air Base was just a few miles from Yokota and had the heavy lift mission with the C-124 Globemaster. Since that time, Tachikawa has closed and Yokota has absorbed their mission, only now it is accomplished with large turbine aircraft, such as the C-5 Galaxy and C-141 Starlifter.

Initially, I started flying the C-47 aircraft with Base Flight. After several trips to Korea and Hong Kong, I was able to transition into the T-33 (T-Bird) aircraft, also assigned to Base Flight. One of the missions that the 'T-Bird' had was to exercise the Air Defense F-102 aircraft by flying out to sea then approaching Tokyo at low level over the water. As the Air Defense system picked up the 'intruder' aircraft, they would launch the interceptors and attempt to 'shoot' us down electronically.

'T-Birds' over Mount Fujiama, west of Tokyo. Note the Chaff Dispensers under the wing

We carried Chaff Dispensers under each wing and, as the intercept was taking place, would drop chaff (aluminum strips) from the dispensers in an attempt to confuse the radars.

*We had only been at Yokota a few months when I suddenly got the urge to buy a sailboat. Now, I loved boats, but with one exception had never been on a sailboat. But this urge came over me and I was determined to learn how to sail. I went to Yokohama, an area that I was pretty familiar with, and toured the boat builders there. I met an aging Japanese man, a Mr. Okamoto, who owned a yacht building business just south of Yamashita Park. After looking at several boats that didn't fit, he said that his son had a friend who came from a wealthy family and was trying sell his boat. It seems he wanted his father to buy him an airplane but his father wouldn't buy the airplane until he sold his sailboat. Mr. Okamoto thought that we might be able to get a pretty good deal. His company had built the boat and he knew it to be a good, solid and well-built vessel. It was sloop rigged, 28 feet long, the hull was double planked Philippine Mahogany. It had a reliable Yanmar diesel and it was only one-and-a-half years old. That all sounded pretty good to me, so I went back to Yokota and talked Jack Lindsay, a fellow pilot and Det 407 teammate, into becoming a partner in the boat with me. He didn't know a thing about sailing either, but the challenge turned him on.

'TAKA' at Yokosuka Naval Base

We contacted the owner, cut a deal and met him in Aburatsubo Harbor, South of Yokohama, to take possession. He gave us a thirty-minute tour of the boat, showed us how to raise the sails and turned us loose. Between the two of us we sailed out of that harbor into Tokyo Bay and tied up at Yokosuka Naval Base, where we would keep the boat for the next four years. We named her 'TAKA,' the closest Japanese word we could find for Falcon, the Air Force mascot. That was the beginning of a love affair that has lasted over 40 years.

After I had practiced a few times, it was time to take the family out. Now, the family at this time consisted of Colleen, who had never sailed, and the four boys, ages one through eight. So, one Sunday, with Colleen and the three older boys, we drove to Yokosuka and got underway in TAKA. It was a nice sail and, when we returned to the pier, I noted all of the Navy guys sitting on the lawn of the club watching this Air Force guy flailing about into what was historically their territory. I was determined to put on a good show and, after close calculation, figured out that under the existing wind conditions I could sail to the dock without having to use the engine. That would impress them!

I lined everything up, came into the small harbor, tacked a couple of times to get the boat turned around, pointed into the wind and did an absolutely superb job of sailing the boat to the dock. As I eased the sheets and brought the boat to a stop at exactly the right spot, I pirouetted to the pier and turned to ensure that everyone was watching. As my back was turned, a gust of wind hit the mainsail, the main sheet fouled and hung up, and the boat started sailing away from the pier.

When I turned around, there was Colleen and the three little boys, headed back to Tokyo Bay. I had three options: 1) Run like hell and try to make a massive leap back on board; 2) Try and commandeer a chase boat and chase them down; or 3) Go up on the lawn with everyone else, have a drink and see what happened. Actually, I chose the first option, made a mad leap and just barely got back on board. I dropped the sails, started the engine, humbly motored back to the dock and chalked that up as a learning experience.

One weekend, when we were going sailing in Tokyo Bay, I invited another couple to go along. When they showed up at the house, I was startled to see that our friend's wife was in a full leg cast, from her toes all the way up. I suggested that a small sailboat on a windy day might not be an appropriate place for a full leg cast and recommended that they put off their sail till another day. But she was the type who would try anything and insisted that she could handle it. Her husband was the same type. So, in spite of my reluctance, we took off for Yokosuka. We were able to get her on board and settled in the cockpit OK. When we got underway, I knew it was going to be a wild ride and hoped she'd stay put. Everything was going fine until she finished her second beer and needed to use the head (toilet).

We had an enclosed head and I helped her below, got all the valves in the proper place, left her on her own behind the closed door and went topside to wait until she was finished. The head was on the port side and we were on a port tack, so she was sitting on the high side of the boat holding on to the seat for dear life with her leg in the cast sticking horizontally straight out. With a pretty stiff breeze blowing, we were making good time with a substantial heel. The little bolts that hold the seat to the commode apparently couldn't stand the strain anymore and both let go at the same time. The noise attracted my attention and I saw her come through the door, her leg acting like a battering ram. With wild eyes, she was still sitting and holding on to the seat with both hands as she shot from the port side to the starboard side. Fortunately, she wasn't hurt, but that vision of her coming through that door on that toilet seat, eyes and mouth wide, holding on for dear life, still sticks in my mind.

*Her husband, Dick, was as much a character as she. When one of the Bomb Squadrons disbanded, it was a big deal. A lot of big brass came to Yokota for the ceremony. We all attended the formal Dining In, attired in our Mess Dress Uniforms with all decorations. The head table was huge and ran almost the full width of the room. The rest of the tables ran at 90 degree angles off the head table and were jammed with eager faces in their splendid uniforms. These ceremonies are often used to present individual awards and Dick, who had already had a few drinks, was slated to receive one. As we toasted the President, Chief of Staff and any other thing that moved, each of us took a sip of wine at each toast. Not Dick! He didn't do anything halfway, and downed his glass at every toast. I was seated close enough to Dick, who was at the head of one of these very long tables, to tell he was going down fast. I started to worry, for I knew he was going to receive a decoration and would be required to perform. When Dick's turn came, his name was called and he struggled to attention at the end of his table. He tried very hard to assume the position of attention, but his thumbs, which should have been at his side, aligned with the seams on his trousers, were desperately clinging to the table in an attempt to hold himself up. I could tell he was in trouble and I had a bad feeling about this. As the elements of the award were read, every eye in the place, including the big guys at the head table, were riveted on Dick. I could tell he was having a little trouble finding vertical and watched horrified as his eyes rolled up under open eyelids and he went over backwards, still at attention! The problem was that he forgot to let go of the tablecloth and wine glasses and bottles and salads and everything else went everywhere. It was hysteria. However, in true Air Force tradition, Dick was removed without ceremony and the festivities continued.

BOEING B-50 'STRATOBOMBER'

George was a good friend. He was also the Flying Safety Officer for the 41st Air Division at Yokota over this period. He had gone sailing with me on TAKA several times and I always enjoyed his relaxed way. George didn't get ruffled.

One day, George was assigned as observer on a KB-50. His task was just to observe the crew's performance. The mission was a daylight refueling of several F-100 Fighter Aircraft. At the completion of that mission, the KB-50 recovered at Misawa AB on Northern Honshu to prepare for a similar mission, to make a night refueling of additional F-100 aircraft. As it turned out, the weather prevented the night refueling mission and the F-100s aborted, so the KB-50 headed south toward Yokota AB, just west of Tokyo. Enroute, the #3 engine (inboard, starboard side) failed and was shut down. Sometime later, the #2 engine (inboard, port side) burst into flame and, after discharging both banks of fire extinguishers, the fire continued to burn.

The Aircraft Commander elected to dive the aircraft in an attempt to blow the fire out, which in several instances has been successful, but more often not. As the speed reached over 300 knots for this old bomber, the airframe couldn't take the strain and pieces of the aircraft started coming off. They believe that one piece hit the elevator, which then made the plane uncontrollable. The Aircraft Commander elected to evacuate the aircraft and initiated bailout procedures. With the bailout bell ringing, George was the last of four people to bailout. Within two to three seconds of George leaving the aircraft, it slammed into a mountain, killing everyone remaining on board. George said that he only swung two or three times in his parachute before touching down, he was that close to the ground when he bailed. Of the eleven personnel on board the KB-50, only four made it out.

George (waving) and two other Air Force friends on a sailing Trip on 'TAKA'

*One of the saddest events of this time was the death of a good friend, Fred Stoss, who I worked with in Detachment 407. Fred had flown multi-engine airplanes most of his flying career (mostly the C-124 Globemaster), and at Yokota had the opportunity to fly the T-33. He was not really keen on flying single-engine jets and I always felt that he flew the bird reluctantly. One night, not too long after his checkout, a bizarre series of events took place.

I happened to be Airdrome Duty Officer (AO) that night and so was on duty when the accident occurred. Fred and a fellow named Black, who had a lot of T-Bird time, had just made a practice instrument approach and were climbing back out for another. They think that at about 12,000 feet climbing, there was a fire and explosion on board and neither pilot got out. The Accident Investigation Board, with assistance from the Tokyo Crime Lab, put together the following cause: A fuel line that ran to the Low Pressure Fuel Filter in the Plenum chamber (intake area) of the engine ruptured. When that happened, raw fuel sprayed into the compressor section of the engine, causing the fire. The fire light then illuminated in the cockpit. At the same time, the raw fuel was picked up in the pressurization system, which pumped these very heavy fuel fumes in the form of mist into the cockpit with the pilots. Black initiated the ejection sequence and, when he did, the aircraft blew up. The Tokyo Crime Lab later proved that the nut that carries the hot gases to the expander tube to jettison the canopy was loose, and when Black initiated the ejection sequence, the hot gases got into the cockpit, now filled with explosive fuel fumes, causing the explosion. We believe that Fred and Black died at that moment.

All aircraft components have a time change or inspection that is required at specific intervals. As a result of this accident it was discovered that the time change for the four-inch line going to the fuel filter was inadvertently left out of the manual, so none of the lines were ever checked during the life of the airplane. All T-Birds were grounded until those fuel lines were changed. The manual was also revised to include a routine inspection and replacement.

*When we first arrived in Japan we lived off-base in a place called Old Tanaka Heights. The living in those places was tough, especially with four young children. The streets weren't paved, so the kids stayed dirty all the time. The only heat during the cold Japanese winters was from a single-burner kerosene heater, which received fuel from an F-86 drop tank on a stand alongside the house. We tried to move what little heat there was around the house with fans. One of the boys had an inherent ability to stay dirty, and most of the time his face looked like a bowling ball with eyes. So it was a big deal when, after two years, we finally got base quarters.

Our neighbor in the duplex was an Air Force Captain with a beautiful wife and young children. Although we didn't become close friends, we had a relationship that was close enough to know that these young people were very much in love. It showed. Not too long after we moved in, action in Vietnam became the major topic of discussion, and it wasn't long after that our neighbor was sent for a 'short' Temporary Duty (TDY) in F-100s to Vietnam that turned into an extensive stay. Somewhere in this period something happened at home. I'm not sure what, but our friend got a "Dear John" from his lovely wife. The next thing we heard was that during a ground support mission, he flew his plane into a hill. They were pretty sure it was suicide because more than one person saw his afterburner light just prior to impact.

Friday's Happy Hour at the Yokota Officers Club was always well attended and I, when in town, rarely missed it. One afternoon I found myself sitting next to one of the Captain Nurses, who was aptly nick-named Sadie Hawkins due to her voluptuous build. It was generally known that Sadie had a reputation to be a bit wild. All of a sudden, the light bulb came on and I saw a chance to be a real wiseguy. By now, I had transitioned from the 'T-Bird' to the T-39 Sabreliner, the first passenger-carrying airplane the Air Force had that could struggle up to 50,000 feet, although it was illegal to do so. So, assuming that Sadie knew what the Mile High Club was, I said, "Sadie, how would you like to be the first woman in history to join the over 50,000 club?"

Without batting an eye she fired right back, "You talkin about feet – or times?"

The T-39 Sabreliner came into the inventory while I was at Yokota.

Another time while at the Yokota bar, I wound up talking to a young Captain, and during the conversation he asked me if I'd like to flip for a drink. I said sure, and with that, he got off his bar stool and did a flip, landing right on his feet. Needless to say, I bought him a drink. "I get a lot of free drinks that way," he said.

* On one trip to Hong Kong the crew went out together to have dinner.

We went to a restaurant/bar and had a drink in the bar prior to eating. Sitting in a booth I noticed that there was a young man, who appeared to be an American listening intently to our conversation.

Finally he came over and asked if we were Air Force and I replied yes we were. He sat down and told us this story: He was a young Captain/ Pilot, stationed at Kadena Air Base in Okinawa in a F-100 Squadron. The F-100 at that time was a front line fighter. He loved the Air Force and especially loved the fighter business, flying the F-100.

He didn't get along with his Operations officer and one day got into a big argument with him. As a result of the argument he elected to resign form the Air Force and did so at Kadena.

A friend of his said that he was building a sailboat in Hong Kong and asked him if he would help him sail the boat back to the west coast of the United States. The young man said that sounded like an adventure and besides his argument with the operations Officer, was probably one of the pieces of the puzzle that convinced him to resign his commission.

As it turned out, the sailboat never materialized, his friend never showed up in Hong Kong, he was broke, didn't have a job and didn't know what he was going to do next.

I felt really sorry for him but I didn't have any answers either. From that point on I always used that story to council young people who were having a difficult time. I would point out that the young man in that story made a decision that effected a long time career based on a short time situation.

In the military if you have someone in the Chain of Command that you can't get along with, very soon either you or he will transfer and that situation will change. That's the way it is in the military. I caution them not to make decisions that affect long term plans based on short term situations.

I'm sure that when the heat from that argument with his Operations Officer cooled down that young Captain regretted his decision to vacate that prestigious and most desirable position as an Air Force Fighter Pilot, many times over.

While stationed at Yokota, I spent a lot of time TDY at other locations. Besides traveling all over the Far East, flying Base Support Missions in the T-39, I went TDY in my Primary duty. One of these TDYs was an entire summer at Pago Pago (pronounced Pongo Pongo), in American Samoa.

Pago Pago is actually a very small town on the island of Tutuila, one of five islands that make up American Samoa. Tutuila is about 25 miles long with a hogback of mountains right down the center of the island. The harbor of Pago Pago is supposedly the crater of a volcano, of which one side has fallen away and allowed the ocean to come in.

When we deployed as a small Air Force unit to Samoa, I managed to smuggle a Honda 90 motorbike onto the plane in a crate disguised as mission equipment. Although I caught a little flak for that, I was the only one of the group to have personal transportation and so got to see a lot of the island.

The south side of Tutuila was the populated side, and at that time there were no roads on the north side of the island. All the villagers who lived on the north side had to hike over the mountains to get to civilization and/or home. However, a road had just been built over the hill behind Pago Pago to the village of Fagesa (pronounced Fangesa. The 'G' in Samoan always has an unseen 'N' preceding it, therefore g is pronounced ng). On one excursion with the Honda 90 over the hill to Fagesa, I met a local fellow called Auvasa Matau. As it turned out, we became very good friends. Auvasa (pronounced Oww-vasa) was the principal of a school located on the north side of the island, and every day he rowed an hour in his Pow Pow (one-man outrigger canoe) to get to school and another hour to get home. While he was at school, his wife ran their one-room store in the village of Fagesa, and that provided some income for them. That is some commute.

Auvasa invited me to his daughter's birthday party one day, and I showed up on my Honda 90, not really knowing what to expect. I found that the birthday party was really more of a religious eating and drinking ceremony (with no booze). In attendance was the local priest, the grandparents, the family and me. I was told that I was the guest of honor. When the food, consisting of potatoes and hot dogs, was brought out it was explained that the guest of honor ate first. I had heard that in different parts of the world it was an insult not to eat what you were given, so I attempted to eat everything that was laid out in front of me. But they kept bringing more food.

After I was full, they continued to bring me food, which I ate and ate until I absolutely was gorged and could eat no more. I did notice that the children kept peeking around the corner to see how I was doing and looking inquisitively at what I had eaten. Auvasa later explained to me that the guest of honor ate what he wanted to first, and everybody else got what was left over. The pecking order (literally) was guest of honor, priest, grandparents, parents, and, lastly, the children. By the time I had gorged trying to be polite, there wasn't much left, and that's why the kids were peeking around the corner, to see if they were going to get anything to eat. I was really embarrassed.

Fagesa is located on a beautiful keyhole harbor surrounded by lush jungle-covered hills and is really a picturesque spot. Auvasa explained that before the road was built, people didn't go over the mountain much and Fagesa was really an isolated village. One day, all of the water in the harbor emptied and the harbor stood dry. The villagers, not knowing why this happened, all went down into the harbor to catch the stranded sea life on the harbor floor. When the tidal wave came back into the harbor, many were drowned. They just didn't know about the water receeding before a tidal wave.

Max Haleck was the major importer for goods on the island. His store and warehouse were located in the building group that formed a major house of ill repute during the war, when 10,000 Marines were stationed on Tutuila. Legend has it that the famed Miss Sadie Thompson was a primary participant/owner of that establishment.

Auvasa was an intelligent man. All of the goods that he got for his one-room store came through Max Haleck at a price that was obviously bumped up. As I was getting ready to leave Samoa, he asked me if I could contact an exporter in the States and check on the price of having goods sent directly to his store, eliminating Max Haleck and his fee from the loop. He gave me an extensive list of goods to check on. Remember, he asked me to "CHECK" on the price of importing goods directly to his store.

Mom was deeply involved in the apple business in Sebastopol, back in California. Since she dealt with exporters, I asked her if she would follow this up for me and gave her the list. Something was lost in the transmission, either in the way I said it or in the way she heard it, and instead of just getting prices, as Auvasa had asked, $2,000 worth of goods showed up on the dock in Pago Pago marked for him. Of course, along with the goods came a bill.

Auvasa would have a difficult time getting $200, much less than $2,000, and I received a letter from the export company shortly after I got back to McClellan AFB in California asking what type of person

Auvasa was. They had shipped him $2,000 worth of goods, had received $200 in partial payment with the promise to pay the rest off. The export company explained that they normally did not do business that way and wondered if they would ever see their money. Of course I gave them a good character reference for Auvasa. I've often wondered how that turned out. Auvasa is either in jail or owns most of Pago Pago by now.

Having been bitten by the sailing bug in Japan, I was genuinely excited when the beautiful 50' gaff-rigged ketch, Ta Aroa, came sailing into Pago Pago harbor. I immediately went down and introduced myself and offered my services. Since I had access to an Air Force truck, I was well received.

There were three girls and two guys on board, and they were on their way around the world. Jack Sederlund, the owner, had bought the boat from a couple who had sailed on their dream cruise from Los Angeles to Mexico, run into some heavy weather and couldn't get rid of the boat fast enough. He had bought it for a song. Jack took it back to L.A. and spent a year outfitting it for the round-the-world sojourn. We became fast friends and I had a great time during the week they spent on Pago Pago. We went on picnics and excursions on the island and I was asked to dinner several times aboard the Ta Aroa.

I was invited to make the 24-hour sail with them on their next leg to Apia, on the island of Upolu in Western Samoa (owned by New Zealand). However, because of mission constraints, I could not make the sail. I did, however, fly over later and spend some time with them in Apia. I stayed at Aggie Greys hotel, a wonderful place with a homey outside bar underneath the hotel. Aggie Grey is allegedly the Bloody Mary of the South Pacific depicted in the famous Broadway show and movie. After spending some time at her bar there in Apia, I can believe it.

After seeing the Ta Aroa off on their next leg, I returned to Pago Pago. Other than one card, I did not hear from them again. For years after that, every time I breezed through a yacht club or marina I would always ask if anyone had heard from or seen the Ta Aroa. The answer was always negative.

Then, one day, years later, while we were in Key West, Colleen was reading the Sunday Miami Herald and came upon a story in the paper titled "The Last Voyage of the Ta Aroa." It was Jack Sederlund's boat, and it chronicled how they had made their dream voyage around the world, gone through the Panama Canal and stopped in Costa Rica, preparing for the last leg back to Los Angeles. With all the stops they had made, it had taken them five years.

The Ta Aroa Crew

Jack Sederlund on the left, the three girls, Alan on the right, and two Air Force friends.

Before they left on their last leg, Jack was befriended by a German man, Wolfgang von Morgenland, who claimed he knew where some underwater artifacts were. Jack loved to dive on wrecks and so he and Yvonne Hackett, an Australian girl who had been sailing with Jack, sailed with Wolfgang on board to show them where the artifacts were. When they got to the spot, the German took out a gun and shot and killed Jack and Yvonne. He then stole the boat and went to pickup his girlfriend, his wife's sister, with the intent of taking off in the boat with her.

Within a few days, Wolfgang ran the Ta Aroa onto a reef and she broke up and sank. The girlfriend went to the police, Wolfgang disappeared into the jungle and, as at the time of the article, had never been found. Apparently, Wolfgang had surveyed a number of boats prior to the arrival of the Ta Aroa and, when he saw her, she was the one he wanted.

I was mesmerized and saddened by that story. To think of the adventures and hazards that Jack had gone through over those five years and to have him, the girl, and the boat end up that way was truly a human tragedy brought about by the greed of one individual.

*I learned a little bit about American Aviation History while at Pago Pago.

Each year, the Ford Motor Company takes 500 of their top salesmen on vacation somewhere in the world. This particular year, 1966, they came to Pago Pago. They took over the entire Intercontinental Hotel, the only large hotel on the island. When they found out there was a small Air Force contingent on island, we were invited to one of their cocktail parties.

Ta Aroa and crew leaving Pago Pago for Apia, Western Samoa

During the evening, I found myself at the bar, engaged in conversation with a retired former officer who claimed that he was very close to Henry Ford during the blossoming years of the company and now hosted these annual vacations on behalf of the company for the salesmen and their wives. He said that after Henry Ford had established himself as an industry giant in the automobile business, he recognized the potential of the airplane and was determined to be a major force in the aviation industry. Ford dedicated a good portion of his company's resources to the development of an airplane, producing the Ford Tri-Motor. With the success of that aircraft, plans were laid out and the process was started that would see the Ford Motor company dominate the aircraft industry.

But one day, a very close friend of Henry Ford was killed in an aircraft accident and Henry was devastated. In his grief, he decided that his company would not be involved with airplanes. From that point on, he scrapped any plans to move the company in the direction of the aviation industry and, with the exception of producing B-24's under Government Contract at the Willow Run plant in Michigan during the Second World War, he backed away from any further attempt to involve himself in aviation.

I am always taken how single events can change history. Because of that single aircraft accident, the entire course of American aviation history has changed. Instead of flying around in Boeings or Lockheeds today, we may have been flying around in Fords.

Some years later, the Pilot of a Navy P-3 Orion Aircraft flying into Pago Pago decided to make a low pass along the harbor. He was unaware of the heavy cable that ran across the harbor for the cable car that ran to the television station. When they hit the cable, the aircraft crashed into the Intercontinental Hotel with a great loss of life. It did considerable damage to the hotel However, it has been rebuilt and is operating under another name.

McClellan Air Force Base
1966 1969
Sacramento, California

*Each year, Air Force Pilots are required to attend an Annual Instrument Refresher Course. This is used to refresh pilots on the complex flying regulations they use and to bring them up to date on changes in regulations and techniques. One year at McClellan AFB, the FAA was invited to attend the refresher course and brought with them two incidents they had recorded on tape and were delighted to play for us.

The first incident takes place in the early days of the Boeing 727, when the airlines first started using jets, and involved a controller(s) at O'Hare Airport, in Chicago, who was not used to the difference in speed between props and jets. The Radar was down so manual control was in use.

It starts out with an Ozark DC-3 asking for taxi, takeoff and went something like this:

"O'Hare, this is Ozark 534, ready to taxi."

"Roger Ozark 534. You are cleared to runway 04. Are you ready to copy your clearance?"

"Roger. Ozark 534 is ready."

"After takeoff, Ozark 534 is cleared a right turn direct to the Poppa Yankee Radio Beacon, maintain 2,000 feet, contact departure control on 125.4."

While Ozark 534 was running up and preparing for take off, a Boeing 727 (I'll use that as the call sign) was preparing to leave.

"O'Hare, Boeing 727 ready for pushback."

"Roger, Boeing 727. You are cleared for pushback and taxi to runway 04."

"Boeing 727 taxi."

"Boeing 727, are you ready to copy your clearance?"

"Boeing 727, ready."

"Roger. After takeoff, Boeing 727 is cleared a right turn direct to the Poppa Yankee Radio Beacon, maintain 2,000 feet, contact departure control on 125.4."

Note that the clearance for the much faster Boeing 727 is the same as for the slower DC-3.

Ozark 534 completed his runup. "Ozark 534 ready for takeoff."

"Ozark 534 is cleared for takeoff. After departure, contact departure control."

Ozark 534 departed.

The 727 arrives at the end of the runway and, because he's a jet, does not need a runup. His before takeoff checklist is complete and he's ready to go. "Boeing 727 ready for takeoff."

"Boeing 727 is cleared for takeoff. After departure, contact departure control."

The Boeing 727 departed, made a solid right turn and proceeded inbound to the Poppa Yankee Radio Beacon.

When the near-miss occurred, the DC-3 pilot later said that they were in a cloud so dense he could hardly see his own wingtip. The 727 wing went over his cockpit close enough to see rivets on the belly – then they went through the wash.

The controller, suddenly realizing what he had done, but not realizing that the near-miss had already taken place, leaped to his microphone and commanded, "Boeing 727, do an immediate 180-degree turn and proceed to the Yankee Zulu Radio Beacon. Maintain 2,000 feet!" The 727 complied.

This put the 727 on a reverse course, headed directly back toward Ozark 524.

After some time, the Ozark pilot finally regained his ability to speak and now, in and out of the cloud, directed the Co-Pilot to report that near-miss. This is what was recorded on the tape.

"O' Hare Departure, this is Ozark 534. I'd like to report a ne ... – LOOKOUT, CHARLEY! HERE COMES THAT SON-OF-A-BITCH AGAIN!"

The second incident took place at Los Angeles Airport, LAX. Again, the radar was down, the fog was in, and departures were manual-control at the busiest part of the day. Manual-control means that instead of the positive control that radar provides, departures were controlled by time, causing major delays when the traffic was heavy. Keep in mind that it is a violation of the FCC Regulations to use profanity over the radio. Violators may be heavily fined.

The first call: "TWA 672 ready for pushback."

"Roger, TWA 672. You are cleared for pushback. Be advised you are number 34 for departure."

Silence on the frequency. Then, after some delay, a very positive, "BULLSHIT!"

The Tower Chief became incensed and was determined to write-up whoever made that profane announcement. He grabbed the microphone. "The aircraft that made that last transmission, identify yourself."

Pan American was at the head of the line of a very weary and agitated group of pilots waiting for departure and started things off with, "This is Pan American 42. Negative on the 'Bullshit'."

Behind him was Hughes Air West "Hughes Air West 583. Negative on the 'Bullshit'."

"Northwest 263. Negative on the 'Bullshit'."

And so it went, down the line, with each aircraft reporting in "Negative on the 'Bullshit'" and the tower chief unable to turn them off. Remember, he had started the whole thing. Our refresher course had a few laughs that year.

*Recall that I had been denied the opportunity to fly the F-86 in France because of the accident in which the Pilot ejected in a snowstorm and the Wing was going to Chaumont, not Toul. Spook Medellin and I got stuck in the C-119. I had always hoped that someday that opportunity to fly the F-86 might come. It came at McClellan Air Force Base.

North American F-86 'SABREJET' Tail # 0-25298 **The Last One**

By 1966, all the F-86Fs had been scrubbed from the Air Force inventory except one. That airplane, tail number 0-25298 was kept in the inventory because many of the F-86s were flying in other countries, such as Taiwan, Korea, Turkey, etc., under the Military Assistance program

(MAP). McClellan AFB was an Air Material Area (AMA) and, among other things, responsible for overseeing the F-86s in the MAP.

This F-86F was assigned to the Flight Test Section at McClellan, which also had the overhaul responsibility for the F-100, F-106, F-104, F-105, B-26 and A-1 airplanes. They eventually also picked up the F-111 program. I often flew backseat with the Flight Test guys whenever I could, and when I found that they had an F-86 and no one was flying it, I made the request to get checked out in the bird. They were required to put so many hours per year on the airframe and, because everyone else was so busy with other aircraft, I think they welcomed me flying it.

She had a beautiful paint job, with red, white and blue drop tanks and an accent on the tail. The maintenance guys treated it as their personal baby and put extra TLC into her.

F-86 # 0-25298 and me over the Sacramento Valley

It was probably the highlight of my flying career. I flew the bird basically anytime I wanted to. By taking off at 0600 I could get an hour-and-a-half flight in and still get to work by 0800. And from then on, every time I went TDY, I'd take the F-86.

On every cross-country flight, the center controllers would comment,

"Gosh, is that really an F-86?" or, "I flew F-86s in Korea." On one trip, when I landed at Indian Springs Air Force Auxiliary, just North of Las Vegas, a grizzled old Master Sergeant Line Chief came out and wouldn't let the younger airmen near the airplane. He came out of his office, chocked it, fueled it and serviced it himself. He explained that he had been a crew chief in Korea on F-86s and hadn't seen one since then. As I pre-flighted the bird, he walked around with me and would stick his hand into an opening, such as the wheel well, and say, "Now there should be a check valve here. Ah! There it is." I saw just the hint of tears in his eyes as we pre-flighted the F-86 together.

It is illegal to fly formation in the USAF without proper authorization and a pre mission briefing to discuss all facets of the mission.. While I was flying the F-86 locally at McClellan AFB one day, two Thunderbirds came into the pattern in F-100's. Before landing they made several passes over the field and without saying anything, I joined on the right wing of the wingman. After a minute or two I said to the lead," Check your right wing." He went ballistic and shouted, "Get the hell out of there!" I did. But now I can say I have flown with the Thunderbirds, even for only a couple of minutes..

Many years later, after I had retired from the Air Force, I did some research on her whereabouts, with the thought that perhaps I might be able to obtain her for our local Aviation Museum, which was becoming very active. Research showed that she had been turned to scrap on the 28th of January, 1971. How sad.

*Flying has always fascinated me. Not only from the point of the challenge it presents, but also what it can do. This point was driven home on a T-39 flight out of McClellan AFB one day. The mission was to go back to Andrews AFB, Washington, D.C., and return with several intermediate stops.

I had breakfast at home and got to the airfield for a scheduled 0700 departure. As we climbed through 20,000 feet to the west, in the distance, I could see the Pacific Ocean, and then we turned toward Texas. We made a quick stop to drop some passengers and pick up fuel at Kelly AFB at San Antonio and on departure I could see the Gulf of Mexico. The next stop was Andrews. On the descent over the Chesapeake Bay, I could see the Atlantic Ocean. We had lunch at Andrews. The next stop was in the hand of Michigan, and with a beautiful and clear day, I could see all five Great Lakes. A quick stop there, then on to Offutt AFB, Nebraska, for fuel, then back to McClellan AFB and dinner.

It was a routine flight, just very long and very busy, and I didn't think much about it until I was driving home from the base and started to recount what I had done that day. In one working day I had breakfast in Sacramento, had seen the Pacific Ocean, the Gulf of Mexico, Chesapeake Bay and the Atlantic Ocean, all five Great Lakes, and then back to the Pacific Ocean and dinner in California. Even with the years and experiences that I had to that point, the realization of what had transpired on that day boggled my mind.

As I drove home, I wondered what a civilization from two or three hundred years ago, just a blink of an eye in human history, would have thought about that day's activity. And I thought of the endurance of the pioneers who slogged their way across this country. What would they have thought?

Chapter 6

1969 - 1970

Tan Son Nhut Air Base
Saigon, Vietnam

It's a shame that wars can't be decided by the side that sings the best songs!

Ashleigh Brilliant

*I had received an alert for a Vietnam assignment while stationed at McClellan AFB, so I wasn't too surprised when one day I got a call from the Air Force Personnel Center. I was surprised at what transpired after that. The voice on the other end said, "Major Reed, we need pilots in two separate assignments for Vietnam, and you are qualified for both. We couldn't figure out the one that best fit, so we thought we'd do something different and let you decide." I went into shock. This had never happened before. I covered the mouthpiece and told Major Joe Skiera, sitting across the desk from me, what the Personnel Center had said. He suddenly got interested. I asked the voice on the other end what the two assignments were and he said that one was in C-119 Gunships. There were few pilots around who had a C-119 background, and I was one. What was the other assignment? I couldn't believe my ears when he said that the second assignment was flying T-39s out of Tan Son Nhut. I told Joe and he listened as I, in my excitement, blurted out "I'll take the C-119 assignment!"

"NO!" Joe said. "You mean T-39s."

"I mean T-39s!" I shouted into the phone.

And that's how I got into SCATBACK. If Joe Skiera hadn't been sitting there, I'd have wound up in C-119 Gunships. Not that it would have been a bad assignment. I enjoyed flying the old C-119, but there were a lot more trips to Bangkok in the T-39. I found out later that the urgency to get a T-39 pilot over there was that several of them had been killed in the crash of a C-47 en route to Hong Kong on an R&R flight. That made them really short of pilots.

When the orders finally came through assigning me to SCATBACK in Vietnam with an en route stop in the Philippines for Jungle Survival School, I got a wild hair. I knew they had T-39s at Yokota and some other bases in the Far East and thought it would be great if one of the birds that was coming out of overhaul in the States might coincide with my transfer and I could ferry it over rather than go across the Pacific via commercial or with the Military Airlift Command. I called the Air Force Command Post and found out that there was a bird going to Yokota that would coincide with my tour in Vietnam. So the orders were cut and, with my crew, I proceeded to Lincoln, Nebraska, where the overhaul facility was for Air Force T-39s. The T-39 is a relatively short-ranged aircraft, so it would be an island hopping trip over to Japan. We flew from Lincoln to McClellan AFB, where all Air Force birds are processed before going overseas in the Pacific. Then we flew to McChord AFB, near Seattle, and on to Elmendorf AFB, at Anchorage, Alaska. From Elmendorf we flew out the Aleutian chain to Adak, where we spent the night to prepare for the toughest leg of the entire journey. The leg from Adak to Midway Island is 1,436 nautical miles long.

Scatback T-39 'SABERLINER'
In a revetment at Tan Son Nhut Air Base, Vietnam

The T-39 has no real way to navigate over water and, depending on variables such as winds, load, altitude, etc., has about a 1,600 nautical mile range to dry tanks. This gave us a planned 20-minute fuel reserve, if everything went right. In the morning, after getting the Air Force Command Post to authorize our Flight Plan (necessary because we had to violate Air Force fuel reserve requirements in order to make the trip), a four-engine Navy P-3 turbo-prop, capable of giving us a position and which flew at about half our speed, took off.

We took off an hour later and flew the same track as the P-3, passing him at the approximate halfway point to Midway. After we lost the TACAN (about 200 nm South of Adak), we were strictly DR (Dead Reckoning) from then on until we could receive the TACAN about 200 nm north of Midway. At the halfway point, the P-3 gave us a fix that enabled us to confirm our fuel burn and we were exactly on schedule, so we pressed on.

We arrived at Midway with exactly 20 minutes fuel reserve, as planned. That poor P-3 crew flew eight hours simply to give us one fix. A quick turn at Midway, then on to Wake Island, Guam, and Yokota AB in Japan. On the leg from Guam to Yokota, we passed directly over Iwo Jima, which happened to have been turned back over to the Japan Self Defense Air Force (JASDAF) the day before. I got the towers attention when I made our position report in Japanese from a USAF airplane.

*SCATBACK,in Vietnam, was a great outfit. Each of the pilots in SCATBACK T-39s were chosen because they were either an Instructor Pilot (IP) or Flight Examiner (FE) in the airplane. Partly because of the difficulty of the mission, and partly because of the fact that we flew a lot of Generals; they didn't have to meet flight currency requirements and, therefore, had to have an IP along if they were at the controls.

*We had two scheduled trips a week to Clark AB in the Philippines. These were great trips because we got out of the war zone, had some good food at the club and got to see what the real world was like. It allowed us to maintain perspective. On one of these trips I got cleaned up and headed for the bar in the Officers Club before getting some good vittles. I sat beside a dapper old gentleman who turned out to be a 72-year-old retired Army Colonel. He told me that he had been living in Florida with his wife and mother-in-law – she had to be in her nineties – and those two old women just got on his nerves. So he packed up and he was going around the world, space available. I asked him how long he had been on the road and he said three months. My comment that he wasn't making too good a time was met with, "Oh, yes, I'm making great time. But I met a nurse in Tachikawa and spent two months there."

*One memorable mission was a scheduled trip from Saigon to Clark AB to airlift Admiral Elmo Zumwalt, when he had command of the Naval Activities in Vietnam. As we approached the Philippines with Admiral Zumwalt in the back, we were advised by center that a severe squall line was going over Clark AB and that they were evacuating the tower. That sounded strange to us, but we could see the towering cumulus in the distance, indicative of some tough weather. We advised the Admiral that Clark was hopeless and he said to divert to Cubi Point and he'd get a staff car over to Clark. So we changed our flight plan and got in ahead of the squall line as it approached Cubi. By this time it was getting dark, and we could see the violent lightning inbound to Cubi. When the Admiral deplaned, we tried to get off and head back to Saigon before the squall line got to Cubi, but after the first engine was fired up, I had my hand on the starter button for the second when a massive lightning bolt struck the ground and all the runway lights went out. So we shut down and headed for the club.

Gabby Haynes, the other pilot, and I sat down for dinner. Normally we flew in flying suits, but because this was a VIP mission, we were in our summer khakis and, therefore, suitably dressed to eat in the dining room. I noticed that while we were eating, two Navy guys kept looking over at us and whispering. Finally, as we finished dinner, one of them walked over and said, "Hey, you guys are Air Force, aren't you?" We replied yes, and with that he said, "We'd like to buy you a drink." And that's how I found out about the Animal Room.

It seems that during the Vietnam debacle, the Navy ships would sit off the Vietnam Coast for six months at a time. When they finally got off station and came to Subic Bay/Cubi Point for Liberty, the guys were so pumped up that they would destroy the Officers Club. After the Base Commander had had enough, they built a special room adjacent to the club, complete with a simulated cockpit of an A-7 Navy Fighter, and called it the Animal Room. In the Animal Room, they could break glass and furniture to their hearts' content and the club would just bill the ship.

These two Navy guys that wanted to buy us a drink had an ulterior motive, and I should have figured that out. What they REALLY wanted to do was get these two Air Force guys to ride the A-7. As we walked through the broken glass, pushed aside the numbed bodies and waded through the scotch spilled on the floor, I saw a wonderful sight. There, in the Animal Room, was the mockup of an A-7 cockpit. It sat on tracks that went through a makeshift hole knocked out of the brick wall and ran down into a shallow pool. The object was to strap in and go through the rev-up motions for a carrier shot and then someone on the side would hit the button and a 3,000 pound nitrogen charge would propel you on the tracks through the hole and into the pool. As you went out the hole in the wall, you pulled a lever that dropped a hook in an attempt to catch the wire that prevented you from going to the bottom of the pool. Just before the wire there was a ramp. So if you dropped the hook too soon, it bounced over the wire. Too late, and you missed. Either way, you wound up in the pool and then it was a survival situation to get unstrapped and back to the surface. To catch the wire the timing had to be perfect. At that time, there had been 3,000 shots and only 12 guys had ever caught the wire.

The drunks were having a wonderful time, but they couldn't wait to see these two Air Force guys make fools of themselves. Gabby asked what would happen if he caught the wire. A Navy Captain who appeared to be the leader of this motley crew said that anyone who caught the wire would get their name on a plaque. By this time, Gabby had a few drinks under his belt and boasted, "Get the plaque ready."

I was first and, when the shot hit, was propelled to the bottom of the pool. Gabby was next and, again, boasted that he'd get the wire. When his shot came, it was a cold shot that barely moved him along. He dropped the hook early and it merely went up the ramp so slow that instead of bouncing over, it caught the wire. Gabby jumped out and shouted, "I caught the wire! Where's the plaque?" Well, you can imagine that there was a very irritated bunch of Navy guys. The one in charge got right in Gabby's face and said, "You don't get your name on the plaque with a cold shot!" Gabby snapped right back, "You didn't say anything about a cold shot. You said if I hooked the wire I'd get my name on the plaque. I hooked the wire. Now I want my name on the plaque!" I tried to shut him up, but it was hopeless.

Things looked as if they could turn ugly, and we were certainly outnumbered. But, as it turns out so many times with drunks, we wound up singing songs at the bar.

*On a late night courier mission in Scatback, we departed DaNang at 2330 hours for Nha Trang. Besides the courier material we had on board, we had an Air Force Colonel who had been shot down earlier that day in an F-4 over North Vietnam. After his medical checkup, he was returning to 7/13th Air Force to brief the brass.

Somewhere in flight, either on takeoff at Da Nang or when we put the gear down for landing at Nha Trang, we lost the right main wheel, the whole works, hub and all. The only thing that was left on the right side was the gear stub. The aircraft Commander on this particular trip was a good friend, Britt Glover. However, as usual, we traded seats, and this leg happened to be mine.

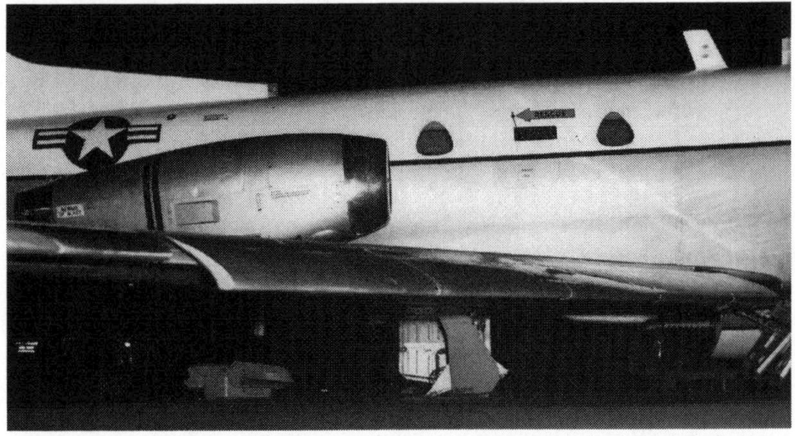

Landing the T-39 at Nha Trang with the gear stub on the right side, minus the wheel.

The gear warning lights will tell you if a gear is not locked either up or down, but they won't tell you that the wheel has fallen off, so we had no clue. We landed at Nha Trang right at midnight, and the thing that saved our butt was a call from the tower advising us that there was construction on the right side of the runway over run and that we should land on the left side. Being the type I am, I didn't lose an opportunity to play around, so I landed on the far left side of the runway. That saved our lives.

As soon as the gear touched down, it was obvious something was seriously wrong, and with the use of all controls – nose wheel steering, brake (left side only) rudder and aileron – we were able to keep the bird on the runway, although we had transitioned from the far left to the far right side, grinding down the gear stub as we went. When we came to a stop, the crew chief put out the small fire under the right wing where the grinding wore up through the brake lines and we were OK. The tower really saved us because had we landed in the center, as usual, we'd have drifted off the runway into the soft sand and probably cartwheeled when the gear stub dug in. In talking to the tower guys later, they said that we had a rooster tail of fire coming from the right gear as we went down the runway.

The Colonel that had been shot down earlier in the day walked up to me and said he wasn't flying anymore that night and was headed for the nearest bar. I joined him.

Trip to Katmandu, Nepal, with Ambassador Bunker:

*Of the nine T-39 Saberliners that we had in SCATBACK, one was dedicated to Embassy Support. As a result of this, we got some pretty good trips, including several to Katmandu, a number of spots in India and some great trips to Hong Kong. The United States Ambassador to Vietnam at that time was a wonderful man named Ellsworth Bunker. At 73 years old, the word was that he gave the younger guys a tussle on the tennis court. He was married to Ambassador Laise who, also at that time, was the ambassador to Nepal, hence the trips to Katmandu.

Here, I'm briefing Ambassador Bunker that we had good weather all the way from Saigon to Katmandu

In the photo above, I am telling Ambassador Bunker that I received a weather briefing from Strategic Air Command (SAC) worldwide briefer that we would have good weather all the way from our departure point of Saigon to Katmandu. Our route would include a stop at Bangkok and Calcutta, India, for fuel. After our departure from Bangkok, we flew over Rangoon and then out over the Indian Ocean. When I switched our radio frequency from Bangkok Center to Calcutta Center, the first words I heard were from a British airliner with a Speedbird call sign describing the largest eye of a cyclone that he had ever seen. When I asked him what the coordinates were, I was dismayed to find out that the eye was right along our route of flight. A cyclone is the same thing as a typhoon or a hurricane, they are just given different names in different parts of the world.

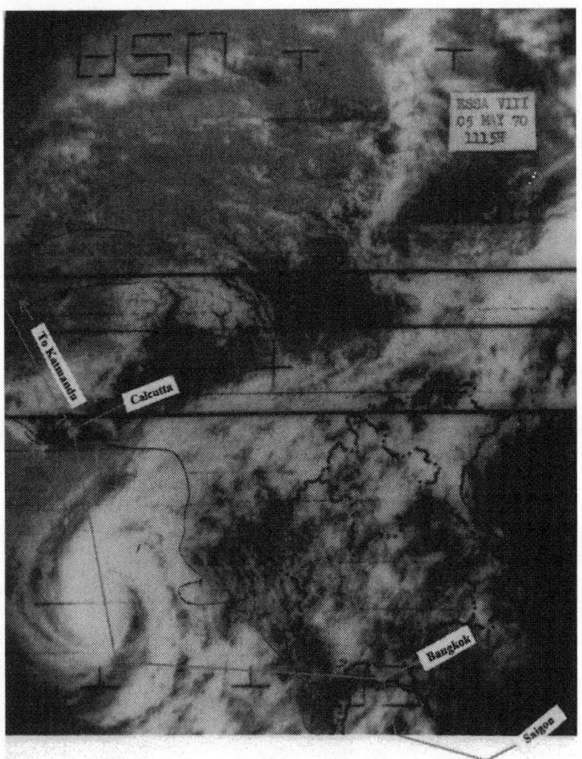

Cyclone over the Indian Ocean about to make landfall in the area of Bangladesh

Circumnavigation of this monster was not an option because of fuel constraints, and also because I had been briefed on the absolute necessity of penetrating the India Air Defense Identification Zone (ADIZ) within the prescribed limits. I tried to climb to see if I could get above the storm, but at 42,000 feet we were still in it. As we passed through what we thought was the eye, we were in heavy rain at 42,000 feet, which seems an impossibility because at that altitude the temperature is generally in the minus 40s or 50s range, and I can only surmise that the warm Indian Ocean air was being pumped up to the higher elevations by this huge storm.

When I returned from that trip to Nepal, the weatherman at Tan Son Nhut had saved the satellite image of the Cyclone for me (photo above).

*Whenever we flew Ambassador Bunker to Hong Kong, we always landed at Phu Cat for fuel, even though we had enough fuel on board to make Hong Kong. The reason for this was that in the event we could not land at Hong Kong, we had to have enough fuel to get back to Clark Air Base in the Philippines, for security reasons.

On one trip to Hong Kong, I was inbound to Phu Cat in some pretty heavy weather when I got a strange message from my Operations Officer, relayed through Saigon Center, that I was not to land at Phu Cat under any circumstances. I could land at any field that would work, except Phu Cat. I got out the charts and determined very quickly that if we went to Tuy Hoa we could still make Hong Kong and use Clark as an alternate. So we had minimum ground time at Tuy Hoa, then on to Hong Kong.

When we got back, I went to the Operations Officer to find out why he sent us that screwy message. He said while we were en route, intelligence found out that the Vietcong had planned to rocket the VIP parking area at Phu Cat as we pulled in with Ambassador Bunker in an attempt to assassinate him. I don't know who those intelligence guys are, and will probably never meet them, but whoever, wherever you are – THANKS!

*In SCATBACK, everything we did was done with great aplomb. In the true tradition of a great outfit, we worked hard and we played hard. There were two parties a month. One was with the FAA guys in Saigon and one was a dance at the SCATBACK lounge across from our hanger at Tan Son Nhut. The monthly dance was well known throughout Vietnam and we had no trouble getting every available nurse, embassy secretary and any other female to come. They loved it. We always did it up right. We all took turns putting the monthly dance together and, when it came to my turn, I was going to make it a special one that everyone would remember.

First, I rationalized that we needed more room. Normally we had the dance in the lounge, but we had all of our beautiful lawn area outside. SCATBACK had a full-time gardener on the payroll to take care of the front lawn, so it was really beautiful. I figured that if I could get two ten-foot high curtains strung on wire from our lounge to the hanger across the street, we could use the manicured lawn in front of the lounge and dance in the street that went between the hanger and the lounge and have complete privacy from the rest of the guys on the base. Six cases of San Miguel beer to the parachute shop took care of getting the curtains made up. Tiki torches from Clark on the front lawn and a great band flown in from DaNang on one of our C-118 runs was going to make this a memorable occasion. After a lot of effort, the big night finally came. But after we had sent the buses out to pick up all the nurses and secretaries, a crisis occurred. I suddenly discovered that we had no tiki torch fuel.

While I was wallowing in despair, someone said, "Hell, tiki torch fuel is just kerosene, and we have a whole ramp full of it across the street."

I was saved! After draining enough JP-4 out of a T-39 to fill all the pots on our tiki torches, the final act was accomplished to make this the most memorable occasion that ever took place at the SCATBACK lounge. The busses filled with nurses showed up and, as the band played on, everyone danced to the light of the tiki torches and I felt a great sense of accomplishment.

What I didn't know was that JP-4 burns a lot hotter than the standard tiki torch fuel and soon the pots full of jet fuel started to boil and pressurize. The tiki torch flames started to grow and, pretty soon, ten tiki torches were a mass of two-foot wide flames shooting into the air, threatening to blow up and burn everyone there. They made a horrible hissing sound. People were running everywhere and shouting, trying to escape.

By this time, the majority of SCATBACKERS there had been imbibing somewhat, and it must have looked like a Chinese fire drill trying to get all those blossoming tiki torches put out. We finally got some fire extinguishers from across the street and were able to douse them.

It was a great party!

*The monsoon in Southeast Asia made flying very challenging. What a sterile word "challenging" is. At times it made it terrifying. I could never understand why the Air Force did not put radar on the T-39 aircraft. Some of the little bug smashers even had radar. But the T-39 didn't, and with the kind of flying that they did, and as cheap as radar had become, it didn't make sense not to have it.

We sure could have used radar during the monsoon in Vietnam. During monsoon, the thunderstorms would saturate the place and, without radar, you couldn't stay out of the thunderstorm cells. We would stumble from one cell to the next. For departures in and out of Saigon, the Cagers (FAA guys) would give aircraft with radar clearance to deviate as necessary to avoid thunderstorms. Because the FAA departure radar was set on secondary returns (IFF transponder) they could not see the weather, so they would give the aircraft authority to use their own radar and deviate as necessary.

As these aircraft deviated, the Cagers would draw the route they took in grease pencil on the scope. Then, if we could get off in a reasonable time, say 10 or 15 minutes, they would run us up the grease pencil line and we'd have a pretty good chance of missing most of the cells. If there was a cell of B-52s en route,we'd follow along behind them to miss most of the thunderstorms. Ingenuity prevailed.

On one of our weekly trips to Clark Air Base in the Philippines, we had a secretary from the Embassy on board. In the climbout from Saigon, I decided to play a little trick on the Cager who was working Saigon Center. He was a good friend who stood well over six feet tall and had a voice like Paul Robeson in the 1936 version of the movie 'Showboat'.

In those days, in the war zone, there were scant few females, and you never heard a female voice on the radio. I decided that when we reached our assigned altitude, which required a mandatory call to departure, we would have the secretary make the call and see how he reacted. I asked her and she agreed.

During the climb, we had her practice on interphone with the headset. "Saigon Center, this is Scatback Hotel, level at Flight Level 290." She practiced until she had it down perfect. When we arrived at the assigned altitude, we gave her the headset and she made the call.

"Saigon Center, this is Scatback Hotel, level at Flight Level 290."

Without hesitation, my friend came back with "Uh, Scatback Hotel, better check your Co-Pilot, I think he's got his seat belt a little too tight."

On another trip, probably the toughest mission we had, I had another occasion to tweak him.

The SCATBACK Delta Mission was an all-night mission that landed at many of the bases throughout Thailand. It was a grinding flight, in which during the monsoon, you bounced from one thunderstorm to the next, trying to maintain a split-second schedule. Departure from Saigon was 2100 hours daily, and you didn't get back until about 0600 the next morning. The only blessing was that around 0300 all of the thunderstorms would begin to dissipate and, by the time you were returning, most of the cells had stratified (died) out.

When we made the mandatory inbound call, 100 miles from Saigon, it was beginning to get daylight and I recognized my friend on the radio and could hear the fatigue in his voice. He had obviously been on shift for some time and was probably as worn-out as we were, coming back from the all night SCATBACK Delta mission.

After the routine calls I said, "Hey, Paul, look at the size of that cockroach over on the right-hand side of your console." After a short time I asked, "Did you look?" His response was a weak, "Yeah." I guess that's the kind of stuff you do to break the monotony.

*We were fortunate to have air-conditioned quarters for the SCATBACK Pilot billets. As we were stationed on Tan Son Nhut, we were able to avoid having to quarter in "Camp Alpha," where processing for R&R was accomplished and where people stayed while waiting for R&R transportation. Camp Alpha was so bad that whenever we had friends come through for R&R processing we could always find an empty bed in the SCATBACK billets so they wouldn't have to endure the horrible conditions of Camp Alpha. I avoided Camp Alpha as much as possible but, as I understand it, they had dirt floors, bunk beds and all the rest of the grunt stuff.

As an example of the various levels of living in Vietnam, when I got on the Pan American Charter Flight for my R&R, I was seated next to a young grunt, just out of the jungle and still in his grungy fatigues. As we taxied out we struck up a conversation and he said to me, "Boy, wasn't that Camp Alpha great?" I almost gave up my R&R and stayed there.

*Our route on one evening SCATBACK mission took us north out of Saigon to DaNang and then across Southern Laos, with the first stop in Thailand, at Nakhom Phanom, commonly referred to as NKP, or Naked Phanny. As we left the DaNang area, we heard a mayday on Guard channel, which we always monitored. Some poor bloke had gotten shot down in an A1E and bailed out, coming down on a sandspit in the middle of a jungle river with the bad guys on both sides. He had dug in under some logs and his buddies, also in A1s, were making strafing passes to keep the bad guys off of him. We were up at 28,000 feet and couldn't provide any assistance, but listened with intensity as this scenario was played out.

Somewhere, someone managed to scrape up a Jolly Green Rescue Helicopter and, as his buddies flew strafing passes, the chopper came in to pick up the stranded pilot. We heard the chopper come under withering fire from both sides of the river and, with the Co-Pilot's windshield shot away and one engine shot out plus many more hits, the chopper had to abort the rescue attempt. Flying down the river below the level of the triple canopy jungle, he was barely able to get above the trees and make it home on one engine. No other choppers were available.

With dark settling in, his buddies continued to make strafing passes until they ran out of ammo. Then they made dry passes until the Vietcong (VC) figured out what was happening. As it finally got dark and they were all out of ammo and with no other resources available, the last transmission to the downed pilot was, "We'll come back and check in the morning. Good luck." That was the last we heard.

I guess that was only one of many sad stories to come out of Vietnam. I've thought of that Pilot often and wondered what happened to him.

I made some very close friends while assigned to SCATBACK. The missions were demanding and you were frequently called upon to use all the training and experience as a Pilot to safely accomplish them. I have stayed close to a number of my SCATBACK Colleagues over the years since we flew through that war. I believe that each of the individuals who spent a tour in Vietnam, regardless of the job they were in, took something special with them when they left. I'm not sure how to explain it, but it seems to be an extra sense of patriotism or a greater love for our beloved country. It was a very special time.

When I returned home from Vietnam, and even before I left to go to that war, I knew that the American public considered it a "bad" war. But I was angry at the way they treated their troops, blaming them for all the things that were wrong with that war. In one of my angry moods I constructed this bit of prose:

I wonder why!

I wonder why in the dark of night
when I feel a chill in the pale moonlight
and my mind does things I can scarcely
tell, as it asks me why my good friends fell
In the lonesome thought that has begged
for light lo, these many years in the pale moonlight
does a nation grieve for her long-lost sons
who have given all so that she might run?

Does the soul regret lost days and nights as it
hangs in space in the pale moonlight? Was the quest
for freedom worth the price?

"**Yes! I'd give my life and give it twice,**" my friends
would say, who have gone away.

But does a nation understand the sacrifice of the
soldier man? The pain, the loss of no more days
to watch his family slowly raise.

Then, how much is a soldier worth when violent people
scorch the earth? We all know freedom isn't free.
And this soldier man is you ... and me.

All are patriots one by one until the call is no more fun
and there where with we all shall stand, the duty finds the
lesser man. So listen up all you out there who go to church
and lend a prayer, think more of what your freedom cost,
who paid the price and what was lost.

And lend a prayer for those out there who duty found the
greater man, so those of us who breath free air will live
a life free from despair.

I believe a nation does have a conscience, and the up-welling of support for the troops in Iraqi Freedom, in part, was due to the guilty conscience they had for the way they treated the troops coming home from Vietnam.

Chapter 7

1970 - 1975

Air Defense Command Headquarters
Colorado Springs, Colorado

**Napoleon once told his Generals:
"There are three types of officers that will serve you:
There is the lazy, incompetent - He merely takes up space.
There is the ambitious and competent - He will win the wars for you.
and
There is the ambitious, incompetent;
You must rid yourself of him for he will surely destroy you!"**

*After Vietnam, we were fortunate to be assigned to the Aerospace Defense Command (ADC) Headquarters at Colorado Springs. Because of my now extensive time in the T-39 Sabreliner, I became the Command Flight Examiner for ADC in that bird and in addition to my other duties, continued to fly it out of Peterson Field right there at Colorado Springs. The T-39 line chief at Peterson Field was a good friend with whom I had served in SCATBACK in Vietnam.

On this particular mission, he came out to the airplane to say hello and we swapped stories before it was time to go. As I started to taxi out to the runway, I noted with dismay that there were spider web-like cracks in the lower left corner of the pilot's windshield. Now, at altitude, the pressure differential between the outside atmosphere and the inside of the pressurized hull of the T-39 is 5.6 pounds per square inch. This doesn't sound like much, but I had previously calculated that 5.6 pounds pressure differential puts over 2,000 lbs of pressure on each of the pilot's windows. So a cracked windshield was nothing to fool around with. As I taxied back to the ramp, my Line Chief friend was in the typical Line Chief hands on hips stance when an airplane of his is returned to the ramp. "What's the problem?" he asked as I shut down the engines. I told him that there were spider web cracks in the lower left-hand corner of the pilot's windshield. He said that they were aware of that, had checked it out and determined that the cracks were in limits according to the manual. I had never heard of such a thing, cracks in a windshield of a pressurized airplane having limits. I said that I would have to see the manual myself, and so he proceeded to get it.

After much discussion, he convinced me that there were specified limits in the manual for windshield cracks in the T-39. I was baffled. I said, "I'm going to write it up as a discrepancy and you can sign it off in the maintenance log as checked and being in limits." I wrote it up and he signed it off.

Then I said, "O K, I'll fly the bird if you'll go with me."

"Hell, no!" he said. "I wouldn't fly in a pressurized plane with cracks in the windshield."

*Late one evening I received a call at home that there had been a T-39 accident at Malmstrom AFB near Great Falls, Montana, with one of the ADC airplanes. I had been named Accident Investigation Officer and the Accident Investigating Team was leaving for Malmstrom first thing in the morning. Because one of the pilots on the airplane was a Brigadier General selectee, the President of the Investigation Board was a General Officer. The President of the board will always outrank the individual being investigated. The airplane was pretty badly beaten up, but there were no injuries among the two pilots and four passengers that were on board although the potential for injury was there.

The accident went something like this:

During gear retraction on takeoff, there was a loud thump, followed by an unsafe gear indication. The pilots then lowered the gear and continued to get an unsafe indication, even though a flyby of the tower indicated that the gear all appeared to be in the proper down position. A T-33 pilot even confirmed the tower's observation by flying formation with the T-39. These observations led the pilots to believe that the gear was down and locked and that the warning system had malfunctioned. When they approached the runway on final approach, as a precaution, one pilot reached up to turn the Auxiliary Hydraulic Power Switch to the "on" position. The Auxiliary Hydraulic Power Switch would provide hydraulic power from an emergency accumulator if the main hydraulic system failed.

When they touched down, the right main gear collapsed, causing the airplane to eventually swerve off the runway, barely missing a collision with the GCA Radar Complex. The crew and passengers deplaned without injury.

As the investigation proceeded, it became apparent that there was a complete loss of directional control after touchdown. The board surmised that had nosewheel steering been available, the pilot probably would have kept the airplane on the runway. Skid marks indicated that in the early stages of the rollout after the collapse of the gear, the airplane started to come back to centerline with only brake and rudder, but as the rudder and brake became less effective they then swerved off the runway. The only way that the nosewheel steering would not have been on would be if the pilot, reaching up to turn on the Auxiliary Hydraulic Power Switch, had mistakenly turned off the Electrical Master Switch. Both are located in the same area on the overhead panel above the pilot's head. Since the fire department had manipulated cockpit switches after the crash, in their attempt to turn off the emergency lights, which had come on, it was not possible to get a true reading of all of the switch positions during the landing.

The board wrestled with the situation for several days. We felt that we knew what had happened; the pilot had turned off the Electrical Master Switch by mistake. But because the Fire Department had contaminated the switch positions, we had no way of proving it. And then, at three in the morning, half asleep in bed, the light bulb came on. It occurred to me that if, in fact, the pilot had accidentally turned off the Electrical Master Switch on final, that would have disabled the electrically-driven compass cards and they would be locked to the runway heading and not have recorded the turn as they swerved off the runway. Since the photographers had taken photos of everything before the airplane was moved, including the instrument panel, I went looking for the photographs. As I suspected, the compass cards were still on the runway heading. They had not recorded the turn off the runway and our conclusions were correct. The only way they could have been disabled was if the Electrical Master Switch had been turned off while still on the runway heading. If that were the case, then nose wheel steering would not have been available.

It pained me to reach that conclusion because the Instructor Pilot on the airplane was a friend of mine, and he was charged with pilot error as a contributing factor. The General selectee became my boss in my next assignment. I must say that I had great respect for him and he never mentioned or even brought up the investigation the whole time I worked for him.

The primary cause of the accident was that, just as they were lifting off, the recapped tire on the right gear disintegrated and six-to-nine-inch chunks of rubber came off, bending the gear actuator and preventing it from fully extending to the locked position.

*I loved Colorado. Since the Air Force Academy is now Co-ed, I'm not sure they still have it, but there used to be a saying emblazoned on a structure at the Academy that said 'BRING ME MEN TO MATCH MY MOUNTAINS'. I always felt that was an appropriate saying for an institution that was developing our military leaders of the future. We need strong men with pure hearts and clear vision. Come to think of it, we set great goals and provide superb training for our future military leaders to ensure their personalities and abilities will meet the task. But where do our civilian leaders get their training? Perhaps there should be an institution for them that would set high standards and high goals for them to achieve before they could be considered candidates to lead our country.

*One of my more memorable flights from Colorado Springs involved taking General Robin Olds, then Commandant of the Air Force Academy, from Colorado Springs to Norton AFB, where he was slated to take over as the Air Force #1 Safety Guy. I had always heard that when General Olds had been Commander of the fighter units in 'Nam that he put out an order that he would court martial any pilot that engaged a MIG under even tactical conditions. In other words, if you did not have absolute advantage, both in tactical position and in numbers, and you encountered enemy aircraft, you had to turn tail and run for home. Sitting there at 35,000 feet with General Olds flying the T-39 and me in the right seat, I asked him if that order were true.

He said, "Yes, Jim, that was correct."

I said, "General, that's not the American way. You were an ace in WWII and you frequently engaged the enemy even though you were outnumbered."

And when he explained it, he made sense. He said that our pilots in

WWII and Korea had to take the risks because we didn't have air superiority and we desperately needed it. That was the goal. The pilots had to take the risks to achieve the goal. In Vietnam, we had air superiority and didn't have to take the risks. He put out the order to prevent jocks from taking unnecessary risks with themselves, their aircraft and the people who would have to come get them – just to get a medal. Then it made sense. By the way, General Olds is a Triple Ace, with a total of 17 aircraft shot down in WWII and Vietnam.

T-39 #10671 and me over the USAF Academy

*The last flight I made in the United States Air Force was from Colorado Springs to the Panama Canal with Major Ted Gesling in T-39 #10671. We airlifted Major General Salisbury there and back so that he could be briefed on South Com, his new command. After 20 years of flying multitudes of aircraft all over the world in the Air Force, it seemed more than just coincidental that the very last flight I made in an Air Force aircraft had the same last three tail numbers (671) as the Squadron that I then took Command of, the 671st Radar Squadron.

Key West Naval Air Station
Boca Chica Field
Key West, Florida 1972 – 1975

*While stationed at ADC Headquarters in Colorado Springs, I was offered a choice of one of three radar squadrons of which to take command. The first was the Radar Station at Mill Valley, California, second was the Point Arena Radar Station, also in California, and the third was the 671st Radar Squadron in Key West, Florida. We wrestled over this for some time. Although we knew nothing about the Florida Keys, and could find very little in the library, somehow Key West seemed to attract us. How fortunate for us that we chose Key West. The people we met, the family adventures we had and the future events that took place as a result of that assignment were incredible.

Shortly after we got settled in Key West, the urge to get another sailboat became very strong. After several months of searching the yacht harbors in Florida, we found "Mirage" a classic 44' Sparkman and Stephens Cutter rigged Ocean Racer. She had a real pedigree and our four boys and I were able to hone our skills as sailors.

She was built as an Ocean Racer and did very well in the monthly races that were held in Key West. She had a great choice of sails which included a very large Spinnaker, which I had no experience with and was reluctant to try.

The first time we launched the spinnaker on Mirage was in about a 15 knot wind in the seaplane basin which was about two miles long and about a mile wide, a fairly confined space to fly a Spinnaker. At this point in our sailing experience we were probably a notch above novice. When the spinnaker blossomed it was an exhilarating experience and the boat took off at a gallop. I underestimated the force of that huge spinnaker and as we bore down on the rip rap that made up the shoreline of Fleming Key, my ill conceived plan was to ease the Spinnaker sheet which would douse the Spinnaker and then turn into the wind.

When it came time to ease the sheet, it was fouled on the winch. Stay calm, don't panic and turn the boat into the wind. When I tried to turn the boat into the wind I moved the tiller and nothing happened! Even with the rudder hard over, the Spinnaker overrode the rudder and the bow of the boat did not turn but stayed on course for a direct hit of the rocks on Fleming Key. The next step was to loosen the guy, the line that went to one of the lower points on the spinnaker, that would douse it.

But the line had been pulled so tight that it jammed on the winch AND I COULD NOT GET IT LOOSE.. As we approached the rocky shoreline, I thought to myself how am I going to explain turning this beautiful boat into a pile of splinters on Fleming key.

Our son Kevin somehow managed to free the Guy which dumped the Spinnaker and the rudder started working again.

Mirage with Spinnaker sailing out of Garrison Bight in light winds

As Commander of the 671st Radar Squadron in Key West, a tenant unit in a dominantly Navy area, I felt that the Air Force should have a little more exposure in town. So one day, never believing that they would come, I wrote to the United States Air Force Aerial Demonstration Team, the USAF Thunderbirds, and asked them to come to Key West. I knew that in order to spark their interest I would probably have to have a gimmick, so I tied their visit to the Blessing of the Shrimp Fleet in Key West and said that if they came, they would be active participants. The Commander and Lead Pilot, Lieutenant Colonel Roger Parish, told me later that's exactly what happened. At the joint scheduling meeting they have each year with the other military demonstration teams to develop the coming year's schedule, participating in the Blessing of the Shrimp Fleet tweaked their interest and so they scheduled a show at Key West.

We planned to have the air show over the water of Key West Harbor, so the maximum number of people could have a good seat. As the date drew closer, it became obvious that this was a major event for Key West. I asked Mel Fisher, who later drew fame when his group located the sunken treasure ship Nuestra De Atocha in the waters off the Key West chain after ten years of searching, if we could use his full-sized replica of a Spanish Galleon to throw a party for the Thunderbirds at day's end. He graciously agreed.

The largest crowd in the history of Key West at that time assembled along the waterfront and in boats for the air show, and it was superb. At the completion of the show, the Thunderbirds recovered at Boca Chica Naval Air Station, about seven miles up the Florida Keys, and were brought to the reviewing stand by boat, courtesy of the Florida Marine Patrol, to avoid the traffic snarls on Highway 1.

Formation shot of Thunderbirds in F-4s over Key West Harbor The Key West Naval Submarine Base is in the background

After the Blessing of the Shrimp Fleet, they had their post mission briefing, then we put the Thunderbirds at the helm aboard five large sailboats and, with Admiral Jason Maurer, the Naval Commander, in his boat 'Inshala' in the lead, we sailed in all the formations the Thunderbirds fly in. Although none of the Thunderbird Pilots had ever sailed before, I was really impressed with their ability to hold close position under sail in these various formations. At the end of the day, all of the sailboats with the Thunderbirds on board tied up alongside Mel Fisher's Spanish Galleon and we had a party that lasted into the wee hours of the morning.

They took the next day off and, when the Thunderbirds left the following day, each of them said they had more personal enjoyment on this trip to Key West than they had on any trip during their tour on the team. They confirmed that when I received a personal note from each of the pilots verifying the same thing. On my next trip to the Thunderbirds' home base, Nellis AFB, Las Vegas, I went to their operations to get a real test of how much they enjoyed their stop at Key West. I asked to see their scrapbook. As I looked through the documentation in the oversized scrapbook of each of their shows during 1973, I found that the regular shows had about half a page of paraphernalia. The really big shows, like Farnborough, Paris or Abbotsford, had a full page in the book. Key West had three full pages! I was satisfied that they had had a good time.

*In 1973, when the Vietnam POWs came home, the city of Key West got together and, through the Chamber of Commerce, made a remarkable offer to any POW and their immediate family. They offered them a two-week, ALL expenses paid visit to Key West. Part of the program included recreational activities and, knowing I had a 44-foot sailboat, they came to me and asked if I could take out sailing any who wanted to. Of course, I said I would be delighted, and got several of my friends who had sailboats to volunteer also.

It was truly a privilege for my family and me. It was also an education on how different people handle the stresses of war. Two separate trips that stand out involve an Army Lieutenant Colonel and his wife on one trip and an Air Force Captain and his wife and daughter on the other. Both had been in the Hanoi Hilton for between five and six years. It was interesting to see the way these two men reacted. The Army Lieutenant Colonel and his wife, who had been married for many years before he went to war, were like newlyweds. They held hands, joked, cuddled and acted as though they were on their honeymoon. The Captain, on the other hand, who had only been married a short time before he went over, and whose daughter had been born while he was in prison, treated his wife and daughter as strangers. Throughout the whole sail he stayed on the front of the boat and they sat in the rear. I often wondered how that turned out.

*In 1973, the 671st Radar Squadron was the only 'Manual' squadron left in the United States Air Force. This meant that intercepts were actually conducted onsite with the radar data being plotted on a large situation board and the fighters given intercept commands from directors taking data from the plotting board. At other radar sites, the data was fed from the remote sites to a central location, where computers did much of the intercept computations.

Our primary function was to watch the southern approaches to our area and, obviously, the area we were most interested in was Cuba. With Cuba being 94 miles south, the curvature of the Earth prevented us from seeing objects close to the surface and, therefore, it was possible for a low-flying aircraft to remain unseen by our radars for some distance. As a result, the Air Force began experiments with a balloon-born radar on Cudjoe Key, located about seven miles up the Keys from Boca Chica Naval Air Station, where the 671st Radar Squadron was located. Although I knew nothing about balloons, I was named Director of the project and tasked to provide support.

Mirage – our 44′ Sparkman and Stephens Ocean Racer

The project was very interesting, and going well, until one day I got a panicked call from the site on Cudjoe Key. "Colonel Reed, you better get out here right away. We've got a problem."

I jumped in my car and, as I approached Cudjoe Key, I could see that something was terribly wrong. The balloon, about twice the size of the Goodyear Blimp, was at an odd angle, with the tail touching the water and the million-dollar experimental radar just barely hanging above the water. I joined the anxious group standing at the water's edge, where the tether from the winch platform snaked out to the stricken craft. The technician in charge gave this explanation: Everything was going fine, with the balloon extended at altitude, when a thunderstorm started to approach. As the thunderstorm approached, they tried to get the balloon down, but since the winch only retracted the balloon at 200 feet a minute, the thunderstorm got over the balloon before they got very far. When the thunderstorm moved over the balloon it was raining and two things happened. First, when the balloon got wet, it got heavier because it had a relatively porous skin and retained the water. Second, it got significantly cooler than it had been in the hot sun and lost lift. These two factors caused the balloon to begin a descent much faster than the winch could retract it. The balloon descended until the tail touched the water and the swirling winds from the thunderstorm caused the tether to wrap around a small mangrove island and get entangled in the mangrove trees about a half-mile from where we were standing.

By the time I arrived, the thunderstorm was moving past, the sun was coming out, the balloon was drying out and heating up and, now, it wanted to go back up. As we stood there trying to come up with a solution as to how we would recover this balloon, we could hear the snapping and cracking of the mangrove trees as it strained to go back up. Every minute that went by, it got more lift and, consequently, more strain. Finally, one particularly large tree stopped its upward progression.

The Balloon at Cudjoe Key. The winch is on the truck underneath the balloon.

As we stood there, a single individual in a small boat came putt-putting along between us and the mangrove island where the balloon was captured. He was unaware of the tether submerged just below the surface of the water and I could visualize a scenario whereby the boater would run over the tether, wrapping it around the propeller, the balloon would break free and begin an uncontrollable ascent, carrying the boat and boater along with it to the heavens. We all began waving to get the boater's attention and managed to get him stopped before he ran over the tether.

We had to do something and do it fast. As the balloon heated and dried, it got more lift. An uncontrolled ascent with full lift capacity would certainly break the tether and we would then lose the balloon and, more importantly, the expensive radar. We made the decision to free the balloon before it got to full lift capacity and risk the tether holding in an uncontrolled ascent.

We talked the individual in the small boat into taking one of our men out to the mangrove island with a chain saw. When he cut the key tree holding the balloon, it broke free and we all held our breath as it began an uncontrolled ascent, snapping the tether from the water as it went up. I had heard stories of runaway balloons being shot down by fighters, and could picture me calling the Base Commander at Homestead AFB and asking him for an F-106 to shoot down my balloon. I shuddered when I thought about that.

As the balloon reached its full extension, I said a small prayer that the tether would hold. It did. I believe the balloon program is still in place at Cudjoe Key as of this writing. However, I've been told that they have faster winches now.

*One evening, while on my way home from work at the 671st Radar Squadron in Key West, I stopped in the BOQ Bar for a quick relaxer. The only other person at the bar was a large Marine Lieutenant Colonel, still in his flying suit, having just landed in his F-4 out at Boca Chica NAS. I ordered a drink. There was a large advertisement behind the bartender displaying a proud Marine Pilot standing at attention in front of his F-4 Fighter with his jet helmet neatly tucked under his arm, along with the caption "THE MARINES ARE LOOKING FOR A FEW GOOD MEN" emblazoned across the bottom. I turned to the Marine Lieutenant Colonel and, pointing to the caption, said, "Hey, have they found any yet?" I was only trying to be funny and perhaps start a conversation, but I soon realized, as the incredible hulk raised up off his stool, that I had screwed up. As it turned out, I told him I was only kidding and we wound up being good buddies and buying each other a drink.

*As the inevitable time for retirement drew closer, I started to search for something to do. I knew we couldn't live on my retired pay, but how can you start a new career at 40 years old? Of course, I planned to pursue flying as a primary means of living, but what would happen if someday my hearing or eyes started to go? So I searched for something to do. I needed a hip pocket career that I could fall back on. If I planned ahead, I could pick what I wanted to do and not be forced into doing something that I hated but had to do because it was expedient. Since I loved boats almost as much as airplanes, the course was clear.

I'm not sure why so many pilots migrate to boats. I've often wondered about this. Perhaps it's because both boats and airplanes operate in a similar medium – air and water. It's different from running a train or driving a car or truck that are tied to Mother Earth. The professional disciplines that each require are very similar, and to function well in either demands a good command of weather and navigation.

And so I chose to get my Captain's License from the Coast Guard. I had the necessary experience because of the sailboats I had owned and my time in the Merchant Marine. And I rationalized that if I had my license I could make a living chartering MIRAGE, our 44′ Sparkman and Stephens sailboat that we owned in Key West. So, after a lot of help from my good friends Chuck Pratt and Bill Conklin, a retired Navy Fighter Pilot, I studied for the exam. Bill and I went together to Miami to sit for our licenses. Both of us were successful and we came back to Key West with 50 ton Captain's Licenses. As it turned out, with several license upgrades, I eventually turned to the Maritime Industry as a primary job, with flying as a secondary job. I had the best of both worlds, airplanes and boats!

*After I retired from the Air Force, things didn't look too good in Key West and I needed a job. So we packed the cars and Colleen drove one and I drove the other. With the four kids and two dogs, we drove to California to look for work. We moved in with my folks in Sebastopol and, looking back on it, I didn't give them much of a chance to say no. In all the resumes I sent out, nothing materialized. The only ray of hope was an interview with a Mr. Hugh Codding, who owned a C-421 and, rumor had it, was looking to replace his pilot. After the interview with him and his wife Nell, a very businesslike woman who had eyes that could look right through you, he explained that although they might be looking for another pilot in the future, they were not quite ready for the change, but to "please stay in touch."

It was about this time that Kevin, our second oldest son, found a loaded shotgun in our bedroom and accidentally discharged it while trying to unload it. Although no one was hurt, he blew a hole in my father's house, blowing away part of the window sill and the drapes. Knowing that I would be furious, Colleen searched for a way to break the news. When I arrived home she said, "Come with me," and took my hand and led me around the path in front of the house overlooking the beautiful valley. I knew something was up. Finally, she stopped, looked me right in the eye and said, "I'm pregnant." My knees went weak. Here we were, four kids and two dogs, living with my folks, me with no job, and she's pregnant. Things looked grim. After giving me a suitable minute to let this sink in, she said, "No, I'm not pregnant. But Kevin shot a hole in your dad's wall." I was so relieved she wasn't pregnant, I couldn't have cared less about the wall. Who says strategy doesn't work?

*With no positive job offers in California, and the fact that my folks were getting a little worn out putting up with us, we returned to Key West. When we got back, I found that a new airline, called "Air Sunshine", had started up, with five DC-3s and two de Havilland Doves and several grandfathered routes, including the route from Key West to

Cuba, which everyone thought would soon open up, so I went to see them. They had all the pilots they needed, and turned me down. They did say that they were going to start an Air Freight service and asked if I'd be interested in operating it while I was waiting for a flying job to open. Of course I said, "Yes," and, before long, I had rented a trailer for an office from Bill Reuter and I was in business. We actually did pretty well and got a good corner on the Air Freight business coming into Key West, even though our cargo compartments were rather small.

It wasn't long before I got into the cockpit.

The DC-3 was fun to fly, and the 55-minute flight to Miami, with an occasional stop at Marathon, was a dream. Eventually, I made Captain and recall that on one flight into Miami we had loaded our passengers for the trip home. When I got into the seat and hit the start switch for the right engine, nothing happened. Tried it again, and nothing. Then I remembered from my C-47 days, basically the same airplane as the DC-3, that the starter solenoid was located in the wheel well directly behind the engine, and with that engine's propensity to leak oil, the hot oil would occasionally get into the starter solenoid, causing it to stick. I told the Co-Pilot what I was going to do, donned my Captain's jacket and, whistling nonchalantly, walked to the back of the airplane and deplaned. Outside, I climbed up onto the right landing gear and started to pound on the starter solenoid, yelling to the Co-Pilot, "HIT IT!" With me pounding the solenoid, it fired up as soon as the Co-Pilot hit the starter switch. I climbed down, nonchalantly walked back to the cockpit and had an uneventful flight to Key West.

What I didn't know, was that there was an FAA inspector on board and he witnessed the whole procedure. He could have nailed me to the cross, because it's against the law to ever take an airplane with a malfunction that's not written up in the log. Had I written the starter solenoid up in Miami, it would have grounded the airplane, and we had no spare. So I was pleasantly surprised when, several days later, a package showed up at Air Sunshine addressed to Jim Reed from the FAA and inside was a rubber mallet with "DC-3 STARTER" engraved on it. Another soul with understanding and compassion. Shades of old Mr. Gambrell.

Air Sunshine DC-3 at Key West International Airport

*Things were going rather well at Air Sunshine. Our primary competitor, SouthEast, was losing a good percentage of their market share. We didn't want all of the business, just enough to take away the profit margin of SouthEast to the point that the environment was not profitable for them to operate. We tried very hard to keep expenses down. Those DC-3s were a lot less costly to operate than the Martin 404s that SouthEast was operating, and their salary scales were much higher. We started our Co-Pilots at $425 a month and flew them the maximum allowed by the FAA. Most of them had to get money from home in order to survive. We had one pilot who didn't get money from home and he fished in the evening to eat. If he didn't catch a fish, he didn't eat. On one early morning flight to Miami, where we had a layover, I said to him, "Lets go to breakfast."

"Nah, I'm not hungry," he replied.

When I said, "I'm buying," he beat me to the counter.

Then one day, one of our birds lost an engine. Since the plane was not in a critical phase of flight when the loss occurred, it was no big deal. The DC-3 was comfortable on one engine, if it didn't happen at the wrong time. The most significant thing was the expense. For an airline operating on a tight budget, an engine change was costly. We had to ship the engine to our overhaul facility in Oklahoma, absorb the down time for the aircraft and endure the expense of the overhaul. Then, several weeks later, we lost a second engine. More expense, more down time. Within a few more weeks, a third engine failed.

All of these engines failed well before Time Before Overhaul (TBO) and we, besides being very unhappy, became suspicious of the overhaul facility. The losses threatened to put us out of business. So we asked the FAA to be present at the teardown of the third engine. The teardown and subsequent FAA investigation revealed that, to save money, the overhaul facility had been using truck bearings for the main bearings in our engines. The FAA shut them down on the spot.

*When the Chief Pilot's position opened up at Air Sunshine, I was offered the job, although the company's first choice was another pilot who had been with them much longer than I and was probably more qualified for the position. When his name was submitted to the FAA for their approval they turned him down because his background (and also that of the other pilots) was primarily light aircraft. They said that because of my background in heavy airplanes, Jim Reed was the only one in the company they would approve as Chief Pilot. Eventually, I filled both the Chief Pilot and Director of Operations positions and, as such, had my office in the Key West Terminal.

I frequently had lunch in the terminal snack bar and, on one occasion, while walking through the terminal to lunch, the janitor intercepted me and excitedly pointed toward the ramp saying**, "Captain Reed, should that airplane be doing that?"** I looked to the ramp and there was one of our Air Sunshine DC-3s merrily rolling down the ramp, engines not running, boarding door open, not a soul aboard and headed for the general aviation area, where all of the light aircraft were parked. I burst through the doors, hopped the concrete wall that separated the waiting area from the ramp and raced full speed to catch up with the errant DC-3. Reaching the door, I managed to get on board, made my way to the cockpit and noted the hydraulic pressure at zero. I quickly pumped up enough pressure to get the brakes working with the hand pump and got the DC-3 stopped just before it wiped out the first line of parked aircraft in the General Aviation area.

It seems that one of our crew had landed, set the parking brakes on a windless day and the ground crew failed to put the chocks in place. As the airplane sat there, the pressure to the brakes bled off and eventually one of the typical noonday thunderstorms moved over the field, preceded by gusty winds of up to 25 or 30 miles per hour. This got the chockless DC-3 moving and, had the janitor not been alert, this incident could very well have shut down the airline.

*Part of the adventure in aviation is the people you meet. After years and years you begin to recognize that any group of individuals who are accomplished professionals have an ego system that provides their driver. In each group there always seems to be basically the same cross section of personalities. There's the complainer who constantly finds something wrong with whatever is going on; the serious one who digs out the regulations and keeps everyone straight; the romancer who thinks that every woman who passes by has her eye on him; the organizer, trying to get everyone together to stand up to management, whether or not it's needed; and then there's the professional, who comes to work each day, does the best he can, makes suggestions for improvement where they may be needed and then goes home. And that's the kind of a pilot Carl was. Carl was originally from Holland and told me an incredible story about his parents during the Second World War. When the Germans invaded Holland, his parents, who were both doctors, became active in the underground resistance. The Germans discovered his father's connection with the underground and, one day, sent a German officer and two enlisted men to their farm to arrest him.

When the Germans arrived at the farmhouse, Carl's mother told them that his father was not at home, which was true. The Germans waited for him to come home and, during that time, told the mother that they were there to arrest her husband for his activity in the underground and that he would most likely be shot. As time dragged on, they demanded that she feed them. While preparing their meal, she was able to get poison from her medical supplies and poisoned all three of them to death. When Carl's father came home, they packed, got out of Holland and, through the underground, made it to England.

Bill, the Chief Pilot for Air Sunshine when I came on board, was originally from Cuba. He had been a pilot in the Cuban Air Force and, when Castro took over, Bill's family "exhibited anti-Castro sentiments" and the whole family was thrown in jail for 30 days. Of course, they threw Bill out of the Cuban Air Force and, in order to support his family, he got a job as a crop duster, flying a biplane. Through connections, he made arrangements to fly himself, his wife and child over the fence to Guantanamo in the single placed biplane. He was successful and was given asylum in the United States.

But Bill was a Latin Don Juan. Although he was a good stick and rudder man, his judgment sometimes kept him barely one step ahead of trouble. Everything he did was done with flamboyant aplomb. If there was a good-looking female passenger in the DC-3, he would don his Captain's Jacket and hat with the scrambled eggs, get the stewardess to invite her to the cockpit and impress her with his explanation of the instruments and radio navigation. Invariably, he would get to the engines and, since we flew with the side cockpit windows open, the low pressure that existed at the window snatched several of his $50 hats when he turned to explain the workings of the Pratt and Whitney Engine. We always said that if the navigation radios went out, we could find Miami by following Bill's hats.

The one thing that did worry us, however, was the potential for a hijacking, which in that proximity to Cuba was very high. Before the 9/11 terrorist attacks, the seriousness of resisting a hijacking was stressed over and over again by the FAA, as it was thought that the danger to the aircraft and passengers was just not worth it, and so the airlines developed a "rollover and do whatever they want" attitude. Take them wherever they want to go without resistance or even the impression of resistance. And that's the plan we adopted at Air Sunshine. But I always worried about Bill. Because he was a defector, I knew that even if hijacked, he would never go back to Cuba. Fortunately, we never had to see what Bill's reaction to a hijack would be. Air Sunshine was bought out some years later by a larger airline.

*On this particular morning flight to Miami we had a full load of passengers aboard that old DC-3. The flight had been smooth and the morning air was crisp and clear. We were about the only ones talking to Miami tower as we turned a long final and dropped the gear and partial flaps for the impending landing. Something caught my eye and I looked up. With disbelief, I saw the burning fuselage of an airplane, with flames and smoke coming out both ends and tumbling down **RIGHT ON TOP OF US!**

I snapped that DC-3 into a 90-degree bank to the right in an effort to get out of the way. When I looked back, the fuselage was still there, tumbling and burning. It continued to tumble and burn and, finally, it sunk in on me that it wasn't an airplane. What it turned out to be was a missile that had been fired from Cape Kennedy and destroyed at some point after liftoff. The crisp cold air and the initial startled look against that clear blue sky had made it appear to be directly overhead and very close. After a profound apology to the passengers, I continued a shallow banked turn back to final. For some reason, nobody congratulated me on the grease job I made at Miami that morning.

*I have to be a little careful as I chronicle this flying career. Each time I put pen to paper, the thoughts that emerge are the ones that are spectacular, either because they involve situations that bring on great stress or close calls or, even worse, a crash. But the hours and hours of boredom had their particular moments also. Those beautiful sights or wonderful scenes or experiences that flying presents, such as:

That night in the C-119 going south across the Mediterranean to Wheelus Field in Libya. The full moon reflecting off the black, romantic waters of the Mediterranean illuminated each of the small, fair-weather cumulus below and made each cloud appear as if it had its own neon light shining from within.

or

Descending in a T-39 across the Sierra Nevada Mountains into Sacramento late on a summer's afternoon and penetrating a deeply reddish/golden towering cumulus. I had often wondered what it would be like inside of a cloud that captured the deep reddish colors of a sunset. Everything inside the airplane was red. The instrument panel, was red, the Co-Pilot was red and I was in a deeply red world until we popped out into the deep blue evening sky.

or

Flying across a Germany that was completely white below against a brilliant blue winter sky, with outside temperatures so cold that you expected the wings to crack.

or

A low level flight across the Bering Sea, passing over the Alaska Coastline and looking down on a ghostly still winter trapped village where, because of the cold, there was no movement except for the thin, vertical towers of smoke rising in the still air.

or

Climbing vertically in the F-86 up one side of a towering cumulus over the Sierras, rolling inverted over the top and then plummeting straight down on the other side. Being close to the cloud gave some perspective on speed and motion and distance or

On a clear winter's day, diving from 15,000 feet and crossing at 100 feet and 400 knots the full length of a glistening Lake Tahoe that lay in a bowl of white sparkling mountains; drinking in that beautiful view from the bubbled canopy of the F-86.

or

Taking off in zero-zero fog at the Sonoma County Airport and bursting into a clear blue sky as the fog, looking like a field of snow that you could walk on, dropped away below. And feeling sorry that the rest of humanity trapped beneath in the gray drizzle couldn't experience what I was feeling.

or

The personal feeling of accomplishment of landing with a 100-foot ceiling and ¼-mile visibility or less. Bringing together all of the training and experience and pressing the system to the limit and safely landing an airplane under the most difficult of conditions.

or

On a <u>night</u> flight to Roi-Namur in the Kwajalein lagoon, seeing a fully developed rainbow created by moonlight, with all of the colors of a rainbow except that they were pastel against a pure black sky.

or

To use your airplane to ease suffering or to save a life. This, perhaps, is the most rewarding of all of the thrills that flying brings.

But, as great as those memories and experiences are for a professional pilot, there is the serious and, sometimes, deadly side of flying.

I suspect that anyone who has pushed airplanes around the sky for 45 years, as I have done, would have several stories to tell about near misses or close calls to a mid-air collision. As I write this, I recall that sick feeling I had one night at Webb AFB when two T-28s went belly to belly while entering initial approach at night. Both Instructor Pilots and students were lost in that one.

I have two recollections of what were true near misses that were close to the extreme.

The first near miss took place in a T-39 near Edwards AFB. We had just dropped someone who had business there at Edwards and we were going to wait several hours until he was through for the return trip to McClellan AFB. Since I had a Co-Pilot on board getting ready for a check ride to upgrade to Aircraft Commander (A/C) in the T-39, I elected to do some air work while we were waiting.

We had flown several instrument approaches to Edwards AFB and were climbing out with a clearance from Edwards Approach Control for another approach. Somewhere around 12,000 feet, the radar controller advised us that we had traffic at 10 o'clock and closing. Both the student pilot and I looked to 10 o'clock for the traffic. Again, the call that we had traffic at 10 o'clock closing. I looked to the left and couldn't see anything.

As I turned my head back, I saw two Navy A-7s flash from our right to our left at our exact altitude, so close that I looked, for just an instant, into the eyes of that A-7 Pilot and heard the scream of their engines as they passed by just a couple of airplane lengths in front of us.

The controller had gotten his O'Clocks mixed up and gave us 10 o'clock when it should have been 2 o'clock, thereby diverting our attention from where it should have been. Had we not been on radar, I'm sure that our visual scans would have detected the traffic. If we had collided, that would have been a radar assisted collision.

The second near miss took place after I went to work flying for Hugh Codding.

I was inbound to Las Vegas from Orange County, VFR, under radar advisories, in a C-421 twin engine airplane with a full passenger load at, as I recall, 17,500 feet. A Boeing 747 inbound to Los Angeles (opposite direction) was cleared from FL 240 down to 10,000 feet, through my altitude. We were both given each other's traffic at 12 o'clock by center, and the 747 pilot was told he could level at FL 180 or above until we were clear. I saw the 747 from a long distance away, but I didn't think he could see me because the afternoon sun was right in his eyes. I assumed he would level at FL 180. He didn't.

I suddenly realized that he didn't level at 18,000. Just before impact, the features of another airplane become very big, very fast. The number three engine on that 747 got awful big, awful fast, and I rolled to nearly inverted in order to miss him. I don't believe the 747 pilot ever saw us.

If I were told that I had another airplane at 12 o'clock and didn't have the other bird in sight, I believe I would have leveled at 18,000 feet or above until I was clear. Oh, well.

*For those who have mixed flying with other things and then returned to it, as I have done over the years, I would like to share a personal observation that might be helpful. When you have been away from a task for a while that requires judgment, good hand-to-eye coordination and lots of personal confidence, it has been my observation that you lose your confidence to perform much earlier than you lose your skill to perform. And the confidence returns very quickly when you have the opportunity to perform the skill. I believe this observation applies to any complex task, whether it be flying or running boats or anything that requires a great deal of confidence in one's self.

And as long as a little Philosophy is being passed around, let me share a personal experience.

When everything is looking grim and there seem to be more bad days than good and the problems don't seem to have any solutions, here's a little advice: Go take a walk in a graveyard! Preferably an old one, say from the 1800s. That may sound a little nutty, but as you go through the graveyard and look at those old headstones, remember that all those people had the same problems, some, perhaps, much worse. The world continued to turn and they all wound up in the same place, whether the problems got solved or not. And so will we.

A walk through an old graveyard puts everything in a little better perspective. Try it.

A postcard advertising Air Sunshine

Chapter 8

1975 - 1980

The Codding Years
Santa Rosa, California

How deep you fish
is not as important
as
how your worm wiggles!

*One day, when I returned from work at Air Sunshine, my son Chuck told me that Mr. Hugh Codding had called and asked if I would call him back. Recall that I had interviewed with him on an earlier trip back to California. To stay in touch, each time I was promoted within Air Sunshine, I would drop Mr. Codding a note advising him of that promotion. That contact strategy must have worked as they were ready to change pilots and he wanted to know if I would be interested.

It's strange how events in life have a way of starting a domino effect that changes everything that happens in the future. That phone call led not only to over 20 years (five of them full time) of great fun flying for Hugh Codding but, because of that move, to many other incredible events.

Hugh was a very successful land developer in Sonoma County, in Northern California. He had come up through the ranks, as contractors go, starting out as a Seabee during the Second World War and pounding nails in the construction business after he got out. Through several ups and downs in both his business and personal life, he managed to beat the odds and make it to the top.

Flying for Hugh Codding was a marvelous experience, partly because of the type of flying we did, but primarily because of the type of man Hugh is. He is a shrewd and cunning businessman, a masterful outdoorsman, an excellent judge of character, and has an uncanny ability to eliminate all the dust and smoke and get right to the heart of a subject.

His annual flying schedule had been developed through many years of experience. In the summertime we went north to places like Tsuniah Lake in British Columbia, an isolated spot in the mountains that, until just recently, was accessible only by plane. And in the wintertime we went south to many different destinations in Mexico. Hugh loved to hunt and fish, and those were always delightful trips. And there were many other destinations: The Northwest Territories, Wyoming, Montana, Nevada, and just about any other place you can name. And they were all fun trips. Hugh always went first class and loved to have a good time.

Originally, Hugh flew for himself. However, it didn't take him long before he found that flying was not one of his many attributes. Shortly after obtaining his Private Pilot License, he departed Salt Lake City in his new Cessna 180. There was an overcast, and Hugh's intent was to get on top for the trip back to California. Since he had never flown instruments before, he decided that he would concentrate on the airspeed and gave the job of watching the attitude indicator to one of the passengers.

Cessna 421 - N 421 AE 'The Abalone Express'

Hugh poked his head in the clouds and drove up through the murk until they got on top. The passenger marveled at how steady Hugh kept the wings, and it wasn't until they broke out on top that Hugh realized that he hadn't uncaged the attitude indicator. They could have rolled inverted and the attitude indicator would never have moved! This incident, plus several others, prompted Nell, his wife, to decide they needed a professional pilot. Over the years they went through several professional pilots before I came along.

The first challenge was Sea Ranch. Hugh had a home at Sea Ranch, a private development encompassing a ten-mile stretch of the California Coast, about 80 miles north of San Francisco. It's a beautiful place. From Santa Rosa, the drive is about two hours, but by plane it's only about 12 minutes straight across the Coastal Range.

The primary purpose of maintaining the house at Sea Ranch was the diving and fishing available there. Diving for abalone was a new experience for me. I was used to the warm, clear waters of the Tropics, and the cold, dark waters of the California coast presented a new challenge, with far greater demands. Hugh enjoyed watching my struggles.

The flying there also presented a new challenge. I was used to runways that were anywhere from 5,000 to 12,000 feet long. Sea Ranch was 2,600 feet, with hills at both ends. And it was just a strip – no tower, no weather advisories, no nothing. We depended on a phoned-in weather report on the existing conditions before we left Santa Rosa from Jeff or Judy, the folks who took care of the house for Hugh. But being on the coast, with the coastal fog, the field could go from sunshine to zero-zero in a couple of minutes. Frequently, I would make a straight in rather than the required pattern because the fog advancing over the hill would have shut the place down before I could make the circuit. And I can't count the number of times I followed the Russian River to get to the ocean and fly up the coast under the fog at 50 feet, hoping the ceiling would get to 350 feet by the time I got to Sea Ranch and hoping that there wasn't anyone else out there as dumb as I was coming in the opposite direction.

Shortly after I went to work for Hugh, a very difficult experience occurred. Codding Enterprises owned the Merced Mall in Merced, California. One weekend, there was a display in the mall in which the Military Services took part. One of the displays included a board showing the different weapons the service used, including, unfortunately, a live incendiary grenade which they had failed to disable. They placed the display board in the storage room overnight and, as luck would have it, the security guard, a young local boy, was curious and started to play with the items on the board. The incendiary grenade went off, burning him severely. He ran screaming into the mostly-closed mall and people in the barber shop, which was still open, ran to help. By the time he got to the hospital in Fresno, things were pretty bad.

After several days, the doctors decided that the only way to save him was to transport him by ambulance plane to San Francisco. But because of his weakened condition, that was a risky move. The doctors were afraid they might lose him during the move, but they felt sure they would lose him if they didn't get him to San Francisco.

Hugh offered to fly the family to San Francisco in the company plane, so they could be with him at the hospital in San Francisco. The mother also insisted that she wanted to ride with her son in the ambulance from the San Francisco airport to the hospital. When the boy arrived at the ambulance plane at the airport in Fresno, I took off with his mother and sister in order to be at SFO in time to allow the mother to ride in the ambulance, as she had requested.

We arrived on time at San Francisco and waited for the ambulance plane to show up. After 45 minutes, I called the Fresno tower to find out what had happened. The ambulance plane was still on the ramp at Fresno and had not yet taken off. They said that the doctors were on the plane working on the boy, but knew nothing else. After another 30 minutes, and at the mother's and sister's prompting, I called the tower again. They said the ambulance was just leaving the plane and they heard that the boy had died on the plane.

It must have been the look on my face, because when I turned around the mother said, "He died, didn't he?" I did not want to pass on unsubstantiated information about her son, so I told her that the ambulance had gone back to the hospital and that she should talk to the doctor. Although she did call the doctor, she already knew that her son had died, and broke down completely when it was confirmed. It was a sad flight back to Fresno.

After I dropped them off, I returned to Santa Rosa. Although I felt confident flying the C-421, I only had a minimum of night time in the bird, and things always look a little different at night. As I passed Merced, heading north, Oakland Center started getting reports of flocks of Snow Geese everywhere from the airliners descending into San Francisco. As these reports came in, you could see the airline pilots turning on landing lights as they started their descent into SFO. Reports of planes flying through flocks of Snow Geese from 6,000 to 24,000 feet were being received by center.

I began to get worried, because if I were to hit a 10-pound Snow Goose at 180 knots, it would come through the windshield and probably take my head off. There has been more than one instance of pilots being killed from bird strikes in the windshield. As the reports increased, you could hear the tension in the pilots' voices. Bird ingestion in a turbine engine is a serious problem and has been the cause of more than one crash.

This is what can happen when a small plane tangles with a large Bird, such as a Canadian Snow Goose

I got really worried when a report came in of a flock of Snow Geese over the Napa VOR at 6,000 feet, which was right where I was heading. I thought of landing at Modesto or Stockton and spending the night, but instead I put the plane on auto-pilot and got down behind the instrument panel in case one of those babies came through the windshield.

Oddly enough, the airline procedures for deterring bird strikes is to turn on the windshield heat, which make the windshield more pliable and better able to deflect a strike, and to turn up the ship's radar to full gain.

Apparently, Snow Geese will sense the RF energy, fold wings and fall out of the way. I got back to Santa Rosa in good shape.

*Shortly after the Fresno and the Snow Geese experience, we took off with a planeload of hunters for a small strip on a ranch in Wyoming. Hugh has gone to the Marquis Ranch in Wyoming on opening day every year for the past 20 or so years. This was my first real cross-country and, as we departed the Sonoma County Airport, I was a bit keyed up. We stopped at Salt Lake City for fuel and lunch and then on to Wyoming. As we approached the ranch (I had no idea where it was), Hugh came up to the cockpit and tried to help me find it, having been there many times before. With his help, we found the strip.

I took one look and had strong reservations. It wasn't really what you'd call an airstrip. It was just a bit of dirt leveled off in the field and, because of the recent rains, had puddles of standing water everywhere. It was impossible to tell how deep those puddles were, and I was truly apprehensive. I told Hugh that perhaps there was too much water there and that we should land somewhere else, like Gillette. He said something that I was destined to hear over and over in the coming years. "Well, all the other pilots would do it." I figured it was his airplane, I had voiced my reservation and, if he was willing to try it, so was I.

As we touched down, my boating experience came in handy and we slogged our way to the end of that muddy strip. I turned the aircraft around while we still had some forward motion, for fear that we'd get bogged down facing the wrong way. When everyone got off, I then deplaned and took a look. The entire fuselage and tail was solid mud from the wing back. We offloaded and then, as planned, I took off for Rapid City, South Dakota, to spend the night with an old Air Force buddy and his family, Gerry Teachout, whom I had known from France and Randolph.

The next morning, I called back to the ranch to see how everything was going and talked to Jeanie Marquis. The first words out of her mouth were, "Boy, are you in trouble. When you left, you took all of the hunting licenses with you, and everyone is out hunting illegally."

I told her that I'd fly right back with the licenses, but she said that was impossible. It had rained all night and the strip was a lake. Besides, although it wasn't raining now, there was a low ceiling and she didn't see how I'd make it. I told her to go outside when she heard an airplane and I'd airdrop the licenses to her. I could hear her gulp over the phone and she came back with a weak, "OK." I wrapped the licenses in four plastic bags and took off on an IFR clearance for Wyoming.

I filed for Casper, which was IFR, and, when I got in the area, told the controller what I wanted to do. I needed descent as low as he could get me at a specific bearing and distance off the Gillette VOR. Then, if I could get under the stuff, I'd go short term VFR until complete, then take my IFR back to Casper. I believe that I happened to get the right personality for that situation. Most controllers wouldn't be part of such shenanigans, but he understood my predicament. He cleared me to 2,000 feet above the terrain in the vicinity of the coordinates I had given him and I was still in solid clouds.

Just as I was about to give up, there was a break and I could see the ground, so I dove for it and cancelled my IFR. The next trick was to find the ranch that I'd been into only once under a 700-foot ceiling in the middle of Wyoming. I flew back and forth for about six or seven minutes, then spotted a building that looked familiar.

Taking off from the Marquis Ranch in N 421 AE (Abalone Express)

As I flew over, a figure dressed in black came out and waved. Using the eyeball', that I developed dropping things out of the old C-119, I flew over and dropped the licenses out of the small triangular window at the pilots position. After one more pass, the figure waved with the licenses in hand and I called up Denver Center for my clearance to Casper, poked my head back in the clouds and proceeded there. When I got to the hotel in Casper, I called Jeanie and she said the licenses landed almost at her feet. When he got back that night, Hugh was impressed and I was off the hook.

But there was another side to Hugh. On one hunting trip into Broadus, Montana, the left engine started running a little rough. After landing, a mag check showed that I had a problem either with the magneto or plugs. The ranch we were going to was about ten miles away from the airport and I told Hugh and the group to go on ahead while I fooled with the engine. I had trouble locating a mechanic, so started to pull the plugs myself. About two hours later, Hugh showed up at the airport. Instead of going hunting, he got worried about me and came back to see if I was okay. That impressed me.

*One of our trips took us to Ruidoso, New Mexico, where Hugh hired a guide for a hunting trip out in the boondocks. I stayed behind, as I'm not so inclined as a hunter. One evening, Hugh returned very excitedly and said that he believed that they had found parts of an airplane crash deep in the woods, south of Ruidoso. He described the wreckage as probably a military plane, because there were rounds of ammunition everywhere and what appeared to be a large container housing a gun. As he continued his description of the pieces they had found, it sounded to me as if it might have been a gun pod housing a Gatling Gun of the type that the Air Force was using.

The next morning I called the Base Commander at Holloman Air Force Base, not too far from Ruidoso, and described what Hugh had found. He got very excited and said that was probably the gun pod that had pulled off an F-4 fighter, and they had been looking for it for the past year. The F-4 was originally designed and built without a gun, depending on its missiles for offensive and defensive weaponry. The fighter pilots in the Air Force raised such a stink that the Air Force added a pod under the nose that housed a Gatling gun. Apparently, during a high 'G' maneuver, this pod had come loose, scattering hundreds of 20mm shells throughout the Ruidoso woods.

The Base Commander said he would send a helicopter with a group of men over to retrieve the gun and shells and asked if he could use Hugh's guide to show them where it was. Hugh said that the guide could show them where the gun was but said he had paid the guide through Friday and that they could use him after that. The Base Commander agreed and sent over the helicopter with the clean-up team on Saturday. It was cutting it close, because on Sunday, Ruidoso got a foot of snow.

As a result of that event, the Base Commander invited Hugh's group to dinner at Holloman AFB with a tour of the Base and all of its functions. That chance finding in the woods led to one of life's more pleasant experiences.

*I've always enjoyed the water, but I must admit that the Pacific waters off the coast of California presented a unique challenge. I was used to diving in the placid, warm and clear waters of the Tropics, which had a friendly personality. The waters off Sea Ranch, where Hugh had a beautiful home, had a different personality. That's where we dove for abalone.

There were times we dove when the visibility was such that you could barely see the end of your arm. And even on the calmest days, there was always a surge. This, coupled with the intense cold and the rumor that Great White sharks spawned in Tomales Bay, just a short distance south of Sea Ranch, gave those waters a very unfriendly personality.

The reward for diving in those conditions were a limit of four abalone. Abalone are actually a snail and spend their life clinging to a rock. The trick is to work through the maze of underwater obstacles – grass, kelp, poor visibility, etc., – pry the abalone off the rock with an iron and get it to the surface. All of this is done free diving, with snorkel and fins, as tank diving is illegal. After the abalone is safely tucked in the bag attached to an inner tube, you can go back and get three more.

On this particular day, I had flown Hugh and five others to Sea Ranch for an abalone dive. The favorite spot to dive was in Chicken Bay, next to some distant rocks about 100 to 200 yards from the beach in about 20 to 25 feet of water. Chicken Bay was so named because it was possible to get a limit of abalone fairly close to the beach, in four to six feet of water. It is the next bay over from where we normally descended down a 70 foot cliff, by rope, to enter the water.

After each of us had gotten our limit, we started back to shore, pushing our inner tubes with the abalone safely tucked inside the nets. I had fairly well expended myself and was looking forward to getting in. Trailing slightly behind the group, and still in Chicken Bay, I spotted what looked like a path etched in the sheer wall of the cliff. I had not seen that path before and it looked like an easy way to the top. I broke away from the group and headed for the beach, thinking, "This will be a piece of cake, and I'll be waiting for everybody when they get in." As I started up the path, I congratulated myself on my alertness in seeing this easy way to the top that avoided the long swim back to the other bay. About two-thirds up the cliff, and about 50 feet over the rocks below, I noted with dismay that about six or eight feet of the path was washed out. I was able to throw my inner tube of abalone to the path, past the washout, and gingerly started to transition across the washout.

About halfway across, the sandy dirt mixture that my toes had dug into started to give way and I plastered myself against the cliff. Arms outstretched, I was desperate to find something to grab on to. There was nothing. Spread-eagled against the cliff, the only thing keeping me from plummeting to the rocks below was where my toes were digging into the loose dirt. And I could feel the dirt falling away under my toes. I could not move ahead nor could I move back. I was stuck.

As I desperately pressed against the cliff, I wondered if I would scream when the moment came to plunge to the rocks below, as they do in the movies, and whether the rocks were far enough out of the water to keep the tide from washing my body to sea. And what would it feel like plummeting down to the rocks? I have never liked heights. Flying upside down at 20,000 feet didn't bother me, but looking over the edge of a twenty-story building gave me the willies.

As I waited for the inevitable, I thought about the group. By now they would have finished pounding the abalone and be headed for the bar. I knew that Hugh would not miss me and wondered if anyone else would. I thought, with all of the narrow scrapes that I've had in airplanes, with all of the times I've cheated the Grim Reaper, this is going to be a hell of a way to end it.

Sam Gordon has been Hugh's Construction Superintendent for many years and, because of his tenacity, efficiency and ability, was one of the many pieces of the puzzle that has contributed to Hugh's success. Sam wondered what happened to Jim and came looking for me.

The dirt was oozing out from under my toes and I knew I didn't have much longer when I looked up and saw Sam Gordon's head peering over the Cliff. "Sam, get a rope, quick," I begged.

Sam ran back to the house, got a rope and wrapped it around himself and laid down to get a better hold. With the rope taking my weight, I was able to swing to the other side of the path and I was saved from the horrible plunge to the rocks below.

I believe there is someone or something, somewhere, playing out the great events that take place in our lives. Some great plan all laid out that dictates everything that we do. If that's the case, perhaps someone up there decided that it was time to get my attention. They did!

*One morning, after an early flight, I stopped off at D's Restaurant at the Sonoma County Airport to grab some breakfast. I happened to sit at the counter next to Kentucky Pentegrast, a man whom I had met through Hugh. He owned a small twin and told me that he hadn't made a decent landing in six months and asked if I would be willing to go along with him someday and try to figure out what he was doing wrong. I said sure I would, and that, in fact, I wasn't doing anything at that moment. So after breakfast, we went out to his plane and took off north to a small landing strip next to the lumber mill at Cloverdale. As we came down final, I watched to see if I could detect anything that Kentucky was doing that might aggravate the landing, but everything looked pretty good and we made a satisfactory touchdown.

We made the touch and go and I sat there with my arms folded looking at the surrounding scenery as we made a right turn and thought, "Gosh, those hills are awfully close for us to be turning into them." I looked at Kentucky and could not believe what I saw. Although he had all of the control inputs for a left turn, WE WERE TURNING RIGHT. His mouth was open, his eyes were wide and he had a look of terror on his face.

I instinctively reverted to the training the Air Force had drummed into me – if you've just done something and everything starts to fall apart, put everything back where it was! Since we had just made a touch and go and had retracted the gear and flaps, I reached over without asking Kentucky and extended the gear and flaps. The controls started working again and, after some experimentation, I determined that only the flap on one wing had retracted from the full flap landing.

The other had stayed full down and we had experienced a split flap. Kentucky told me later that throughout all of his training, he had never even heard the term 'Split Flap'.

We left the flaps down, returned to Santa Rosa and landed. His problem with landings over the past six months was obviously a result of that flap partially hanging up either going up or going down. This time it decided to hang up while it was full down, and I'm convinced that if

I hadn't been with Kentucky that day he would not have survived that incident.

However, if that had happened, two other people might be alive today. Some years later, in a jealous rage, Kentucky shot his girlfriend and was deemed by the court to be responsible for a second death. At this writing, he is currently in the State Prison at Vacaville.

*Hugh's relationship with his employees was evident in one memorable flight to Merced. On this day, Hugh and I flew to Merced to meet with Paul Newman, the famous actor of stage and screen. Newman was looking for an investment and was flying up to meet Hugh and take a look at the Merced Mall.

We met at the Merced airport and went to lunch in Merced. Newman's Pilots stayed at the airport and waited for their Boss there but Hugh's Pilot (me) was invited to go along. We had lunch in downtown Merced and Hugh sat on one side of Newman and I on the other. After lunch the Mall Manager drove us to the mall and the three of us started to walk the length of the mall with Hugh on Newman's left and me on his right..

As we passed one of the stores that had a popcorn machine visible from the mall concourse, Newman took a sharp left, proceeded to the popcorn machine and asked the girl behind the counter for a bag of popcorn. I thought the girl was going to have a hissy fit when she recognized this famous actor.

Back on the concourse we continued our tour of the mall with Newman offering popcorn to Hugh and I. About halfway through the mall a lady recognized Newman and came over to ask for his autograph. Paul excused himself and said he was sorry but he did not give autographs and we continued our tour.

But the cat was out of the bag. Before long a group of about 20 women were approaching and we started to hurry down the mall eventually breaking into a full run with the anxious women chasing from behind. Bursting out of the doors at the end of the mall, we ran across a construction site, hopped a small fence and got into a car that was waiting for us.

As we drove away I turned to Paul Newman and said "You know...that happens to me all the time." That got a genuine laugh out of Hugh and Newman.

On the way to the airport Newman graciously offered me the rest of his bag of popcorn and I took it.

When I got home from that flight and told my wife, Colleen, what had happened the first question out of her mouth was "Where is the Popcorn bag?" I said it was still on the airplane. She demanded that I go back out to the airplane and get it before one of the girls from the office snags it.

I believe that some 30 years later she still keeps that popcorn bag in her nightstand.

*One thing that Hugh has is an extraordinarily large ego! It's no secret. He knows it, everyone knows it and they even joke about it. On one trip, coming out of Mexico, we were approaching Calexico to clear customs back into the United States. Customs requires a one-hour advance notice, and I had done that in my flight plan. When we were about 45 minutes out, Hugh suddenly realized it was getting to be lunchtime and Yuma, about 50 miles east, had a better restaurant than Calexico, so he told me to change to Yuma. Reluctantly, I did. A few minutes later, realizing, I guess, that it was a little out of the way, he told me to change back to Calexico. I started to do a slow burn. I explained that customs and the FAA were going to get upset with us for making all of these changes and I did not want to make another one. Hugh explained that I worked for him and not the FAA and customs and to change the flight plan, which I did. Then, a few minutes later, for what reason I don't know, he said to change it back to Yuma.

Flare-ups with Hugh usually only last a very short time, and when he's wrong he will generally apologize. The next morning, back in Santa Rosa, Hugh called me into his office and I anticipated an apology for his behavior. Instead he said, "I had breakfast this morning with the guys who were on the plane yesterday and they told me that I shouldn't treat Jim that way, he's liable to quit. You know what I told them? Pilots are a dime a dozen and pilot jobs are too hard to find. Jim wouldn't quit."

What Hugh didn't know was that I had been offered a job by Global Associates as Aviation Manager at Kwajalein a few days earlier and had turned the job down. When he said that pilot jobs are too hard to find and I wouldn't quit, I excused myself, called Global Associates and asked if the job offer was still good. They called me back in less than an hour and said that it was still a good offer.

I walked into Hugh's office and told him that I had a firm job offer at Kwajalein and that I was quitting.

When we take events that shape our lives into our own hands, who knows whether we've done the right thing or not. A little flare of temper on both sides resulted in a significant change in our lives. Hugh got a new pilot and I got a new job. We are still good friends, and the events of that time are well behind us. I have a great deal of respect for Hugh and I believe he has the same for me. When I returned from Kwajalein, I continued to fly for Hugh for many years as a fill-in pilot, even though I had a full-time job in San Francisco running ferry boats there.

Authors Note: Years ago, in theaters, the main feature was preceded by newsreels. When I was very young, perhaps 10 or 12 years old, I watched a newsreel story about a developer who built a house in one day. For some reason that newsreel stuck in my head over the years. That developer was Hugh Codding. Little did I know that one day I would be his pilot. Sam Gordon was Hugh's Construction Superintendent who coordinated the event.

Chapter 9

1980 - 1986

Bucholz Army Air Field
Kwajalein, Marshall Islands
Micronesia

**The only difference
between men and small boys
is the price of their toys!**

*Kwajalein is the terminal end of the Western Test Range for the United States. As the world's largest lagoon, it is the perfect place to test this nation's evolving missile gear, among other things. The remoteness of the lagoon, its shape and the fact that there are numerous islands surrounding the lagoon on which to mount sophisticated radars, make it ideally suited as a target at which to aim our strategic and tactical missiles. Missiles are fired periodically from Vandenberg AFB in California at the Kwajalein Lagoon. The re-entry vehicles from these missiles splash down on targets either in or near the lagoon. When I got to Kwajalein as the Aviation Manager, responsible for all the flying activities on the range, and got a feel for the enormity of the operations there, I felt I was in my element. Although the Kwajalein Missile Range is an Army facility, there are few Army people there. The majority of the functions within the range are conducted through civilian contract companies. My company at the time was Global Associates, which I felt did a masterful job in the conduct of their contract with the U.S. Army. The few Army personnel stationed there were primarily contract evaluators.

The Aviation Department consisted of about 150 people, of which about 26 were pilots. Flying equipment consisted of two Lockheed Electras (which we transferred early on), seven DHC-4 Caribou (Military designation C-7A), a 28-passenger high wing aircraft built by de Havilland and five U.S. Army single-engine Huey Helicopters on floats. These aircraft were primarily used to transport people and equipment to their work areas on the many outer islands forming the Kwajalein Lagoon.

Kwajalein Lagoon, showing the East and West Reefs and the Island of Kwajalein

We had a daily flight schedule, as would any small airline, and were evaluated on, among other things, our on-time performance. I acquired and retained my currency in the DHC-4 to provide an extra pilot in the event we needed one, but also because I didn't think that I would be able to survive in a flying environment unless I, too, were flying. In that time, the DHC-4 aircraft flew a morning and afternoon schedule to Meck Island, about 17 nautical miles north of Kwaj, and to Roi-Namur, about 43 miles north. Since our first takeoff was at 0520, I normally showed up for work at 0500 so I could jump in the cockpit if, for some reason, the scheduled pilot didn't show.

I'm not sure why I was flying this particular morning, but with Tom Barrett in the right seat and 27 passengers on board, we departed into the oncoming morning for Meck Island. When the gear was extended for the landing on Meck, we got an unsafe warning and aborted the landing. Investigation revealed that although the right main gear was down, it was not locked and would collapse upon landing. As the sun came up and daylight became a reality, we tried everything in the book to get it locked down.

It was so close to being in the locked position but refused to lock. We worked for an hour-and-a-half pulling 'Gs,' activating emergency hydraulic systems and even tried some unorthodox suggestions from the maintenance guys on the ground. Nothing worked, and I could see myself being the first gear-up landing in the outfit. I had heard that in some instances pilots have been able to land and bounce the gear in place and suggested that as something to try. The answer was a resounding no.

And rightly so.

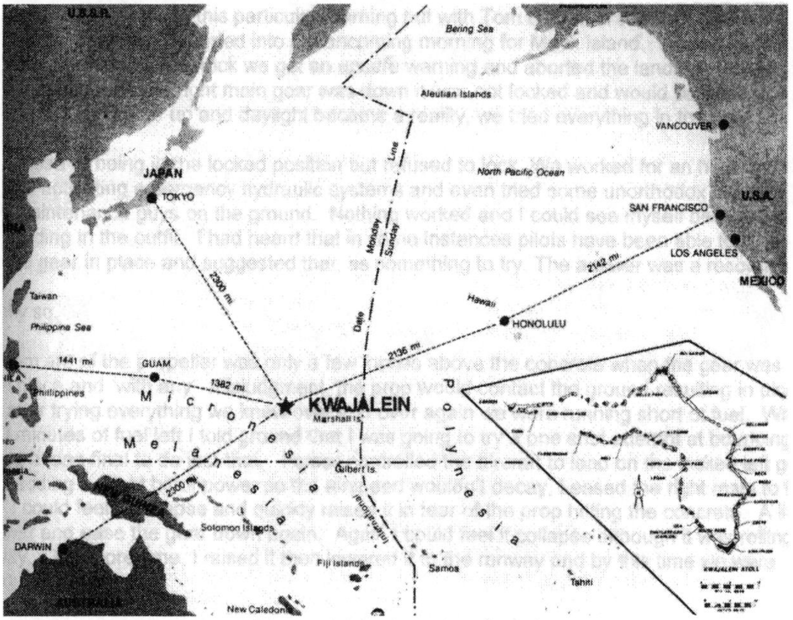

Map of the Pacific showing Kwajalein's location
The insert shows the shape of the Kwajalein Atoll, with the Island of Kwajalein at the bottom

The bottom arc of the propeller was only a few inches above the concrete when the gear was locked in place, and with any misjudgment the prop would contact the ground, resulting in disaster. Finally, after trying everything we knew over and over again, we were running short of fuel. With about 20 minutes of fuel left, I told ground that I was going to try a one-shot attempt at bouncing it in and set up a long final to do just that. I cross controlled the aircraft to land on the locked left gear and then, adding a slight bit of power so the airspeed wouldn't decay, I eased the right main to the runway. I could feel it collapse and quickly raised it in fear of the prop hitting the concrete. A little more power and I eased the gear down again. Again, I could feel it collapse, although it was rolling on the runway. One more time, I raised it then lowered it to the runway and, by this time, we were running out of runway.

Due to the fuel situation and the reluctance of the powers that be, I knew I wouldn't get another chance at getting the gear down and I could see a belly landing coming up. Suddenly, as we were rolling the unlocked gear down the runway for the final time, and with the end of the runway getting ready to disappear under the nose, the light bulb came on. TOUCH THE RIGHT BRAKE! Since the landing gear retracts forward and extends aft and the wheel was rolling on the ground, perhaps the brake would drive it in place. I did, and it did. **Three green!** I added power for the go around and announced to some very relieved people (including me) that we had all gear down and locked.

Because the landing gear on the Caribou is too long to fit in the gear well, it has a shortening mechanism to shorten it as it retracts. A linkage actually pulls the two-piece gear strut up inside itself. There is a canvas cover between the two pieces of strut to keep debris from getting down inside. Investigation showed that the hard steel ring that gives the cover its shape had worked its way out of the cover and fallen down inside the two struts, jamming the mechanism from going into the full down position. When I touched the brake, the force overrode the jam and locked the gear in place.

de Havilland DHC-4 'CARIBOU' and me with Roi Namur in the background
(Photo Credit: Bruce Trombecky)

*After landing the C-7A with gear problems, a Mrs. Chu came up to me while we were standing on the ramp, with the mechanics briefing me on what they found had caused the unsafe gear. She asked to see my hand. After studying my hand, she said it was OK for her husband to fly with me because I had a long lifeline. When I started to pull my hand back she grabbed it, studied it for a second time and then exclaimed "Oh Mr. Reed, you have no lust in your heart" I became very indignant for her to utter such a private matter in such a public place. Apparently we all have a Lust Line located somewhere on our hand.

When I got back to the states I told my 90 year old Mom that story and jokingly took her hand and said "Gee Mom, you have a very active Lust Line. She asked "Is it at the beginning or the end?"

One day, as Thanksgiving was approaching, several of the young pilots came to me and asked if, on Thanksgiving, we could drop a few frozen turkey's and a stack of Playboy magazines to the crew of the Russian Spy ship that hung off the shoreline of Kwajalein to watch the missile shots. I pointed out that the Russians (at that time) were the enemy and if a frozen turkey were to hit a crewmember or damage a critical piece of equipment, it could cause an international incident.

In earlier days, before I arrived, I was told that the crew on the Russian ship, which would sit off shore from Kwajalein for months at a time would put their personal mail in a sealed container and drop it over the side. The trade winds and the current carried the container onto the Kwajalein shoreline and the American kids would take the letters and money to the Post office for mailing. There was always money left over to reward them for their trouble.

*Considering all of the things that had happened to me over the years, the incident I most treasure, and is perhaps most significant, certainly the most significant event in my eight years at Kwajalein, was recovery of the Designating Orbital Tracker (DOT) Missile. This event made me proud of the American men and women that I worked with and created a success story that I wish every American could have read about, because they would have been proud of their fellow Americans who pulled it off.

It happened that the Lockheed and Boeing Corporations were jointly contracted to develop a tracker that would guide an interceptor missile to destroy an incoming re-entry vehicle. If successful, this program would demonstrate our country's improved intercept capabilities to destroy incoming missiles. I had worked with the Boeing representative to ensure the safety of the delicate tracker during its shipment through Kwajalein and up to Roi-Namur.

Through many different stages of development, the time had come to have a live firing of the tracker. The plan was to fire the interceptor missile from Roi-Namur, an island on the north reef of the Kwajalein Lagoon, at an incoming Minuteman Missile of opportunity for another program fired towards the lagoon from Vandenberg AFB California. The interceptor missile would simply make a close flyby of the incoming missile and then parachute to a soft landing about 200 nautical miles north of Roi-Namur. The trick was to recover the interceptor missile in the broad ocean area as soon after splashdown as possible to preserve the data.

With their massive capability, the United States Navy was chartered to provide retrieval of the interceptor missile and subsequent return to Roi-Namur. Everything was in place and going well until about three weeks before the firing, when the Navy pulled out to go to a crisis somewhere in the world. Panic set in. Without the capability to retrieve the missile, the shot could not take place and Boeing could see that by losing the incoming missile of opportunity, eight years of work would go down the drain.

All of the managers on Kwajalein were called to a meeting at Range Operations to discuss the problem. A message from the Army Ballistic Missile Command asked us to take a close look at our capability and see if we could provide a solution to the problem. As Aviation Manager, I reviewed my resources and, try as I might, couldn't figure out a way to help. We had seven DHC-4 Caribou and five single-engine Huey Helicopters. The Marine Department had a couple of old tugs and some landing craft, and none of this added up to a miracle. So the joint response of all of the members at that meeting was that the capability at Kwajalein was not sufficient to mount an effort to save this program. And that was the response sent back to the Ballistic Missile Command.

After the meeting, I got into the operations van and took a ride around the island, just to think. I parked on the west end, looking back at the lagoon (Kwajalein Island is in the shape of a boomerang). As I sat there, I spotted the remnants of some old DeLong barges. These barges were actually a bridge that had, at one time, spanned a river in Vietnam during the war. There were four sections of this bridge, each 120 foot x 60 foot, and after the war they were being towed back to the States. Upon arrival at Kwajalein, the tugboat Captain, for whatever reason, left them there and proceeded alone. Kwajalein inherited them. I had heard that they were so unseaworthy that he felt it dangerous to take them any farther. And, sure enough, they were sitting in the lagoon, constantly sinking, with the Marine Department pumping them out every so often to keep them off the bottom.

Single-Engine Huey with practice DOT missile inside on a sled

But as I sat there, a plan formulated in my head. Our single-engine, float-equipped Huey Helicopters only had a range of about 200 nautical miles. But if one of our old tugs could tow a DeLong Barge to the area and I put a fuel truck on the barge, the helicopter could land on the barge, refuel, pick up the missile and carry it back to Roi-Namur.

Now excited, I found Jim Brown, a close friend and Chief Pilot of the helicopter section. We went to my quarters and sat in the living room to develop a potential plan to pull this thing out of the fire. Jim said that he would be willing to fly to the barge, pick up the missile and carry it back to Roi. That could be done. But fuel constraints would not permit him to sling load (hang below the chopper) the missile, and to reduce drag he would have to carry it inside.

After coming up with what we thought was a workable plan, I excitedly went to Don MacAfee, General Manger for Global Associates, and laid the plan out for him. The first words out of his mouth were "BULLSHIT! Those DeLong barges are sinking and wouldn't make it out of the lagoon. Besides, it's too tight on fuel for the Huey. You'll wind up dumping it in the drink."

I explained that Jim and I had everything worked out and we thought it would work. "BULLSHIT," again. I could tell I didn't have Don MacAfee convinced, so I went to the Boeing representative and he immediately responded positively. Here was a way to save his program, and everyone else would be taking the risk. He went to work advising everyone that we had a plan and the thing gained so much momentum in the first day that Don MacAfee couldn't stop it, even though he wanted to.

And it was risky. Don was right. To fly a single-engine helicopter to the limit of its fuel endurance, 200 miles over the water (we couldn't put extra tanks on because of the weight) to a barge whose location we were not really sure of (our tugs were equipped to flail around in the harbor, not navigate at sea), find and pick up a 1200-pound missile and carry it back 200 nautical miles was kind of ridiculous. But this was the kind of thing that I loved. Hang everything out on the edge and see if you can make it work. Sometimes it works and sometimes it doesn't. <u>That's</u> the challenge.

What happened over the next two weeks was astounding. The entire island population got hyped. There was a 24-hour-a-day, seven-day-a-week effort to prepare the equipment and make this program work. The best DeLong barge was selected and brought into the pier for repair. Patches were welded over the holes to limit the amount of water intake. A small city started to appear on the barge. As it turned out, facilities for 16 men were prepared on the barge for this operation. Water tanks, generators, radios, trailers, a mess hall with cooking facilities, etc., sprung up. A second barge was selected and used for practice helicopter landings in the lagoon. I don't believe I have ever seen such enthusiasm to make an impossible situation work as I witnessed on this project. If the comment was made that "Gee, we should take off the bits on the stern to make more room for the chopper," the bits disappeared, without reams of paperwork, normally required.

We were within one day of departure of the tug and barge and the landing area for the helicopter had not yet been painted. Torrential rain had precluded painting the deck, and one of the absolute requirements was that the deck MUST be painted with a grey, non-skid paint and, because of the close quarters, an outline in yellow was required for the floats as a guide for landing. As I stood on the helicopter landing area in the torrential downpour with Dick Timas and German Rodriguez, two wonderful guys from heavy equipment, I bemoaned the fact that if we couldn't get this area painted, we may have to cancel. I left, came back about two hours later and, to my amazement, with that torrential downpour still taking place, the deck was painted non-skid grey and the yellow outline was in place. When I asked Dick Timas how he did it, he explained that they took the huge air compressors from the sandblast area, disconnected the sandblasting gun and connected the paint gun just below the sandblast nozzle and blew away the water and painted at the same time. How's that for American ingenuity?

During this time, a lot of training was taking place. Besides our helicopter pilots training on the barge, the Navy had sent their Seals down to provide assistance in retrieval of the missile from the water. They would be in the helicopter as it left the barge to retrieve the missile. When they got to the missile, they would go into the water, cut the missile from its parachute and attach the sling to the chopper. A small boat would be dispatched from the barge to pick them up. Because of the safety zone, the barge could not be closer than 17 miles from the missile landing area, and I was concerned about losing track of the Navy Seals who would be left in the open ocean after the chopper departed.

In addition, when the Army helicopter guys in Hawaii heard what was going on, that civilians were going to pull this thing off, they cried like squashed cats. They wanted in. Things had progressed too far along for them to be the primary pickup helicopter, so they shipped a couple of their Hueys down to Kwajalein to take the backup position. They would be in a position on the island of Rongerik, north of Roi-Namur, that would permit them to get to the barge in the event something happened to our Huey.

There was no landing area for a helicopter on Rongerik, so Mel Carr, the Port Captain for Global at Kwajalein (and a close friend of mine), took an LCU, our large Landing Craft, along with a bulldozer, road grader and other equipment and spent a week creating a helicopter landing area at the old weather station on Rongerik. We felt that the Army guys should have a practice landing on Rongerik and checkout the site, so Dick Evans and I accompanied them on a practice trip in a Caribou. They landed and were greeted by Mel Carr and taken for a tour of the site. That was OK. But the only time I really got upset at this lifelong friend was when I saw him invite the Army Pilots aboard his boat for lunch, which left us circling on a sky hook overhead. I know what a gracious guy Mel is, and when I saw them walk aboard that LCU, I knew what was going on.

About three days before the shot, the barge was ready, the 16 men boarded and the tug set sail for sea. The tug had no way to navigate, so once or twice a day I'd send a DHC-4 Caribou out, find the tug and give them a position. When shot day came, Dick Evans and I flew the Caribou to accompany Jim Brown and Steve Dougherty in the Huey. We provided the navigation assistance for them to find the barge (hopefully in position) and had Navy Seals aboard our aircraft who could deploy in the event the single-engine chopper went down.

As we went over the North Reef inbound to the barge, I noted the Russian Tracking Vessel that normally hung around Kwajalein to observe the lagoon impacts appeared confused. He would usually stay just outside the advertised hazard zone to watch the incoming re-entry vehicles impact the lagoon – but what was all the traffic heading north? In addition to the two Huey's and Caribou, the Navy had provided a P-3 Orion to assist in tracking the DOT missile as it parachuted to its soft landing in the sea. So with all this traffic heading north, the Russian started in that direction, then changed his mind and returned to his normal position.

When we got to the area, the barge was right where it should be and Jim landed aboard and started refueling. We listened on the High Frequency radio as the countdown progressed for the launch. There were a lot of people who didn't think we could pull this complex mission off, including the guys at the Pentagon who said "we were nuts to even try." But when the shot went off, we were as ready and as pumped as any men could be. Jim Brown was supposed to wait aboard the barge after missile impact and until released by the Range Safety Officer, but instead took off and headed for the impact area based on the impact time.

As it turned out, those few minutes made the difference. After the intercept in space took place, our missiles chute opened, but the radio beacon that was to give us a fix during descent, didn't work. Fortunately, the P-3 got a radar fix on only one sweep of its radar, and that provided enough information to find it. The P-3 hit the landing site with a smoke flare, which guided Jim to the missile. When they arrived on site, the Navy Seals got into the water, cut the missile from the chute and attached it to the Huey. As it turned out, one of the doors hadn't closed and the missile was taking on water. Instead of the 1200 pounds it should have weighed, we believe it weighed well over 2,000 pounds, and the Huey couldn't pick it up. (I'm trying to remember those weights. They may be off a bit).

This photo of the first MX Peacekeeper on October 1, 1984, appeared on the cover of "Aviation Week" magazine. It was taken from a Navy P-3at 8,000 feet approximately 80 miles north of Roi Namur. (Photo credit: Bruce Trombecky)

Rather than cut it loose, as might be the tendency of most pilots, Jim Brown elected to attempt to drag it the 17 miles back to the barge, where we had a floating rack in the water that could capture it. As he progressed back towards the barge and the water drained out, it became light enough to lift from the water and Jim got it airborne and sling-loaded it back to the barge. After getting it aboard the barge, the missile was placed in a locally designed and constructed sled and, with a come-along, was coaxed into the helicopter. The flight back to Roi-Namur was uneventful, and with Dick Evans and I flying alongside the Huey on that gorgeous day, we felt mighty good.

My only regret about this whole thing was the lack of character that the Boeing people showed after the event was over. They took credit for the entire program, never recognizing or even thanking the Global people who provided the idea, the energy and the force to make it all happen. After I got over my anger, not only for me but for all the other Global people who made the program work, I felt sorry for the people in Boeing. After saving their bacon, Global never got so much as a thank-you.

*We had seven DHC-4 Caribou to perform the mission at Kwajalein. These planes were used primarily to airlift people to the islands of Meck and Roi-Namur. Occasionally, we became involved with other specialized missions in support of the range. We had no hanger facility and the airplanes spent their entire life at Kwajalein in the salt-laden atmosphere created by the trade winds stirring up the ocean. As the waves broke on the reef, just a few feet from the ramp, the salty mist floated across the airplanes. As a result, corrosion was a major problem.

We had a very active corrosion control program but that wasn't enough. The Army recognized, through years of experience there, that the only real way to control corrosion was to put the airplanes through an overhaul every two years.

And so our contract read that we would send each aircraft through an Inspection and Repair As Necessary (IRAN) program every 18 months to two years. As a result, of the seven aircraft we had assigned, one was always at the overhaul facility. Every so often we would re-bid the overhaul contract. Oakland, California, procured the contract on one occasion. Birmingham, Alabama, got it another time. It was a long haul, flying at 135 knots in a Caribou back to Oakland or Birmingham from Kwajalein. Flight time from Kwajalein to Honolulu was about 16.5 hours, then another 16.5 hours to Oakland. Since we didn't need the heaters for the low level work we were doing in the Tropics, the ferry flights back to the States were mighty cold. Initially, we were installing three large rubber bladder tanks to provide the fuel range for these long flights. The problem with the bladder tanks was that there was no way to dump fuel. For the first five or six hours after takeoff, the gross weight would not permit flight on one engine. If you lost an engine with no way to dump fuel – bang – you're in the drink. Eventually, we switched to the Benson tanks, which had a dump capability, and I felt much better.

We had two close calls while we were using the bladder tanks. Both were on the Oakland to Honolulu leg on the return from overhaul. It was strange, but we never had a problem with our airplanes en route to overhaul. It was always on the way back.

On one of the trips back from overhaul, they had just passed the Equal Time Point (ETP) between Oakland and Honolulu and someone made the comment, "Well, we're by the ETP. Time to lose an engine." No sooner had they gotten the words out when the right engine failed. With the engine shut down, they were not able to hold altitude and started to drift down toward the sea, anticipating that when they got a little lower the bird would hold altitude. It didn't, so they started throwing stuff out.

Eventually they got down to about 50 feet and the descent stopped, probably because of ground effect. They spent the next ten hours between 50 and 200 feet, at night, on one engine. As soon as the Coast Guard notified us that they had gotten a mayday call from our bird, I gathered up the Operations and Maintenance brains in the outfit and set up a Command Post in my office to provide any assistance that we might be able to muster. The Coast Guard launched a C-130 and intercepted our bird, flew alongside them through the night and provided a direct relay from the Caribou to the Coast Guard and to us in the Command Post. For some reason, I had a bad feeling about this one.

The Pilot advised us that they had used up much of the oil in the reservoir located in the fuselage on the engine that eventually failed. On long flights such as this we carried spare oil on board that could be transferred to the engine reservoirs as needed. Each engine reservoir held 28 gallons. Shortly thereafter they transferred the last of the spare oil to the good engine and reported that with their flashlight they could see a pretty good oil leak on that engine. There are no oil quantity gauges on the Caribou, only a low oil level light that illuminates when the oil quantity in the reservoir gets down to about 11 gallons. Their low oil level light for the reservoir in the good engine came on with fully five hours yet to fly before reaching Maui, their new destination. The ante had certainly been raised.

Another three hours transpired and we kept waiting for the call that would say they were losing oil pressure on their left and final engine. Suddenly, the pilot called and asked a very interesting question. They had five gallons of hydraulic fluid on board and he asked if they could transfer that to the reservoir on the good engine. All of us in the Command Post got our heads together. Hydraulic fluid is petroleum based, but would it provide enough lubrication? The fluid we had on board was flammable, not the non-flammable type widely used today. Although it would provide some temporary help, we felt that it would soon wipe the cylinders of lubrication and eventually result in engine failure.

This is what we told them: If they had the lights of Maui in sight when they started to lose oil pressure, put the hydraulic fluid in the reservoir. With no oil the engine would fail very quickly. The hydraulic fluid might just provide enough lubrication to get them there. If they did not have the lights of Maui in sight and the oil pressure started to drop, don't put it in. Go ahead and ditch. The hydraulic fluid could cause an engine fire and then he'd be facing that along with the ditching. As it turned out, they landed in Maui with just under two gallons of oil left in the reservoir. We wound up changing both engines on that airplane because they had worked that good engine beyond its limitations in order to make their destination.

As a result of the two close calls on our ferry flights, we took a very close look at the ditching section of the Pilot Handbook for the Caribou. Some of the things in the ditching procedure baffled us, so the Chief Pilot, Norm Splitstoesser (a good friend and excellent pilot), got hold of the Air Force Safety Center and asked them to send us any information they had on ditching experience with the Caribou. They had only one ditching incident with Caribou and sent us the following accident report. I have heard two versions of this story and will include both here. The reason I am including both versions is that version #1 is such a good story, but version #2 is more likely to be the accurate one.

Version #1:

Four Caribou were being ferried back from Vietnam. They had gotten to Hickam AFB in Hawaii and all four were preparing to depart on the leg to California. The Flight Leader noted that one airplane was 400 pounds over maximum allowable weight and ordered the pilot to download 400 pounds of fuel. The basic weight of this airplane was just heavier than the others. So the pilot downloaded 400 pounds of fuel and the four-aircraft flight took off for California.

Sometime into the flight, and beyond the equal time point, the aircraft that downloaded the fuel lost an engine and, as the flight progressed, it became obvious that they may run out of fuel before reaching their destination. The pilot started hollering mayday, so the Air Force launched a helicopter out of Hamilton and the Coast Guard sent a boat to intercept them. The ditching took place between the Farallon Islands and the Golden Gate Bridge, with excellent ditching conditions. The helicopter had made the intercept and flew formation with the Caribou as it ditched. According to the observers, it was a good ditching and the Pilot did an excellent job. As the aircraft ditched, the nose buried and the front of the cockpit collapsed in on the pilots. Although the Co-Pilot was able to get up and he and the others escaped out the rear of the aircraft, the Pilot, though not badly hurt, was trapped in the seat and could not get out.

As the Helicopter Pilot hovering nearby saw the airplane start to sink with the Pilot trapped in the seat, he sent two paramedics into the water in an attempt to get the Pilot out. They entered through the overhead hatch and, once in the cockpit with the water rising, tried to free the Pilot from the twisted metal holding him in the seat. As the water rose, the two rescuers struggled. Quickly, the water was over the Pilot's chest, then his chin, then mouth, then nose, and the rescuers realized that if they didn't get out that they, too, would go down with the plane. So they abandoned their rescue attempt and turned to leave.

The Helicopter Pilot, realizing the situation, knew that he had to do something, but what? And then, drawing on that something inside that makes people who don't give up an edge on death, he went to the rear of the Caribou and hovered over the tail. The rotor wash from his helicopter drove the horizontal stabilizer down, which in turn brought the nose up. As the water momentarily receded from the Pilot's face, the two rescuers went back to their struggle and were, in that extra minute or so that the Helicopter Pilot had given them, able to free the trapped Pilot. All three of them made it out of the airplane before it sank.

Version #2:

The Commander of the Helicopter unit at Hamilton AFB, where the rescue helicopter and crew were stationed, read Version #1 above and contacted me to make some corrections to that story, which I had been told came from the USAF Safety Center. First, the primary cause of the ditching was that the aircraft had lost an engine and the increased fuel consumption caused it to be short on fuel to make the destination. Concerning the helicopter, that portion was true except the Helicopter Pilot did not extend the rescuers' time by placing the rotor wash on the horizontal stabilizer to bring the nose up. He did emphasize the heroic efforts of the two Para Rescue men who went into the sinking aircraft and freed the trapped pilot.

And that answered the question that we had concerning the ditching procedure in the Pilot's Handbook for the Caribou. In the procedure it said, "In the event of a ditching, one Pilot should go to the rear of the airplane." Now we knew why. The front end could collapse, trapping one or both of the pilots. That procedure was most likely placed in the Handbook as a result of that ditching.

*One evening, shortly after I got home from work, I received a call from the Base Communications Center saying that they had received a call for assistance from the Department of Energy (DOE) Contract Vessel the M/V LIKTANUR. They were at the island of Likiep, about 130 nautical miles northeast of Kwajalein, and one of the DOE women had suffered a heart attack. They needed an immediate Air Evacuation.

The Island of Likiep had a new landing strip, but it was just a strip, no lights or any other approach aids. Strictly a daytime VFR operation. And I could not launch an aircraft off site without the Army Commander's approval. I knew that would take a while, and sunset was almost upon us.

Our last flight of the day had just landed at Roi-Namur Island, about 42 nautical miles north of Kwajalein, and I knew that he would not have a lot of fuel on board, having already made several trips to Roi-Namur. After a quick mental calculation on time, distance and fuel, I called Dudley Nichols, the Aircraft Commander, and told him to make an immediate launch for Likiep, gave him the approximate heading and distance as I remembered it, and told him that I would go to Operations and refine the heading and distance, get approval for the flight and pass that all to him on the radio. I knew that Nichols had not been to Likiep and didn't even have so much as a chart on board to help him find it or to know what the runway heading was.

I notified (then) Major Jake Starr, the Army Government Flight Representative and the Commander's contact with the Civilian Aviation Department, told him what I was doing and asked him to obtain approval for the flight. I said I would meet him in Base Operations in a few minutes.

When I got to Base Operations and plotted out the course and distance to Likiep, I found, to my dismay, that although the heading I gave Nichols was right on, I had underestimated the distance by about 30 miles. That doesn't sound like much in an airplane, but we only cruised at a little better than two miles a minute, so that was almost an additional 15 minutes. With sunset almost upon us, that could make the difference between making it or not. I passed the corrected distance and the runway heading to Nichols, who by now was almost halfway there.

Major Starr joined me at Base Operations and said that he had obtained approval for the flight with the stipulation that the aircraft **must** land before **official** sunset. Official sunset is always 20 or so minutes before it really gets dark, and I knew that we were pushing dark time, much less official sunset.

As it turned out, when Nichols showed up at Likiep, it was way past official sunset and was, in fact, dark. John Vissat, a close personal friend of mine, was the Mate on the M/V Liktanur and a sharp individual. He knew that the plane could not land without some kind of a reference for the runway. He had on board his vessel an entire carton of Cylume lights, the chemical light that you break and shake to illuminate. He broke out the carton of Cylume lights and passed them out to the local island residents, who lined the runway with about 200 of the lights.

Nichols landed, but when he attempted to turn around on the runway, his nose wheel dug in to the loose coral and he got stuck. All of the island people got together and literally pushed the airplane out of the hole. This delayed Nichols about 30 minutes.

In the meantime, Jake Starr and I went to the Base Communications Center because their VHF Radio had more range than the one in Base Operations. We had lost radio contact with Nichols when he started his approach to Likiep and would not have contact again until he was back in the air. My concern now was his fuel. I computed that to make it back to Kwajalein, once he got off Likiep (there were no alternates), he needed a minimum of 1,000 pounds of fuel per side to have any margin of safety. If his fuel state was any less than that, I would have committed a major mistake sending him in the first place. So, it was with ragged anticipation when we finally regained radio contact with Nichols shortly after he reported airborne from Likiep with the patient.

As I asked him what his fuel state was, I prayed that the answer would be at least 1,000 pounds a side. I was shaken when he reported back that he had only 800 pounds of fuel per side. I could see this great rescue going sour and literally ending up with a splash.

But Nichols was an old Military Airline Transport Service (MATS) Pilot and had flown a lot of overwater flights where he had to stretch fuel. And he knew how. He slowed way down, pulled the power and RPM back to where he was just barely hanging in the air and, although, it took a little longer, he made it back to Kwajalein, no sweat!

Although this story had a happy ending, it is indicative of the many times in aviation that life or death decisions must be made in an instant, many times with only the minimum of information on which to base a decision. And many times based just on what your gut tells you.

When the M/V LIKTANUR finally returned to Kwajalein, John Vissat told me that after Nichols took off, the local children picked up all the Cylume lights, cut them open and poured the illuminated chemical over each other. Apparently, the chemical was not harmful. John said it really looked weird, 50 illuminated kids running through the nighttime jungle.

*It has always amazed me at the variety of ways different people can have different views on specific circumstances. Let me give an example. The crew of the Caribou consisted of three people: the Pilot, the Co-Pilot and the Kicker (similar to a stewardess on a small airliner). All three were on interphone during takeoff. On one early morning flight from Kwajalein to Meck Island in the Caribou I made a night takeoff from the left seat. Shortly after we broke ground, all of the lights started to flicker and I noted the ammeters were throwing the load back and forth between the left and right generators, with the left ammeter surging very high. I needed an immediate scan on the left engine. If the generator was tearing itself up, the problem was serious and I needed to make an immediate return to the field. If it was simply an electrical problem, I could resolve it by turning the generator off and continuing to Meck Island, only 17 nautical miles away, with one generator. It was, therefore, urgent that I get an immediate scan of the left engine to see if any sparks or hot pieces of metal were coming out, which would indicate that the generator was tearing itself up.

The kicker's name was Richard, so I called him up on the intercom. "Dick, give me a scan on the left engine." Silence. Again, with a greater sense of urgency "Dick, I need an immediate scan on the left engine!" Again, silence. Finally, getting a bit upset, I called, "Kicker, this is the Pilot!"

Then I heard, "Oh, were you talking to me? Most people call me Richard." There were only three people on interphone, and the Co-Pilot's name wasn't Dick. That's what I mean about different people having a different view of specific circumstances. By the way, it was only an electrical problem and I isolated the generator and continued on to Meck, being careful to address all comments for the rear to Richard.

*Kwajalein was a closed site. That meant only aircraft that had been approved by the US Government (or a bona fide emergency) could land there. So I was surprised one day to receive a message authorizing an old Lockheed Lodestar to land and refuel at Kwajalein. The Lockeed Lodestar is a twin engine tail dragger (tailwheel) of the 1930s vintage, about half the size of a DC-3. It being a Sunday, and not having seen one in a long time, I went down to the flight line as it pulled in to Base Operations. When it stopped, the reardoor opened and a tall skinny fellow in a tank top and wide-brimmed Mexican hat got off, followed by six blond headed gorillas (beach boys).

I introduced myself to a Mr. Sticks and asked, "What are you doing in this part of the world in that airplane?"

He said, "Well, it's an interesting story. My nephew is in the process of sailing around the world on a sailboat with three other people and he hasn't been heard from in some time. They were at the island of Ulithi when the local sheriff made them leave in the middle of a typhoon. My mission is twofold: first, to find my nephew; and second, I'm going to have a talk with the sheriff. That's what those six blond headed gorillas are for."

I commented that he certainly couldn't hold out much hope in finding the boat. I had done a lot of over-water searches, and they generally don't work out too well unless you have the target pretty well pinpointed. He said that normally he would agree, but then told me this story.

He came from a rather wealthy family and, when they got news that the nephew was missing, they all gathered to see what they could do. They hired a psychic, the same one who had told the police where Patty Hearst was years ago. She told them that she saw the boat with the nephew onboard 632 miles northwest of Ulithi and that there was a problem with the sail. She said it was a strange boat, in that the mast had no wires holding it up and the sail was all gathered at the top of the mast and they couldn't get it down. Up to that point no one had told her that the boat was a Freedom Yacht, which has a freestanding fiber mast.

The psychic then stopped and asked the gathered group if there was anyone there who didn't believe what she was saying. A grizzled old grandfather in the back stood up and said, "Yes, lady. I don't believe a damn word you're saying."

"I understand," was the reply. "Sir, would you reach in your wallet and take out a dollar bill?" When the psychic read him the serial number on the dollar bill, the old man sat down.

Based on the psychic's information, the family decided to sponsor an expedition to find the boy, and that's what Sticks and the blond headed gorillas in the Lodestar were doing. "By the way," he said, "the day after the meeting with the family, the psychic called the mother up and said she saw five, not four, people on the sailboat. They called out to

Ulithi and that's the first any of them knew that a local native boy had gotten on the sailboat with them."

Despite the fact that I personally don't believe in that sort of thing, the story gives reason to ponder about psychic phenomena. I did find out later, through the person who chartered them the airplane, that the search was not successful. I don't know how they made out with the sheriff.

Several off the wall incidents occurred during my first tour on Kwajalein.

* The first story starts out with me getting an authorization from Huntsville for a Civilian C-310, a small twin engine, 4 passenger plane, to stop overnight at Kwajalein and load up with fuel. When the C-310 landed, I met the pilot, the only one on the plane, and invited him into my office as I was curious as to what he was doing in this part of the world in that light twin.

He said he was a medical Doctor and had contracted Leukemia. He had always had a dream to fly around the world in a small airplane and was in the process of doing that before the Leukemia took over and progressed to the point that would prohibit him from achieving his dream.

I was taken by his positive spirit and invited him to have dinner with Colleen and me at our quarters that evening. He told some of the funniest jokes throughout that evening and Colleen and I laughed until our stomachs hurt.

The next morning I waved to him as he taxied out, enroute to Honolulu and thought to myself that I would never see him again.

About a year later, I received a call from the Doctor that he was in Majuro, the Capital of the Marshall Islands and he was with an expedition in search of Amelia Earharts airplane. He explained that his leukemia had gone into remission and he was given a second chance at life. He then went on to explain that the expedition was being funded by a fellow named Bryce who owned a large resort back on the East Coast.

They needed a boat to go up into the Northern Marshalls and the cheapest one they could find was asking $25,000 per day to charter it. He hoped that I might have an in to find a cheaper boat. Further, he went on to say that there was a man named Vincent Loomis with the expedition who had been a Major in the Air Force and who was in the Marshall Islands during the Atomic Bomb tests back in the '50's. His job was to go to some of the uninhabited islands of the Northern Marshalls and lay out colored streamers for some reason that had to do with the bomb tests. He had a boat and helpers to assist him in doing this.

While on one of the Northern Marshall islands, when they went ashore, he found an airplane sitting in the jungle just off the beach with one wing damaged. This seemed rather odd to him because there was no runway on that island.

For several years after that event his curiosity got the better of him and after he got out of the Air Force, he started tracking down all the information he could on Amelia Earhart's disappearance. He went to Japan and studied the Japanese Naval Archives concerning the disappearance of Earhart's airplane. He claims to have found messages that said that Earhart had ditched in the water next to the island of Mili and that a piece of the wing had been ripped off the plane during the ditching. He went to Mili and talked to the man who had possession of that bit of wing, and who stated that the piece was off of Earhart's airplane. The man would not let them take the wing but he took photos and sent them back to Lockheed for evaluation..

Most all of the Lockheed employees that would have been around during that time frame were gone but several of them said that although they couldn't be sure, it appeared to be a part of a Lockheed Electra wing.

Armed with this information Loomis was able to get a backer, Mr. Bryce, and put together an expedition to look for the airplane in the Northern Marshalls. I might add that several of the islands that form the Northern Marshalls are not inhabited because the Natives treat them as home of ghosts and won't go there. Mr. Bryce was an avid aviation buff and always showed up in the operations shack for our early morning takeoffs and chatted with the pilots..

I contacted the man who owned the vessels at Kwajalein that were under contract to the Department of Energy to provide a vessel and platform for the Scientists, Engineers and Medical personnel to determine a way to make the Bikini Atoll and other affected Islands habitable and to treat the natives who had been exposed to radiation. He got very interested and said that if they found Earhart's airplane that he would let them charter the boat free of charge.

I talked the Army into letting the members of the expedition came to Kwajalein and quarter in some trailers that were vacant.

They rented an airplane from the Kwajalein aero club and flew over the islands that might have been the one on which the Major had seen the airplane. None of the islands triggered a memory.

About this time, there was an uprising among the native Marshallese concerning the rent that the United States was paying for the exclusive use of the Kwajalein Lagoon and certain islands in the lagoon. The uprising started to get ugly, the Army had their hands full and as a result, asked the expedition to leave.

That was the last I heard of them or of the attempt to locate the plane that the Major allegedly seen. For my part in assisting them Mr. Bryce paid for my member ship in the (then) Confederate Air Force, which set him back about $500.

* Because I showed up on the flight line at 0500 each weekday morning so I could slip into the seat if one of our pilots scheduled for the 0520 takeoff overslept, it was dark when I peddled my bike to work.

On this particular morning I was peddling merrily away and noticed a very large bird, illuminated by the street lights and about 20 feet in the air coming toward me. As we got closer, I was startled when the bird pulled up, did a wing over and came down on top of me with it's talons in my shirt and tried to lift me off my bike.

With it's wings flapping vigorously, I started hitting the bird as best I could shouting "Let go damn it let go" while wobbling down the street on my bike.

Finally, the bird must have thought it hopeless, let go and flew away.

When I finally got to the flight line , I was still pretty shaken and the mistake I made was telling the pilots about that experience. I was ragged for the next six months about that bird. I did get some redemption when, the day after my bird experience, a large bird attacked a man standing outside his trailer. The bird forced him back into his trailer. Also there was a large number of Cats listed as missing in the local Kwajalein paper, the Hourglass.

Some people surmised it might have been a Kingfisher which have a large wing span and can be very aggressive.

*The United States Air Force, under charter to the US Army, provides airlift support to Kwajalein. The schedules change from time to time, but basically there were two C-141 trips per week from Honolulu that haul cargo, fresh vegetables, newspapers, etc., to the island. During our first tour on Kwajalein, these C-141 aircraft were the primary transportation for most of the civilian contractor personnel transiting between Honolulu and Kwajalein.

Because the C-141 aircraft are primarily designed to haul cargo, there are no passenger windows and so, in addition to the extra noise that you have in a cargo plane, you felt like you were sitting in a large tunnel. The clanging and banging and other strange noises, coupled with the fact that you could not see outside, bothered some people. For those who were already apprehensive about flying, the five-hour flight between Kwajalein and Honolulu became a very stressful situation. Booze, normally used on airliners to calm the nerves of those afraid of flying, was strictly prohibited on Military Aircraft, and so those apprehensive people had to tough it out on their own for five hours.

On one flight, I was seated next to a middle-aged woman in the three-across, semi-airline type seats that the Air Force provided. I wondered why this woman had worn a suit coat in the hot, tropical climate of Kwajalein. Shortly after takeoff, I noticed that she reached inside her coat and, with her thumb and index finger, slowly pulled out a straw just far enough to take a couple of healthy swigs and then neatly and very quietly slipped the straw back inside her coat.

Although we did not converse, I'm certain that she was one of the people who were apprehensive of flying, especially in the C-141, and had devised her own way of beating the no booze rule. She had a very relaxed flight to Honolulu.

*John Vissat was the Mate and sometimes Captain on two boats that were at various times under Department of Energy Contract and home-based at Kwajalein. Their mission was to provide, among other things, transportation for medical services for Bikini and Enewetok. The Marine Department was chartered to provide docking space and support for their vessel. John was also a good sailor and a good friend. His background, experience and personality made him the type of person who can do anything with nothing. There was always a way to fix something that was broken. John came over to the house at different times and told several stories that are worth repeating.

He had built a trimaran at his home in Santa Cruz over a period of about eight years. The dream was to cruise Polynesia, and perhaps the world, in that boat. Eventually, the boat was completed and off they went, jumping off from Cabo San Lucas, in Mexico, for Polynesia. While en route, and about halfway between Mexico and Polynesia, they became aware of a major hurricane that was bearing down on them. A hurricane in a small boat is probably one of mankind's most terrifying experiences. First, because of the sheer violence of it, and second, because it goes on and on over a long period of time. Not like a bad experience in an airplane. Usually that's over pretty quickly, one way or the other. And in a small boat like John's, there is no way to escape. You can't go fast enough to run away from the storm, as a larger, faster vessel can.

About 24 hours before the hurricane was to arrive, a 200-foot seiner (fishing vessel) showed up, saw their sail and came over to them and stopped. The loudspeaker blared, "THERE IS A MAJOR STORM COMING. WE RECOMMEND THAT YOU ABANDON YOUR VESSEL AND COME WITH US. COME UP ON YOUR HF RADIO." John didn't have an HF Radio, so he shook his head. "COME UP ON YOUR UHF RADIO," they said. John didn't have a UHF Radio, and again shook his head. He did have a Ham Radio on board and quickly scrawled "HAM" on a piece of cardboard and held it up for the ship to see. The ship lowered a small boat and the Mate came over to present them with a ham and a dozen oranges. This floored them. But they were still faced with the decision whether or not to leave their sailboat and seek refuge on the larger vessel.

Although he understood the risks, John did not want to lose the eight years of work he had put into building this craft. He knew if he abandoned his sailboat that he would never see her again. But he had his life, the life of his girlfriend and another couple with their young child to consider. With the Mate impatiently waiting, they all agreed they would stay onboard the sailboat and, as the seiner sailed over the horizon, John wondered if he had made the right decision.

When the hurricane finally hit, John realized he had made a mistake. He said there were several moments that he regretted the decision not to leave the sailboat and take refuge on the larger vessel. However, they did stay afloat, he doesn't know how, and suffered only minor damage, and they did make it to Polynesia.

Throughout the months that followed and the many harbors they visited, they found only one spot they could tie to a dock. Every other landing required anchoring off shore. At this particular dock, where they spent a week, a 35-foot Norwegian sailboat shared the dock with them and they became friends, swapping stories. The Norwegian said that they were on a global circumnavigation and this was their second attempt. When asked why, he explained that on the first attempt they were halfway across the Pacific, it was a beautiful day and everything was going well. Coming up from down below he was horrified to see the bow of a large ship about to overrun them. As he leaped for his horn, the ship rammed them, a glancing blow, splitting open the side of their hull. Water immediately started coming in and he leaned on the horn, hoping someone would hear the frantic wail. The ship did hear and the sailors onboard then saw him as he slid down their side. The Master made a short turn and came back alongside the sinking sailboat. The Norwegian was amazed that the skipper was able to maneuver his ship to a stop alongside his sailboat, and even more amazed to see them lower a makeshift sling, pick his boat up in the open sea and set it down on the deck of the ship.

This Russian ship was headed for Vladivostok, and so that's where they took him, his crew and his boat. At Vladivostok, the owners of the ship paid to have his sailboat and his crew shipped across Russia, back to Norway, and for the repair of his boat at the original yard where it was manufactured. And that's why they were on their second attempt. He went on and on about the seamanship the Russian skipper and crew displayed in bringing his boat onboard and the honesty of the company in taking care of their mistake. It goes to show that people can get along even though governments can't.

LANDFALL off Beigi Pass in the Kwajalein Lagoon

There are many stories about small boats meeting disaster in one way or another as they transit great spaces of water between islands or continents. Hitting half-submerged containers that have fallen off ships, meeting up with unscrupulous human beings in faraway places, being rammed by submarines or whales in the middle of the night. And how about the large containership approaching their berth in New York Harbor? As the ship neared the dock, those on the pier were shading their eyes and pointing up at the bow. When the Bosun looked over the rail to see what they were pointing at, it was the first time he saw the aluminum mast and rigging of a sailboat hanging in the ships anchor.

Shortly after our arrival at Kwajalein, I knew that I had to have a sailboat. The lagoon, the world's largest, was the perfect place to sail. The East Reef protected the lagoon from the trade winds so that in the typical 15 to 18 knot breeze that almost always persisted, the water was flat. And the night sails were entrancing. The tropical moon is magic. Imagine seeing the bottom in 30 feet of water at night as clearly as if it were day, illuminated only by moonlight.

While on vacation, we fell in love with "Landfall", in Honolulu. Since I had used up my vacation time, I hired a man and his wife to sail her downwind to Kwajalein. The downwind trip is the easy one. The trades blow out of Honolulu on an almost direct course to Kwajalein. She made those years at Kwajalein a true pleasure.

After Landfall had been at Kwajalein for several months, I detected a strange odor and made a point of searching for it. I found a 10lb. sack of potatoes that the ferry crew from Hawaii had stored in a hard to find locker. That sack of potatoes had been left in the tropic heat and had turned into a caustic, slimy sludge that dripped down on the fuel tank and ate a hole in the top of Landfalls black iron tank. I had no idea that potato sludge was caustic and would eat a hole in a black iron fuel tank When I removed the shelf I found myself looking directly into the diesel fuel in the tank.

I contacted Ron Ami, the designer, on how to get the tank out of the boat. He passed on the information to put a 6" X 6" timber from the entry hatch through the left porthole and it would pass directly over the engine. Use a come along to get the engine out of the engine bay then use a cherry picker to get it out of the boat. Slide the water tank into the engine bay and then remove the fuel tank, sliding it forward into the space for the water tank, then into the engine bay and out of the boat. Although it sounds like a big deal it was a relatively easy procedure.

Another innovation that Ron Ami designed into Landfall, was that the stainless steel emergency tiller was an exact duplicate diameter of the prop shaft. So, if you were in the boondocks with no way to haul the boat and had to pull the prop shaft, you pushed the shaft out through the packing gland with the emergency tiller and no water would come into the boat.

Perhaps Landfall was one of the reasons we didn't get "rock fever" on that island of Kwajalein that measured just 3½ miles by ½ mile. We would load up the boat and leave at about 1500 hours on Friday and sail to the island of Illeginni on the West Reef. By the time we arrived, all the workers were gone, airlifted out by helicopter, and we had the whole island to ourselves for the weekend. At times we felt like the only people on Earth. Then there were sails to other islands in the lagoon that were always magical.

*When we finally made the decision to leave Kwajalein, I was faced with the choice as to what to do with Landfall. The options were to sail her either to Hawaii or Japan. Hawaii was straight upwind to the trades, which involved 1,000 mile tacks if we went the northern route; or south and east until we could get a wind bearing that would carry us north to Hawaii. In either case, it would be a long trip that would test our endurance.

On the other hand, if we went to Tokyo, the wind would be primarily on the beam and we should be able to sail in a straight line right to Japan, a much shorter trip, even though the actual mileage to Hawaii or Japan from Kwajalein was identical, almost to the mile. I had spent some wonderful years in Japan and this would give me an opportunity to go back for a visit. And to sail to Japan versus Hawaii sounded so much more interesting.

Landfall from the Bow Pulpit

The decision was made and, on May 9, 1985, at 0300, Landfall departed the port of Kwajalein for Yokosuka, Japan, with myself, Al Whitcomb, Leo Nolan and Wes Westhafer aboard. The reason for leaving at such an ungodly hour was based on the fact that we wanted to arrive at Bikini during daylight hours. Bikini was directly on our course to Japan and, although it was generally a closed site, we had been invited by Bill Robison of the Lawrence Livermore National Laboratory, to stop overnight. Besides, we salivated at the thought of being able to dive on the Aircraft Carrier Saratoga, which sits straight up at the bottom of the Bikini Lagoon, sent there as a result of the nuclear weapons testing in the '50s. As it turned out, Landfall's engine required realignment and that took up the time that we should have spent diving on the Saratoga.

But we had a wonderful party that night on the island of Bikini, with

Landfall tied up alongside the Egabrag (that's garbage spelled backwards), a ship on the Department of Energy contract at Bikini. She really was misnamed, because she was a wonderful ship, commanded by Keith Coberly, one of the nicest men I've ever met.

The next day we did a realignment on the engine and departed for Japan. The only land we would see for the next 18 days was the one-mile triangular Marcus Island (Minami-Torashima), a Japanese Island that was currently housing a LORAN Station (**LO**ng **RA**nge **N**avigation). This island was directly on our route to the entrance of Tokyo Bay and, although celestial navigation was our only means of knowing where we were and where we were going, we hit this island right on the money, to the degree that we had to turn slightly to avoid it. Al Whitcombe and Leo Nolan were the navigators and did a wonderful job of keeping track of where we were. What a great sight Marcus Island was after not seeing any other human-related object for almost a week. Besides, it was exhilarating to see Marcus Island right where it should be. Although we did not drink the entire trip while underway, I made an exception and broke out a bottle of wine for the crew (Al had a little Bourbon) to celebrate our success in finding Marcus Island. The no drink rule ended as soon as we got to the dock at Yokosuka.

I've got to say that people who are fortunate enough to make a voyage such as this will discover many different aspects of their own ability, and experience first-hand some of the wonderful secrets of nature. I did not realize that, on a moonless night, stars provide enough light so that one can safely walk about the deck. And to watch porpoise come alongside the boat on a pitch black night and illuminate the water with phosphorescent light lines that appear as tracer bullets underwater. Although we were in what could be considered some of the loneliest parts of the ocean, we saw birds every day. And, fortunately, we had four personalities aboard who really got along with each other. We laughed and joked all the way to Japan and only on one occasion was there a semblance of disagreement or serious discussion.

And well there should have been.

As we approached Japan, a typhoon was also approaching from the southwest. We had been watching "Typhoon Gay" for several days and, when it became apparent that we going to meet just outside Tokyo Bay, we made the decision to turn southeast and try to get as far from the eye as possible. So, on May 24, at 2330 hours, we turned to a heading of 120 degrees. The next day, as we tracked the eye, which had now built to 100 mph, it became apparent that she was turning more easterly and bearing down on us. We put all movable gear below and, as evening came on, we all went below and prepared for a rough night.

The only serious discussion on the trip was whether or not the life raft in its canister, should be placed below with us. One argument was that if we needed it in a hurry we might not be able to get it out in time. The other was that if it was below with us, at least we'd know where it was. It was only loosely tied to the forward hatch and the storm might carry it away. The down below argument won.

Another problem that we were facing was that we were fast running out of fuel and oil. Up to this point we had been running the engine in excess of a week due to lack of wind and I had calculated that unless we got some wind, we would not have enough fuel or oil to make land.

Several Japanese fishing vessels, some quite large, made a pass on us as they were making for shore and safe harbor, to let us know there was a typhoon coming. One even offered to put us under tow and tow us to shore. I declined, knowing that he would likely tow at 16 or 18 knots, which would either pull out our bits or sink us, as our hull speed was about 6-1/2 or 7 knots. As another one of them came by, I asked if they could pass us some oil, which they did. The crew filled a large bucket about half full of oil (probably about two gallons) and Hi-Lined it over to us as we motored in formation. Although I have videos of some points of the trip, I was not able to get a video of this maneuver because we were all involved with the passing of the oil.

As the eye approached, I was desperate to get weather information on the location, intensity and movement of the storm. As so often happens when a storm of this size approaches, the High Frequency radio, our only contact with the world, becomes ineffective. I tried every frequency that I knew to make contact with someone, but no luck. And then, as I was spinning the dial, a voice boomed in. **"Continental 187, you are cleared to climb to FL 350, call passing FL 280."** I was listening to Tokyo Center giving clearances to aircraft.

I wondered if perhaps I had gotten a harmonic frequency, kind of a shadow frequency whereby you can receive but not transmit. It was illegal for me to transmit on this frequency because we only had a ham radio license onboard and by law are not authorized to transmit on Aviation frequencies. But what the heck. I considered this an emergency. So I picked up the mike and said, "Tokyo Center, this is Air Force 28756, radio ground check."

Immediately the voice answered, "Air Force 28756, you are loud and clear." It was not a harmonic frequency, and I had made good contact.

I considered my next move and waited a few minutes to act. "Tokyo Center, this is the sailing vessel Landfall. Do you have a discreet frequency?" He gave me another frequency and I retuned the radio. I am certain that every military aircraft and civilian airliner on Tokyo Center also went to that discreet frequency out of curiosity, to find out what was going on. I told Center that we were a sailing vessel about 200 miles south of Tokyo and unable to make contact with any other station and asked if he could give me an update on the typhoon. He said, "Standby," and a minute or two later came back with the best briefing on intensity and movement of the storm that we had the whole trip. I thanked him and left the frequency.

The last report was that the eye should pass within 30 nautical miles of our Dead Reckoning (DR) position about midnight. As the night settled in we all wedged ourselves in our bunks to ride out the storm. As midnight approached it got very rough with the roar of the wind and the crashing of the sea being our total, dark world. From my bunk, I could see the barometer and was severely discouraged when, at 0300 the pressure was still falling. That meant the eye had not yet passed. Although the ride was very bouncy (it might have been a blessing it was nighttime and I couldn't see the conditions outside), I never once felt that we were really in jeopardy aboard Landfall. She was a strong boat.

The rough ride that night tested our morale and we were getting tired of going sideways at a good clip. A drifting boat has a tendency to lay sideways or perpendicular to the wind. We decided that if we put up a storm jib we would be back in charge and, at 0800, Wes and I went to the bow to retrieve the 45-pound CQR (plow-type anchor) we had put out as a semblance of a sea anchor to try and keep our bow to the wind. I might add it had no effect and we made a good speed sideways as the anchor was being dragged at right angles off the bow.

Getting the anchor in proved extremely difficult and hazardous, as Wes and I spent a lot of time underwater each time the bow dipped. I did consider cutting it loose, but after a lot of holding on and pulling, we got it back on board. With the barometer now rising and the winds probably around 40 or 50 mph, we set the storm jib and started sailing on a heading of 310 degrees. Our morale immediately went up. You could feel it. We were now in charge of our own course and destiny instead of drifting helplessly in the Pacific.

We tied up to the dock in Yokosuka at 2230 on May 28, 20 days after leaving Kwajalein. Then we broke out the booze and celebrated our successful voyage. At this point, I must pass on what I feel is an incredible story in Landfall's history.

When Landfall was originally commissioned in Taiwan in 1975, she was sailed from there to Japan and then on to Hawaii. Aboard were the owner and his wife and a ferry Captain and his wife. The ferry Captain's wife was blind and, although this seems highly irregular, it is my understanding that she had sailed with him all over the Pacific. In Japan, the owner and his wife got off and the ferry Captain and his wife began the sail to Hawaii. Somewhere en route, the ferry Captain fell overboard and the wife, being unable to sail the vessel, could not help. As I understand it, she could hear him shout off and on for sometime, however, she was not able to maneuver to get to him. After a while, she could not hear him anymore and, for about 30 days, drifted alone, helpless and blind in the Pacific.

After being sighted by a ship, she was taken aboard a Coast Guard Cutter that had been dispatched from Hawaii with a crew aboard to sail Landfall on to Honolulu. I later met one of the crew that sailed her there. The boat went through several owners before I got her, and enjoyed her for several years at Kwajalein.

When I finally sailed her to Yokosuka, we were told as we approached Japan that we must stay aboard the boat until cleared by Japanese Customs, who would be down at 0900 the next morning. We did as we were told and did not leave the boat. When the Customs people showed up the next morning, we faced them with appropriate hangovers from our arrival party the night before. Although they were very polite, they were also very thorough.

After they left, I got up on the dock and a boat owner who was living aboard his boat introduced himself as Jim and asked if there was anything he could do to help us. I made the idle comment that everything was in order but that the Customs people were a little sticky. Jim said, "The Customs people didn't used to be so particular, but about ten years ago a guy came to Yokosuka, matter of fact tied up on this dock right where you are tied. He cleared Customs coming in, but left without clearing out." At this point the hair on the back of my neck started to tingle because I had a premonition of what Jim was going to say. "Ever since then," Jim continued, "Customs has been very thorough. Matter of fact, the guy fell overboard about halfway to Hawaii and his wife, who was blind, couldn't pick him up and he drowned."

"Jim," I said incredulously, "that was this boat."

He said, "By God, you're right!"

I had come back ten years later to the same spot, on the same dock that Landfall had departed from on that fateful voyage. Anybody familiar with Tokyo Bay and its size and density will understand that the chance of that happening is incredible.

When the Customs people left, we decided to walk to the snack bar, about three or four blocks away from the pier, for some breakfast. Recall that we had a substantial arrival party the night before and none of us were in the greatest of shape. As we approached the snack bar and the discussion had turned to what kind of eggs and sausage we were going to have, one of our crew couldn't hold it any longer and turned to toss his cookies in the street, right in front of the snack bar entrance.

A couple walking by saw, with dismay, the unattractive event that was taking place in front of the snack bar and I could tell by the expression on their faces that they were rather shocked. So I pointed at the crew-member in crisis and then the snack bar and told them, "Boy, I wouldn't eat in there!"

When Landfall eventually was shipped back to San Francisco, I kept her at the Treasure Island Marina at the Treasure Island Naval Base. Eventually, when I went to work for the Red and White Fleet in San Francisco, rather than commuting to Santa Rosa each day, 1.5 hours each way, I stayed in the BOQ during the week at Treasure Island (TI), when space was available, and drove home on the weekends. It was a convenient setup because the few times that space was not available at the TI BOQ, I would stay on Landfall. The Yacht Club there had shower and cooking facilities, so there was everything I needed.

I enjoyed that.

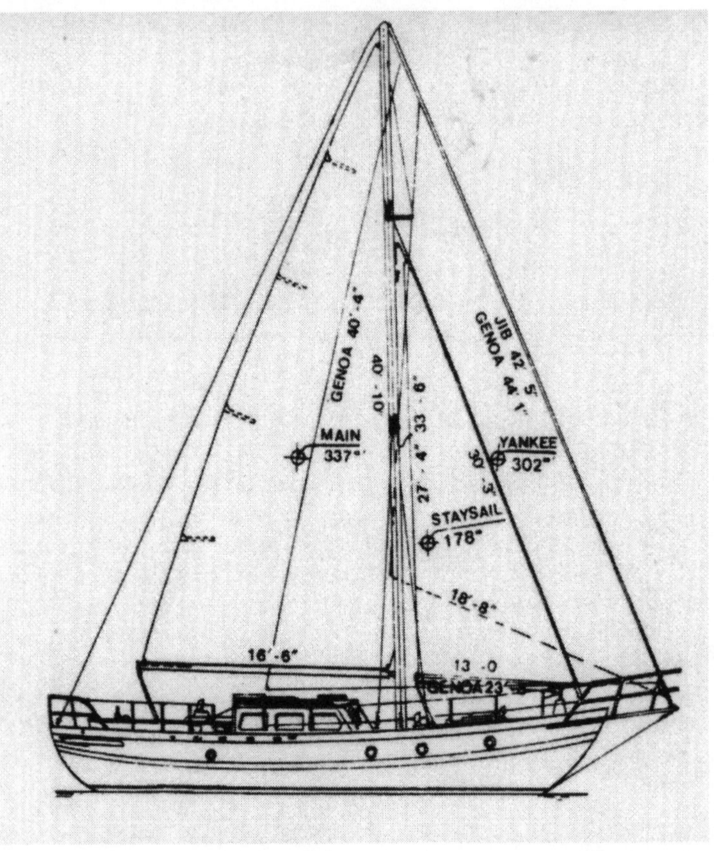

Landfall's sail plan

Chapter 10

1986 - 1993

The Red and White Years
Fisherman's Wharf
San Francisco, California

Can a bruised ego be considered a work-related injury?

*Back in Santa Rosa, we settled into our home, which we had rented while at Kwajalein. I searched for something to do and was offered a part-time position teaching Aviation Courses at the Santa Rosa Junior College, and also teaching the Rapid Radar Plotting Course at the California Maritime Academy in Vallejo. Although I could not expect a serious monetary return from either of these positions, put together, we could make ends meet.

One day, while playing golf with one of the senior Red and White Fleet Captains, he said that they were looking for Captains for their upcoming summer schedule and that I should go down and apply. I did, and since I had a current license and radar endorsement, they put me right to work running ferry boats in San Francisco Bay.

The Port Captain for the Red and White Fleet was temporarily filling that position and, within a year, he went to another job within the Crowley Corporation, the parent company. I was asked if I would take the job as Port Captain and, although not really interested in a management position, I accepted because I was low man on the seniority list and the company was getting ready for the wintertime layoffs, of which I would have been one. Accepting the Port Captain's job would assure me of employment throughout the winter months. That job led to many interesting events.

*You would think that compared to airplanes, things happen slowly on boats. But that's not always true. One morning, we had a very qualified Captain prepare his boat for a day of taking people to Alcatraz, the former federal penitentiary which is now in the possession of the National Park Service and a popular tourist attraction. The Alcatraz run is about as basic and timid as you can get. The first thing he did was to unlock the boat, go to the wheelhouse, unlock the wheelhouse door and deposit his gear there. The doors on this particular boat had buttons in the round doorknobs, so that when you unlocked and opened the door, unless you released the button, the door was still locked even though it was open.

Well, our Captain went below, fired up the plants and got the boat shipshape for the passengers and the coming shift. Finally, the 300 passengers were loaded and the gangway clear and he started backing out of the slip. Once the boat started moving, he stepped out on the wing to ensure the deckhand and lines were clear and the door (not being latched open as it should), reacting to a gust of wind, slammed shut behind him. So now the situation was that both engines were in reverse, 300 passengers were on board and the Captain was locked out of the wheelhouse. He searched frantically for the fire ax to break the window but, as luck would have it, on this particular boat it was stowed in the wheelhouse.

Fortunately , we had several boats in which the front window would slide down to open. The locking latches were worn to the point that by wetting his hands he was able to coax the window down far enough to reach in and take the engines out of gear. I've often wondered what the passengers must have thought as they witnessed the Captain crawling in the front window of a vessel that was underway.

*One night I got a call on my pager at about 2200 hours while I was asleep at the BOQ on Treasure Island. The wind had come up and the boats at piers 9 and 41 were riding hard. I proceeded to pier 9 and with the help of Clint Lindstrom, a Red and White Captain, got that situation under control with extra lines. At pier 41, the Harbor Emperor and Royal Prince were riding hard and pounding the pier and I elected to move them to a safe harbor in Oakland. We called out crews, got the boats secured and got back to pier 41 at about 0300.

With the wind settling down and the forecast for it to continue to abate, I left a deckhand, Bill Elliott, to watch the boats at Pier 43-1/2 (the dispatcher on duty at Pier 41 could not see those boats from his vantage point) and I went back to bed. At about 0500 I got another call to say that I'd better get there right away. The winds had picked up from the worst direction, northeast, and were blowing at an unbelievable velocity. The headlines in the paper later said that they clocked 100 mph on the bay during that period. I believe it.

The boats that we had left at Pier 41 were riding OK because they were sheltered somewhat behind the breakwater, but the boats at Pier 43-1/2 were pounding the dock to pieces. The Harbor Princess had a motion that was difficult to comprehend. Never had I seen so much mass moving around so violently. This 400-passenger boat had parted eight of the ten lines we had on her and, as I watched, she parted another, then being held to the float by only one line. She had tried to jump up on the float and had broken off the end knee, which left a hole in the float. The float was taking on water and sinking, and it was obvious that we had to get her out of there or lose both her and the float. But that takes time.

This photo of the Harbor Queen, sister ship of the Harbor Princess shows the relationship of Pier 43½ to the Submarine Pampanito. The Liberty Ship, Jeremiah O'Brien, behind the submarine, was not there. The vicious wind was from the right to the left looking at the photo.

We struggled across the float, which was partially under water, to get another line on the boat while we got her engines lit off. After the light off, I backed her out of the slip with two deckhands onboard, Bill Elliott and Rich Phillips, against ferocious winds coming from the port side. The Princess was known to be the most underpowered boat that we had, and I prayed as I backed out that I would be able to control her against that brutal wind. She did fine until I came out of reverse on the starboard engine in an attempt to turn her upwind and out of the close quarters we were in. To my amazement and horror, the starboard engine quit and I could not get it restarted.

The wind immediately took over and started setting us down on the Pampanito, a World War II submarine that is on permanent exhibit at Pier 45. One second I was high above the Pampanito and the next second she was high above us. I knew that if I came down on the Pampanito that we'd both go down and, even though we were close to the pier, the violent water made the chance of survival for any of us on board a slim possibility. Instinct is a strange thing. At the same time that I went full astern on the port engine, I began blowing continuous blasts of the ship's whistle to alert all in the area that we were in trouble while at the same time trying to start the starboard engine. As we approached the Pampanito, I knew it would be close, but with our port engine full astern, we missed her stern by a few feet.

As this was progressing, Bill Elliott came to the wheelhouse and stuck his head in the door to ask what was happening. I don't know how he made that trip to the wheelhouse, the way that boat was heaving. I told him the starboard engine had quit and he turned and headed for the engine room to try and start it from there. Now, in my lifetime, I've been in a lot of situations that were falling apart and, when that happens, having people around you like Bill Elliott is a Godsend. They are the ones with cool heads who don't give up. While Bill headed for the engine room, we impacted the dock at Pier 45.

I couldn't believe all this was happening.

Here we were, windlocked against the dock, with the sea picking up this 400-passenger boat and slamming it down sideways on the pier. The only chance I had was to try and back down the pier with the good engine, hope the wind would blow the stern around on the end and be able to head upwind with the remaining engine. About this time, Doug Taylor, the Port Engineer, appeared on the pier. I shouted to him that the starboard engine was out and he took a running leap and dove head first through a broken window on the side of the boat, which had now been destroyed by the pier. All the windows were gone and much of the side of the boat had collapsed. Doug went to the engine room and found that Bill Elliott had gotten the starboard engine going, but the tachometer in the wheelhouse still read zero. Later we found that the pounding had disconnected the tachometer lead from the starboard engine. Finally, with the starboard engine running, I was able to back away from the pier and, with a very bruised boat, headed for Oakland.

The float she had been tied to sank shortly thereafter. Under the existing sea conditions, the Pampanito had begun destroying the pier she was tied to, as well as herself. The heroic efforts of a Crowley Tug Captain (I don't know his name) to tow the Pampanito to safety, as well as Jim Adams and others who assisted in getting her loose from her permanent mooring, were captured on national television and were truly one of the greatest acts of seamanship that I have ever witnessed.

*On the night of the celebration of the 50th anniversary of the San Francisco-Oakland Bay Bridge, the area of San Francisco Bay off the downtown section was completely covered with small boats at anchor, waiting for the ceremonies to begin. That evening was touted to have the largest display of fireworks in the state's history, and it seemed that every soul in the state was there in a small boat to watch.

I was taking the high speed Catamaran "Dolphin" from Fisherman's Wharf to Vallejo, some 25 nautical miles away. But the passengers on board pleaded with me to forget the schedule and delay in the harbor to watch the fireworks. Most of them on board had ridden the boat down from Vallejo in hopes of seeing the display. Since this was the last run of the day, I made the decision to delay so the passengers could watch the fireworks. As I looked at my color radar, the blanket of small boats off the city front made one yellow glob of a radar return all the way from the shoreline of San Francisco to the shore of Treasure Island, the Naval Base in the middle of the bay.

The fireworks were scheduled to start very soon and, while we were waiting, there was a call from Unit Charley to Vessel Traffic announcing his departure from the Port of Oakland for sea. Unit Charley was the radio call sign of the San Francisco Bar Pilot who was taking a very large containership from Oakland to sea and had to transit under the Bay Bridge, where all the small boats were anchored. He was not yet aware of the jam of small boats blocking the shipping lane. As he turned the corner around Yerba Buena Island outbound, the glob of boats blocking his way suddenly came into view.

The Captain of the Port of San Francisco (a Coast Guard Captain) then realized what was going on and the danger that existed if the containership continued. The next transmission was from his vessel to Unit Charley. "Unit Charley, the Captain of the Port directs you to return your ship to anchor."

Already committed and on an Ebb Tide, Unit Charley realized he would place everyone in more danger by trying to reverse his course at that point and replied, "Negative. I am proceeding ahead at slow speed."

The Captain of the Port directed him to return to anchorage for the second time and, again, Unit Charley refused, explaining that he would place his vessel in jeopardy if he attempted to comply.

Realizing that this large containership was bearing down on hundreds of anchored vessels in the shipping lane, the Captain of the Port directed Unit Charley to return his vessel to the anchorage for the third time. Again, Unit Charley said that he was proceeding ahead at slow speed.

I watched my radar as Unit Charley, with the return of the containership on the color radar depicted in bright red, slowly ground his way through the mass of boats showing up in a lighter color as one big yellowish blob. I could feel the boats sliding down the side of his hull and imagined the panic that was taking place on those small boats. It was truly a miracle that no one was killed or injured as the containership finally came out on the other side of the glob. And I marveled at the courage that pilot had to make the split-second decision he made to avoid a tragedy. Especially since he had been ordered three times by the Captain of the Port not to do what he did. The thought crossed my mind that Unit Charley probably would have made a good fighter pilot.

The last transmission from the Captain of the Port's vessel as Unit Charley proceeded to sea was that he was to report to the office of the Captain of the Port at 0800 hours the following morning. Wouldn't you love to have sat in on that meeting?

*The Red and White Fleet ran its seniority system somewhat similarly to the way the airlines do. There are so many jobs (or bids) that change based on the season. Summertime would obviously have more bids than winter because of the increase in tourist traffic. Each bid change, Captains would bid what jobs they wanted based on their seniority. The most senior Captain got his pick, then the next senior got to pick what he wanted out of what was left, and that's the way it went, right on down the line. And so I was happy when I got the evening commute bid. I enjoyed running the High Speed Catamaran and this bid involved a couple of day trips to Sausalito and Tiburon, then four evening commute trips between the Ferry Building in downtown San Francisco and Tiburon.

This particular night was absolutely gorgeous. Folks from Tiburon would come to San Francisco for dinner and ride the last ferry back. As I slowed the boat to start the approach to the Ferry Building Pier in San Francisco, the husbands and wives migrated to the upper deck to get a beautiful view of the lights of San Francisco reflected in the calm bay waters.

Suddenly the deckhand lookout alerted me. "BOAT, NO LIGHTS!" As I strained to see, I noted a target on the radar, then saw the dark outline of a small boat, apparently drifting with the current along the city front. Probably broke loose, I thought.

It is a standard call to report an unlighted vessel at night to Coast Guard, Vessel Traffic and I knew the Coast Guard would want a boat description when I made the report. As I diverted my vessel toward the darkened boat so I could get a look, the passengers on the upper deck sensed something was up. Then one of them saw the boat with no lights and they all crowded the rail to see.

I approached the boat slowly, engines at idle, and, when alongside, flashed the wing spotlight down on it. The first thing I heard were loud gasps from the women passengers leaning over the rail. Below, bathed in the spotlight, were a guy and gal, bare naked, consummating the act. I don't know how it looked from that fellow's point of view but his head was turned toward me and all I could see were eyes and mouth. I mercifully turned the spotlight off and then shouted something authoritative like, "Get some lights on that boat," added power and headed for the pier. As I left the scene, Vessel Traffic asked if they needed any assistance. I told them they were doing just fine.

*One of the runs we had with our High Speed Catamarans was between San Francisco and Vallejo, about 25 nautical miles northeast of San Francisco. Our transit time between these two points was about an hour. In the morning and evening we provided commuter service and at midday we made several trips to provide connector service to Marine World, which was located in Vallejo. Mare Island Naval Shipyard, a submarine repair facility, is also located here and we frequently had Naval personnel as passengers.

During one of the midday runs, I had just dropped the engines in reverse to back away from the Vallejo Pier when a young man in a coat and tie, carrying a suitcase, ran up to the locked gate and shouted to me at the wing controls, **"Does this boat go to San Francisco?"** I replied back that, yes, it did and returned to the pier to pick him up.

After we were underway he came up to the wheelhouse to thank me for delaying our departure to pick him up and, noticing the miniature Submarine Dolphins on his lapel, I invited him into the wheelhouse. On the way to San Francisco, we swapped stories and he related this incredible story to me:

He was on a Nuclear Attack Submarine, west of the Japanese Island of Honshu, in the Sea of Japan, cruising at 110 percent reactor power at a depth of 450 feet. When the skipper retired in the evening, he left instructions in the night orders to the Officer on Watch to bring the boat to 400 feet at midnight. The Watch Officer apparently missed the instruction, remained at 450 feet and around daybreak, the submarine contacted a seamount (underwater mountain) at that high speed. The glancing blow caused a violent pitchup of the sub and they broke the surface, transiting from 450 feet to the surface in about 10 to12 seconds. With everyone aboard stunned, the sub settled back in and descended, uncontrolled, stern first to about 1,200 feet before the crew could respond and stop the descent. They surfaced the second time and then realized they had come up in the middle of a fleet of Russian Naval Vessels conducting maneuvers in the same area. The Russians immediately put two destroyers on them and dogged them for the next several days.

Not knowing what damage had been done, the skipper was fearful of submerging and proceeded south on the surface. Each time they attempted to bring the speed past 6 or 8 knots the boat would start to roll and shake, so they proceeded at a very slow speed, hoping to get to a safe port before something else went wrong.

During the transit, about two days after the impact with the seamount, they ran into a violent typhoon. The weather got so bad and the seas so rough that the Russian Destroyers took off and the skipper elected to attempt submerging to escape the storm's fury. At 100 feet, the leaks were so bad they could go no deeper and so rode out the typhoon at that depth. The young man relating the story to me said that the ride in that storm was the worst part of the whole incident.

When they finally reached port, they discovered that the nose cone had been partially torn away and about 35 feet of the space from the bow, between the inner and outer hulls, had completely filled up with mud. In addition to a myriad of other damage, the propeller shaft had been bent.

To me, this was an incredible story of survival, with the accent on luck. To have made contact with a seamount at the speed they were going, even a glancing blow, and survived, was a miracle.

I kept our sailing vessel Landfall at the Treasure Island Naval Station Marina after she came back from Japan. During the years that I worked at the Red and White Fleet I spent many a night aboard her when I couldn't get a room at the BOQ. It was a convenient setup.

The 'CATAMARIN' and me, passing Alcatraz, in San Francisco Bay

When the Loma Prieta Earthquake struck California in October of 1989, I was standing on the floating pier and sanding her teak aft rail in preparation for varnishing. Suddenly, the dock started to move about and all of the boats in the Marina began rocking. I thought, "Some big boat has run its wake into the marina." Then I heard what sounded like a distant clap of thunder and thought that someone was shooting fireworks in preparation for the World Series, which was just getting ready to start. When I looked up, I was puzzled at the very large stream of water that was coming out of the San Francisco-Oakland Bay Bridge spewing at right angles to the bridge and into the bay. Then I heard someone on the shore shout, **"EARTHQUAKE!"** I then knew, as well as sensed, that something very serious had taken place.

The clap of thunder I heard was the upper deck of the Bay Bridge roadway collapsing down onto the lower deck. When it collapsed, it severed the main water line to the Treasure Island Naval Station. That was the stream of water I witnessed.

My first inclination was that I had to get to the Red and White Fleet at Pier 41. I knew that in a major earthquake scenario in the Bay Area that the Ferry system would play an important role. I jumped into my car and headed for San Francisco.

As I drove up the causeway that joins Treasure Island to the bridge, I had a strange feeling that I could not explain. I could see smoke at several locations and presumed that it was a result of the earthquake. Things got even more weird when I got on the bridge and I was the only car on the upper deck at a little after 5 p.m. The lower deck, which is the eastbound direction to Oakland, was jammed with cars that were stopped. The upper deck, which is the westbound direction to San Francisco, had collapsed on the Oakland side of the bridge, so no cars could get through. In the past, I had driven across that bridge and it was always full of cars, regardless of the hour. It was a strange feeling being the only car on that section of the bridge.

En route to Fisherman's Wharf and the Red and White Fleet offices, again, I was the only car on the Embarcadero Freeway that ran along the waterfront. I didn't know it at the time but that section of freeway was severely damaged. It was eventually torn down. Officials said that had the earthquake lasted five more seconds, that section of freeway would probably have collapsed. I believe I was one of the last cars that ever drove over the Embarcadero Freeway.

When I got to the Red and White Fleet, they had already started mobilizing to provide transportation out of the city. All the bridges were shutdown pending a safety inspection. BART, (Bay Area Rapid Transit), the Bay area subway system, was also shutdown. Other than driving all the way around the peninsula, for those that had cars, the ferry boat system was the only way out of town.

I was asked to go to the Ferry Building Pier, which was the Red and White Pier at that time, and to coordinate all of the Ferry Boats in and out of that pier. All of the Ferry Boat companies had agreed to work together and move as many passengers out of the city as possible to the East Bay, Marin County and Vallejo at no charge to the passengers. All ferry boat rides that first night were free.

By the time I got to the pier, probably around 5:45 p.m., the place was jammed with people. As each vessel came in I would announce where it was going and then let people stream through the gate until the vessel reached the maximum capacity of passengers authorized in the vessel Coast Guard Certificate of Inspection.

As it got dark, things got a little panicky on the pier. The entire city was without lights and a continual stream of people jammed onto the loading area trying to get aboard a boat and get out of the city. At any given time there were probably two or three thousand people jammed into that area. The only light we had was from the searchlights on the vessels, which the Captains shone on the walkway to the pier. The smell of gas permeated the area and I had the Captains make the announcement over their loudspeakers for everyone to please refrain from smoking.

And we experienced aftershocks throughout the evening.

People were coming through the narrow gate with pale, frightened faces and I'm not sure if it was the fear of the aftershocks or what they might find at home or the fact that they were so tightly jammed for such a long time before they could get through the gates. Or just the stress of the whole situation.

We worked throughout the night filling boats to the maximum capacity and turning them around as soon as possible. I was very proud of the crews in our company and in the other companies at the performance they displayed that night. They responded to a major crisis in a calm and professional way to alleviate what could have been a disastrous situation for many people.

And I was proud of the way our company management and the management of the other companies responded. We all banded together in time of emergency for the general well being of the public.

When it became obvious that the Bay Bridge would be shutdown for some period of time, Crowley Maritime, the parent company of the Red and White Fleet, brought four 700 passenger vessels from Southern

California and set up additional terminals in Oakland, Richmond and Alameda to service those areas. In addition, the Washington State Ferry System sent four ferry boats down to San Francisco to help alleviate the crunch that we knew was coming.

Chapter 11

1993 - 1995

Back to Kwajalein

Frequently, the difference between the impossible and the possible is the strength of the will of the person involved!

*Late in 1992, I was offered the position of Marine Manager at Kwajalein and the lure of the island convinced us that we should return. My concern was that I would not be flying. All of my Marine activity in the past had been spiced with flying. When I was chartering MIRAGE, I flew for Air Sunshine. When I worked for the Red and White Fleet, I flew for Hugh Codding. When I went to Kwajalein the first time, it was as Aviation Manager and I was actively flying. This would be different and, frankly, it concerned me. But the lure of the island was too great and we went back to Kwajalein. We had many old friends there and we knew what Kwajalein was and what it offered, so we didn't expect any surprises. We found out differently!

The Marine Department consisted of about 112 people and Mel Carr, my old friend from the previous tour there, was still the Port Captain. The department had a varied mixture of people, a good percentage of Marshallese, some Hawaiians and some from the CONUS (Continental United States). One of our crew members, Primo, boasted that he had a daughter who was 58 years old, another who was 7 years old and 14 children in between.

Equipment in the department had been upgraded and we now had two 120-foot ocean-going tugs and two high-speed ferries similar to, but smaller than, the ones we had in the Red and White Fleet in San Francisco.

There weren't as many missile shots as before and the mission of the range had changed somewhat. It found itself in much greater competition with other National Ranges for its future survival.

*In December 1994 there were two unusual weekends. The first weekend I received a call that a plane had crashed approximately 400 miles east of Kwajalein.

Two twin engine Islanders were being ferried from China back to the States and, on the leg from Majuro, in the Marshall Islands, to Honolulu, Hawaii, one had ditched. The report we had was that, during the ditching, the aircraft had blown up and caught fire, and the pilot, the only occupant, had managed to get into his one-man life raft. This information was relayed by the second aircraft, who was flying with him, and who stayed with him using the Global Positioning System (GPS) to give us positions until he was forced to leave at dark. The ditching took place about 150 miles northeast of Majuro and, we found out later, was a result of a failed engine and the pilot not being able to dump excess fuel that would get him down to a flyable weight because of a faulty fuel dump valve.

As the Marshallese dispatched their Patrol Boat from Majuro, I diverted our LCU 2021 Great Bridge, which was coming home from a trip to the outer islands east of Kwajalein, to the site of the crash. The next morning, the Army initiated an Air Search at first light and, due to the GPS positioning the second aircraft had given the previous day, and a lot of luck, the injured pilot was spotted in his life raft.

Within a few hours, the Marshallese Patrol Boat was alongside the pilot and discovered that besides the burns and injured ribs, he had suffered two broken legs as a result of the crash. His pain was excruciating, to the point that he would not permit them to touch him. As a result, he lay in the raft alongside the Patrol Boat for quite some time until they could figure out a way to get him onboard. Finally, they rigged a sling and took him, still in the life raft, onboard the vessel. He lay on deck in the life raft, still not permitting anyone to touch him, his broken legs skewed at odd angles to the rest of him. Unfortunately, the Marshallese boat had no medication or sedatives on board to ease his pain. I had the Great Bridge rendezvous with the Patrol Boat and pass them drugs that would allow the pain to subside enough to lift him out of the raft and move him to a bunk.

I cannot imagine what this American Pilot, Earl Covell, went through during that night. Alone and severely injured with two broken legs in typical 8 to 10-foot seas. A one-man life raft merely keeps you afloat, it doesn't keep you dry. The constant motion of the raft on his broken legs must have been unbearable. A Coast Guard C-130 met the Patrol Boat in Majuro. After a short stint in the hospital there, the C-130 airlifted him to Honolulu, where we received news that he would recover.

*The following weekend I received a late call from our Marine Department Dispatcher that a vessel had run aground on 'R' coral head in the lagoon, just west of Ebeye, a well-populated island on the East Reef just north of Kwajalein. The morning revealed that the Micronesian Chief, a brand new container ship on her maiden voyage, had run onto a coral head. She was only 2-1/2 months old and did not have a spot of rust on her. The skipper requested assistance and I dispatched two tugs to try and get them off.

When I arrived at the ship, it was apparent they were pressed hard onto the coral head and it would be a trick to get them off. The Skipper, his officers and I met in the wardroom to develop a strategy. He said that he would like to attempt to pull the ship off the coral head with one tug pulling the port bow while the other pushed the stern from the starboard side.

When we attempted to do this, the ship, which had about a 6 to 7-degree list to port at the outset, went quickly to a 16 degree list, with the skipper shouting over the radio, "**Stop! Stop!**"

There was serious concern as to the stability of the ship due to the angle of heel she presented and the height of her load. The concern was that because of her low freeboard, the water was about to come over the rail on the port side. If that occurred and her heel increased any more, there was the possibility that she could roll over. Not a very healthy situation.

We then attempted to pull her straight back with both tugs producing 51 tons of bollard pull apiece. Even with 102 tons of bollard pull and the ship's engine full astern, we were unable to budge her.

It was apparent to me on the tug that the starboard shoulder of the vessel, about one quarter back from the bow, was the only thing holding the vessel on the coral head. Since coral heads are generally curved, I sent the DynCorp Marine Department Divers down in an attempt to find out how far we would have to move the ship sideways before reaching the curved part, whereby the ship would start righting and become more buoyant. The divers reported that we were close to the edge and we would have to move the ship less than 15 feet to reach the edge of the coral head.

The MICRONESIAN CHIEF stranded on 'R' Coral Head in the Kwajalein Lagoon. The coral head can be seen as light green water on the ship's starboard side.

I explained this to the Captain On the radio and suggested that we use the length of the ship as a 600-foot lever arm and attempt to push the stern around by putting a tug on the starboard side, near the stern, and push the stern to port, which should slide the shoulder off the coral head. Since that was how we had increased the list to port to a dangerous degree in the first place, he was adamantly opposed to that procedure. Because I was on the tug and had a different perspective of the situation, I invited the skipper on the tug to look at it from my perspective. After viewing the situation from the tug, he reluctantly agreed that it might work. I suggested to the skipper, that just in case this didn't work, that all unnecessary personnel be moved topside and that they all should be wearing life jackets.

With tensions high, we began pushing the stern to port and immediately the list began decreasing. The length of the ship gave us a tremendous leverage advantage and we slowly pushed the ship through about a 120 degree arc and she righted herself as the shoulder came off the coral head. Then, with only a small portion of the ship on the coral, we were able to pull her straight back with two tugs and refloat her.

The ship then made it to Ebeye under her own power and began offloading. Later that night, actually early in the morning, while back loading the steel containers two at a time (they were empty), the operator managed to drop a pair of containers on four tour busses that were bound for Saipan. He destroyed all four busses. Talk about a Captain having a bad day!

*When our company lost the contract in February 1995, I was offered a contract with the new company but, because of what I felt were unwise and ill-advised changes they were making all over the island as well as in the Marine Department, I declined the contract and we returned to Santa Rosa.

Chapter 12

1995 - ?

Turning Final
Santa Rosa, California

Life is uncertain - Eat dessert first!

*My experience with Crowley Maritime was that they really had an interest in their employees' welfare. Hugh Codding was the same way about his employees. In both of these cases, these men, Tom Crowley and Hugh Codding, felt a personal relationship with the people who worked for them. I attribute this to the fact that, in both cases, the company and the men grew together and they recognized and appreciated the important role that the employees played in making their ventures successful. People who take the reins of a company that is already successful don't seem to have that personal relationship with their employees.

Among many other benefits that the Crowley Corporation provided was a two-day seminar for employees over 55 years of age to help them prepare for retirement. One speaker who stood out in that seminar was a financial adviser who gave advice on how to financially prepare for the retirement years. He started out by saying that it was important for all retirees to understand the National Debt, because what happened to the National Debt could have a direct impact on the worth of their retirement dollars and would affect such important programs as Medicare, Social Security, etc. He said that he searched for a way to put the National Debt into perspective, because most of us have very little concept of millions, billions or trillions. They are just numbers with no meaning. So, in an attempt to put those figures into perspective, he converted them to time, specifically seconds, with which we are all familiar. He did it this way:

1 million seconds would equal about 11-1/2 days
1 billion seconds would equal about 32 years
1 trillion seconds would equal about 32,000 years

So, if we paid back the five trillion-dollar National Debt, not counting interest, at one dollar a second, 24 hours a day, seven days a week, it would take 160,000 years to pay it off. Although it's depressing, I thought that was a good way to put the National Debt into perspective.

Another speaker at this very informative seminar was a prominent physician who had spent his career studying ageing. He chided the medical profession for using a cholesterol figure of 200 as a norm for Americans. He said that he had studied the Serengeti Tribesman of Africa, who have maintained the same diet for thousands of years and have an average cholesterol of 70. He said the figure of 200 was established primarily because it's what the modern world has accepted based on our eating habits. According to him, our bodies are designed to live an average of 120 years, and if we ate properly and took care of ourselves, each of us, marring some other unfortunate event, should live to the ripe old age of 120.

I've heard people say that the best remedy for old age is to stay busy. That's probably true. However, I don't believe that just staying busy is the total answer. I believe that, as individuals, we must face a challenge and maintain a positive attitude toward life in order to preserve our mental and physical capacities. Marring some medical disability, there is no reason not to pursue the challenge. I think of Sir Francis Chichester, who sailed around Cape Horn alone at 73 years of age. And Ambassador Elsworth Bunker, who was ambassador to Vietnam when I was over there. At 73, he gave the young guys a tussle on the tennis court. I think of my stepmom, Connie Reed. When in her 90's, she took several major trips each year and entertained 13 or 14 people twice a week at her home.

The thing that each of these people have in common is that they pursue a challenge and they maintain a positive attitude. Each one of us can't be a Chichester and sail around the Horn, or be a Bunker and be the Ambassador to a country, but what about the other challenges that we can tackle? How often have I heard folks of my generation say that computers are too complicated for them to learn? Computers are a challenge that is not only fun once you get into it, but also very rewarding. And not as complicated as you think, once you get the hang of it.

There are literally hundreds of challenges that we can pursue that will guarantee the best chance of sliding into those golden years with a healthy and happy perspective. Each of us need only find the one that fits.

*It may be appropriate to pass on a few things that I've picked up over the years as concerns some flying and boat stuff. Nothing that's a big deal, just interesting.

THE COMPASS:

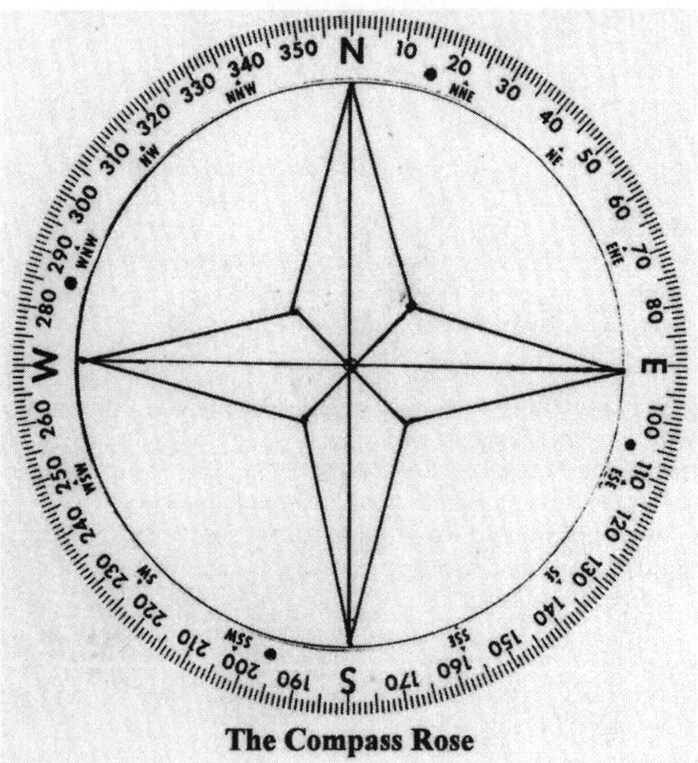

The Compass Rose

We all use a compass without thinking much about it. In aviation, under the current method of navigation, we are frequently required to determine the reciprocal of our heading. As an example,when using the VOR, which is omnidirectional, we may be asked to track inbound on a radial, which always emanates out from the VOR. Therfore, we must determine the reciprocal of the outbound bearing. Most modern instrument displays will have the reciprocal of the selected bearing shown at the bottom of the case, however, pilots have for years used different methods of figuring reciprocal bearings in their heads.

Remember the old method, subtract 180 degrees from the inbound bearing to get the reciprocal? Actually, there is a much simpler method.

Think about this. All Cardinal and Semi-Cardinal points add up to the number nine. That is:

360 degrees 3 + 6 = 9
045 degrees 4 + 5 = 9
090 degrees 0 + 9 = 9
135 degrees 1 + 3 + 5 = 9
180 degrees 1 + 8 = 9

And so on around the compass. But what's really interesting is that all reciprocals add up to the same number. That is:

For 215 degrees, the reciprocal is 035 degrees. Both add up to the number 8.

For 325 degrees, the reciprocal is 145 degrees. Both add up to the number 10.

And so on around the compass. This works for any heading on the Compass Rose.

Knowing that reciprocals add up to the same number makes it rather simple to find the reciprocal of any given heading. Actually, although it sounds confusing, with a little practice it makes it very easy to determine the reciprocal of any bearing.

The Poor Man's Celestial:

For those in small boats navigating the great expanses of the ocean, navigation has, until recently, been one of the biggest hurdles to a safe trip. Electronic Navigation in the form of LORAN, Satellite Navigators and now the Global Positioning System has really eliminated navigation as a problem. **Or has it?** It's nice to be able to crank up the Satellite Navigator and get your position in Degrees, Minutes and Seconds, but what happens if it quits? Suppose it gets wet and cranky, or a diode goes out or whatever. What then?

Most of us in the Northern Hemisphere can find Polaris (the North Star). Remember how you did it? Just line up the two outer stars of the pot on the Big Dipper and there it is. The interesting thing about the North

Star is that it doesn't move in reference to the horizon. All the other stars or celestial bodies appear to rotate around the Earth (we know that the Earth is actually rotating) except the North Star. This is because the North Star is located almost directly on the Geographic Axis of the Earth.

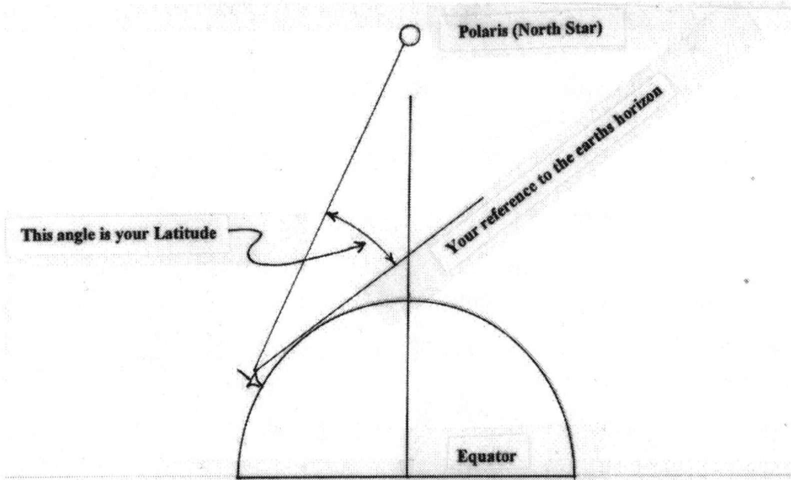

Finding the Angle of the North Star

What this means to us is that whatever angle the North Star is in relation to us and the horizon of the Earth is our latitude on the Earth. With an inexpensive plastic sextant and a little practice it can be very simple to determine this angle.

So, if we are on a small boat going between Hawaii and Tokyo and, halfway across the pond, the handheld GPS gets dropped overboard, never fear. Even if we don't have an intimate knowledge of Celestial Navigation, which most of us don't, there is hope.

We know from our chart that the entrance to Tokyo Wan (Bay) is 35 degrees, 53 minutes north. Therefore, we need to proceed on a generally westerly course and keep the North Star at an elevation of just under 36 degrees. If we find the angle is increasing, that is going to 39 degrees, we need to head a little further south of west. And just the opposite if the angle decreases. Eventually, we will find a heading that keeps the North Star right close to 35 degrees, 53 minutes elevation and we'll tool right into Tokyo. We won't know exactly when we'll get there, but our Dead Reckoning will give us a pretty good idea. Any landfall can be made in the Northern Hemisphere using this simple solution.

*All of us have some days that are better than others. I would like to document a day that was really a good day for me.

On an earlier TDY from Kwajalein to Newport News, Virginia, I had some time to kill over the weekend. Having never been to Kitty Hawk, North Carolina, I made the two-hour drive south of Norfolk to visit the Wright Brothers Memorial at Kill Devil Hills. As a professional Pilot who spent the greater part of his life caught up in the great adventure of flying in so many different forms and challenges all over the world, seeing the place it all got started was something I had always wanted to do.

I can tell you that it was a religious experience for me. Standing on the very spot where two brothers had followed their beliefs and challenged the elements to achieve the first powered flight, and then realizing man's achievements following that historic event, was awe inspiring for me. Oh, I guess if the Wright Brothers hadn't done it somebody else somewhere in the world would have. And there is dispute even today as to whether they were really the first. But that didn't make any difference to me at that moment.

The National Park Service did a superb job of telling the story of the Wright Brothers' achievements and maintaining the simple but authentic memorial and displays there at Kill Devil Hills. I was truly impressed with the entire presentation. To top the day off, when I drove back to Norfolk that afternoon, I was privileged to witness a performance of the United States Air Force Aerial Demonstration Team, The Thunderbirds. On that day, I had been to both ends of the spectrum!

*What does an old Pilot do when he doesn't look forward to Slipping the Surly Bonds of Earth on a daily basis? One of the things he does is to reflect on the era that he has lived in, the people he has met and the adventures he has had.

I guess of all the things I've done, places I've been and things I've seen, if someone asked me what was the greatest adventure of my life, I would say, without pause, "The people I've met."

The people around you have a quality about them that forms the fabric of what we are and influences what we will become. I have been fortunate in the people I've known over the years. The Spook Medellins, the Gerry Teachouts, the Hugh Coddings and C.J. Stephens and so many others. I remember those we lost along the way who were denied, for one reason or another, fulfillment of their lives. My mother, my father, Fred Stoss, Jim Wheeler and others. All of us have someone we care about whose life was ended early, and we grieve for that. Because when someone we care about is gone, a little of us goes away too.

*And I reflect on the era through which my life has spanned. What a spectacular time to live! To share this time with such great human events and such distinguished men and women. In all of human history, if I had to pick the time I would want to live, it would have been the time that God gave me. And the great question always arises. "Is the adventure over, or is it just the beginning?" As we reach that time in life where we are "**Turning Final**," I'm reminded of a poem that is very appropriate as we and our loved ones grow older:

I am standing on the seashore. A ship at my side
spreads her white sails to the morning breeze and
starts for the blue ocean. She is an object of
beauty and strength,
and I stand and watch her until at length
she hangs like a speck of white cloud where
the sea and the sky come down to
mingle with each other.
Then someone at my side says:
"There! She's gone."
Gone where?
Gone from my sight - - - That is all.
She is just as large in mast and hull and spar
as she was when she left my side, and just as able
to bear her living freight to her destination.
Her diminished size is in me, not in her; and just
at the moment when someone at my side says,
"There! She's gone,"
there are other eyes watching her coming and other
voices ready to take up the glad shout,
"There she comes! "
And So, That is Life!

Henry van Dyke

TURNING FINAL
Glossary of Acronyms and Terms

ADF **Automatic Direction Finder**. A device which automatically points to a low frequency radio station to obtain a relative bearing to the station. When this needle overlays a rotating compass card, the bearing becomes a magnetic bearing. The ADF system was unsatisfactory because the radio was difficult to tune and operated in the frequency range that was close to the electrostatic energy produced by thunderstorms.

In addition to producing a lot of static, making it difficult to tune, the needle would, at times, point to the thunderstorm instead of the radio station and lead you into the heart of the storm. In the late forties and fifties it was replaced by the VOR as the primary navigation aid for aviation.

BOQ **Bachelor Officers Quarters.** Military housing.

CW **Carrier Wave**. The method in which trained radio operators send messages on High Frequency radios (HF) with Morse code, which is a series of dots and dashes. Generally more reliable than voice.

DR **Dead Reckoning.** Navigation based upon an aircraft's (or boat's) projected course and speed from a known fix. When either visual, electronic or celestial means are not available to achieve a known position, Dead Reckoning is used to project a course and speed to obtain an approximate position until a known fix by some other means is available.

Feathered On a multi-engine, propeller-driven airplane, when an engine fails the propeller is feathered to reduce drag. That is, each individual blade is turned so that it is streamlined to the airflow, presenting the least amount of surface area. On some aircraft, feathering was accomplished using oil pressure from an electric pump and, through a series of pistons and gears, each blade was turned when the pilot simply pushed the feathering button.

GCA **Ground Controlled Approach.** A radar unit located on the ground, near a runway, that houses radar equipment and radar controllers that talk aircraft to the runway in bad weather.

CONUS **Continental United States.** Includes the 48 contiguous states but does not included Alaska, Hawaii or other United States Territories.

GPS — **Global Positioning System.** A sophisticated Navigation System using Satellite Ranging to provide highly accurate positioning anywhere in the world. Beside the incredible accuracy of GPS, it is not affected by weather and may, in the future, replace the current approach aids for aircraft.

IFR — **Instrument Flight Rules.** Aircraft operate under two basic sets of flight rules: Instrument Flight Rules and Visual Flight Rules. When operating under Instrument Flight Rules, the pilot must file a flight plan, receive a clearance from a controlling agency and follow the clearance instructions from that agency. While operating under Instrument Flight Rules, the pilot is assured of separation from other aircraft operating IFR. The FAA requires all Flag Carrier operations (such as United, Delta,.) to operate under IFR at all times, regardless of the weather. In addition, all operations in the Continental United States above 18,000 feet are controlled and must be operated under IFR.

ILS — **Instrument Landing System.** An electronic system that enables a pilot to find the runway in fog or bad weather. A vertical needle presentation within the cockpit allows the pilot to approach the runway on centerline. In addition, a horizontal needle shows him a glidepath to follow that puts him at the proper altitude over the runway.

Localizer — The part of the ILS system that shows the pilot the centerline of the runway.

PCS — **Permanent Change of Station.** Transferred from one place or job to another.

Pitot Tube — The Pitot Tube is a device generally mounted on the leading edge of the wing or the nose of an aircraft in undisturbed air and is part of the Pitot Static System, which measures the volume of airflow over the aircraft and gives the pilot a readout Indicated Airspeed.

RON — **Remain Overnight.** A term used by aircrews when they are spending the night, usually away from their home station.

VFR — **Visual Flight Rules.** The rules a pilot operates under when he is flying under good weather conditions and is visually providing his own separation from other aircraft. See "IFR" above.

VHF — **Very High Frequency.** The primary communications radio used in aircraft operations. Since range is primarily determined by line of sight, the effective range of the VHF radio is primarily line of site dependent.

VOR **Very High Frequency Omnidirectional Range.** The VOR replaced the ADF in the forties and fifties as the primary navigational system for aviation. The airways structure within the United States and most of the world is based on the VOR. It provides accurate bearing data, basically unaffected by weather. Since the control head, in the cockpit, for the VOR contain preset crystals, tuning is very simple. In addition, most VOR stations also contain Distance Measuring Equipment (DME),which then provide not only a bearing from the station, but an accurate distance, together giving the pilot an accurate fix rather than just a bearing.

On the back cover is the crew that sailed Landfall from Kwajalein to Japan. This photo was taken during a test sail in the Kwajalein Lagoon after re stepping the mast following repair of the top section of mast that had been damaged.

From left to right: Wes Westhafer, Leo Nolan,
Al Whitcombe and Jim Reed

Edwards Brothers Malloy
Oxnard, CA USA
December 1, 2014